EUROPE AND THE AMERICAN CIVIL WAR

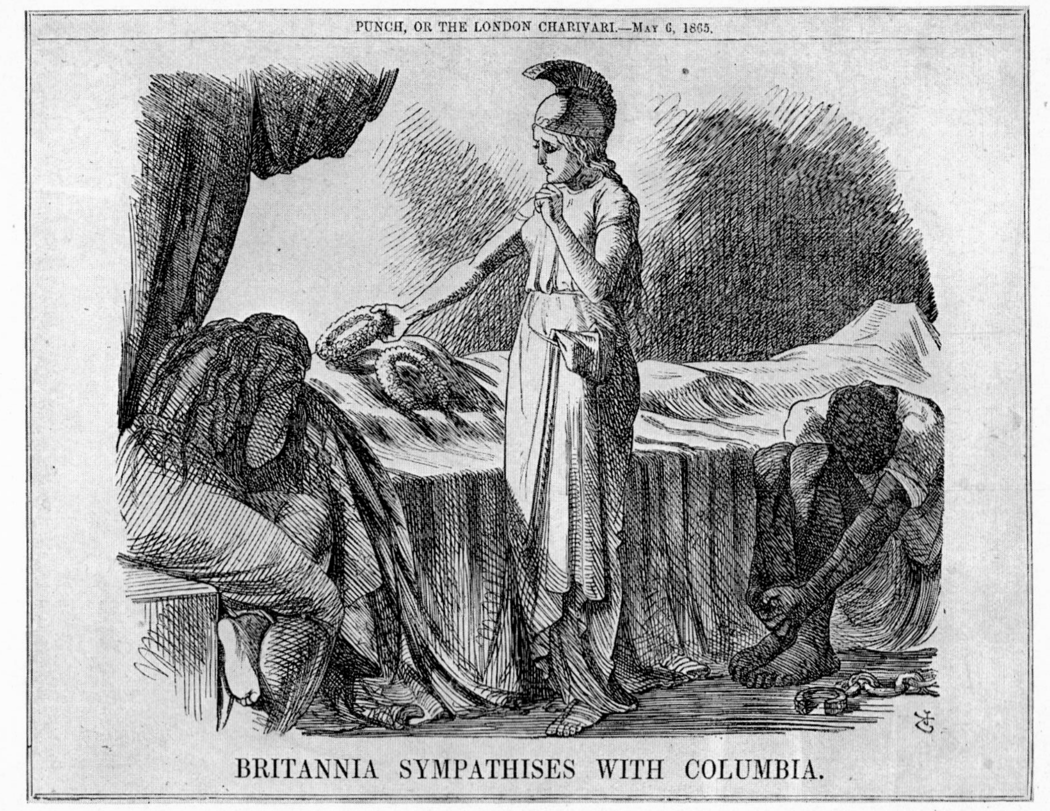

The Cartoon that Accompanied the Poem 'Abraham Lincoln' by Tom Taylor

EUROPE AND THE AMERICAN CIVIL WAR

BY

DONALDSON JORDAN, Ph.D. (*Harv.*)

and

EDWIN J. PRATT, D.Phil. (*Oxon.*)

with an introduction by

SAMUEL ELIOT MORISON

BOSTON AND NEW YORK
HOUGHTON MIFFLIN COMPANY
The Riverside Press Cambridge
1931

The Riverside Press
CAMBRIDGE · MASSACHUSETTS
PRINTED IN THE U.S.A.

PREFACE

THE following essay is written in the belief, increasingly clear, that the relations between the American democracy and Europe have never been so much diplomatic as cultural and economic, and that America has influenced Europe, especially from the mid-nineteenth century onwards, far more than Europe has admitted. Chapters I to VII are the work of Mr. Jordan; Chapters VIII to XI of Mr. Pratt; and Chapter XII is their joint conclusion.

The authors wish to express their gratitude to many friends and teachers who have assisted them. Among these should be especially mentioned Professor S. E. Morison, Professor Edward Channing, and Professor Wallace Notestein. Thanks are also due to Mr. Travers Buxton, M.A., for the use of the manuscript minute-books of the Anti-Slavery and Aborigines Protection Society, and to Mr. W. H. Chesson for the generous loan of the diary of his father, Frederick William Chesson. Not least should be mentioned the courteous authorities of the British Museum, the Harvard College Library, the Library of Congress, and the Archives of the Ministry of Foreign Affairs in Madrid.

H. D. J.
E. J. P.

HANOVER, NEW HAMPSHIRE
and
VIENNA, AUSTRIA
August, 1930

CONTENTS

INTRODUCTION, *by Samuel Eliot Morison* xi

PART I. ENGLAND

1. Secession and the Outbreak of War 3
2. England as a Neutral: The Trent Affair 21
3. The Gentlemen and the Masses: The Keynote of British Opinion 48
4. Personal Influences 72
5. The Dangerous Year: 1862 95
6. Slavery, Emancipation, and the Reaction to the North 125
7. Propaganda and the Failure of Confederate Efforts in 1863 164

PART II. THE CONTINENT

8. The Continent and the War 193
9. Napoleon III and the Confederacy 202
10. French Public Opinion of the Civil War 218
11. Spanish Opinion of the Civil War 245
12. Conclusion 259

BIBLIOGRAPHY 271

INDEX 291

ILLUSTRATIONS

The Cartoon that Accompanied the Poem 'Abraham Lincoln' by Tom Taylor — *Frontispiece*
From *Punch*, May 6, 1865

A 'Punch' Cartoon of 1861 — 22

Cartoon in 'Le Charivari,' Paris, March 6, 1862 — 236

Cartoon in 'Le Charivari,' Paris, October 13, 1865 — 266

INTRODUCTION

HISTORIES of the American Civil War we have had aplenty, even histories of the diplomatic side alone; but of what Europe thought of it we have had only rare glimpses in a page or two of Henry Adams, the memoirs of John Bigelow, and footnotes to James Ford Rhodes. Yet European opinion was one of the vital factors in the outcome of the war. Intervention by Great Britain or by France would have established the Confederacy. It was reasonable to suppose that they would so intervene. Aiding oppressed nationalities to win their independence was a traditional policy of both countries. Governing classes, in England, France, and Spain, thought in terms of balance of power. Given that way of thinking, it was their obvious interest to have two republics instead of one between the Rio Grande and the forty-ninth parallel. If neither government hailed the Stars and Bars as equal to the Stars and Stripes, public opinion was the fundamental reason. Napoleon III, a quasi-arbitrary ruler, dared not flout the liberal opinion which his dynasty was trying to conciliate. Lords Palmerston and Russell dared not flout the English nonconformist conscience; and if O'Donnell had ever brought Spain to the point of recognition, he too would have heard from liberal opinion.

The study of the sentiment of these countries, as reflected in the newspaper press, in pamphlets, and in the writings of contemporaries, is essential to the understanding of our Civil War. And it marks the breaking of a new force into diplomacy. Rulers have always had to respect some public opinion, if only that of their immediate *entourage*; but never before in European history had large masses of opinion exerted such weight in foreign policy as in England and France during the American Civil War. For there was some quality in this epic struggle which even in its earliest stages aroused the keen interest of the newspaper-reading citizen; and interest developed into passionate partisanship. Finally the issues became sufficiently clear to divide public opinion clean-cut into pro-Union and pro-Southern; to array, as the Comte de Montalembert said, 'on the side of the pro-slavery people all the open or secret partisans of the fanaticism and absolutism of Europe — the open or secret enemies of liberty,' and on the other, all who believed in democracy, in the republican idea, and in the dignity of labor. So it is a fascinating story, this development of the public opinion of Europe, and the reaction to Seward's strutting and to Bull Run, to the universal mourning over Lincoln and the wonder at the peaceful disbandment of a nation in arms.

Although this study covers public opinion in the whole of Europe, even such as there was in Russia, the authors have chiefly considered England, France, and Spain, the three countries which had American possessions, American interests, and efficient power to throw into the balance between North and South. There is a curious legend in American history that England as a whole was hostile, positively and mischievously so, to the Union. Professor Ephraim D. Adams has already proved this to be unfounded on the diplomatic side; Professor Jordan shows that it has little foundation in public opinion. When we understand the background and the circumstances, we can even feel a little more kindly toward the offensive condescension of 'The Times.' Both North and South, in the heat of the conflict, expected of their mother country what they had no right to expect, hundred per cent sympathy and unanimous support: exactly what England and Germany expected of America in the early stages of the World War, and with as little justice. Dr. Pratt has done nothing to alter the tradition of the cynical unfriendliness and tortuous diplomacy of Napoleon III, but he has shown that Franco-American amity, in these crucial years, was something more palpable than a tradition; and that liberal France supported the Union cause with as deep a sympathy as liberal England and an even keener intelligence.

These two young American scholars, classmates but each working independently in his chosen field and under different universities, have investigated the subject with fairness, thoroughness, and accuracy. It so happened that I read both their doctoral dissertations, the one at Harvard, and the other at Oxford. Both impressed me as having turned up historical treasures which should not be allowed to lie fallow in the vaults of the Widener and the Bodleian. At my suggestion they have completely rewritten their work in collaboration, discarding the scholarly apparatus and impedimenta which greatly increase the cost of publishing a book, without adding much from the reader's point of view. I can assure the reader that the work is sound; I hope he may share my opinion that their story is one of unusual interest for the history of America, and of democracy.

S. E. Morison

PART I
ENGLAND

EUROPE AND THE AMERICAN CIVIL WAR

1

SECESSION AND THE OUTBREAK OF WAR

SECESSION and the slow drift of the United States into civil war were as puzzling to Englishmen as to Americans. Perhaps the conflict was irrepressible, but during the long and painful months between Lincoln's election to the Presidency and his call for seventy-five thousand volunteers, between November, 1860, and April, 1861, irrepressibility was at a heavy discount on both sides of the Atlantic. With the exception of Southern fire-eaters and a few reckless spirits in the North, Europeans and Americans alike deprecated the severance of the Union and urged the needlessness of civil conflict.

Englishmen, or at least that portion of them who pay any attention to public affairs, have always been interested in the United States and appear to be actuated by a keener sense of cousinhood than has existed for a hundred years on the western side of the ocean. Interest in American affairs, however, had rarely been less than in the year 1860. The United States was in abeyance, and rose to prominence in the newspaper press with some difficulty. European and Indian events had for some years been absorbing attention. The Crimean War had come just in time to increase the popular demand for newspapers which could at last be sold at a price within reach of persons of moderate means, while the potential power of the press had been strikingly demonstrated — and exaggerated — by the extraordinary success of 'The Times' in focussing public opinion on the scandalous blunders in the conduct of the war. Then had come the Indian Mutiny, followed shortly by the remarkable series of events which were fast culminating in Italian unity and a Bonaparte hegemony. In the summer of 1860 the eyes of the world were turned toward Garibaldi, and while the famous Thousand were performing prodigies of the impossible in Sicily and Calabria, there was naturally little cause for interest in the familiar phenomenon of an American election fought with nothing more deadly than the usual big words. As a 'Saturday Review' writer remarked, Garibaldi was 'the subject of more discussion in a day than all the parties and all the orators in America in a year.'

In November the news that the anti-slavery Republican Party had elected its candidate was received with mild satisfaction in England. It presaged something hopeful, though no one knew quite what. The leader writers improved the occasion with little homilies on the institutions of a country which could call such an untrained man as Lincoln to head its councils, or expressed their pontifical conviction that the results of the election were a blow at the supremacy of the 'slave oligarchy.' Only the small group of active anti-slavery workers showed any appreciation of the ambiguous position of the Republican Party. A few politicians were half aware of the critical balance of forces in America, but they did little to leaven the lump of ignorance.

With the news of secession threats which immediately followed reports of the election itself, there was a general pricking-up of ears. The anti-slavery party, men of high unbending principle akin to the American abolitionists, began to anticipate a separation of the sections with something approaching complacency. Others, remembering 1856, were sure that the South would back down. The very violence of Southern denunciations did more than any amount of Northern protesting to persuade foreign observers that the anti-slavery cause had made real progress; and scarcely any notice was taken of the fact that Lincoln was elected by a minority. Hand in hand with an increase of contentment with the Republican victory went a chorus of rebuke and expostulation addressed to the South. 'Punch' as usual expressed the dominant sentiment:

> 'Come, South, accept the situation;
> The change will grow by safe degrees.
> If any talk of separation,
> Hang all such traitors if you please.
> Break up the Union? Brothers, never!
> No; the United States forever,
> Pure Freedom's home beyond the seas!'

It is difficult to judge how much attention Englishmen really paid to trans-Atlantic events during this confused winter before the firing on Fort Sumter. Certainly the press felt a constant duty to comment, but there is very little evidence that individuals saw anything alarming or spectacular. Such opinion as existed followed a definite evolution. As long as the threats of the South appeared to be the disgruntled bluff and bluster of a constitutionally defeated oligarchy, Southern grievances, which were not very obvious, received little or no sympathy. But when secession began to look like an accomplished fact, English advice and prophecy correspondingly changed. In December, the South was told to accept the situation; in March, the North was counseled to do so. The shift was quite candidly made. We had thought, said 'The Times,' 'that instincts of patriotism and private interest would prevail, and that the Yankees and the Southerners would quarrel harmoniously for many years to come.' But when the quarrel produced formal secession ordinances and a dignified call for a constitutional convention of the seceding States, the situation looked quite different. Englishmen could not be expected to judge with much care the strictly constitutional aspects of secession, but it followed naturally from their characteristic respect for the forms of law that secession should appear logical, reasonable, and not improbably legal.

What is striking in this period is the promptness, sometimes amounting to alacrity, with which a number of journals accepted the first secessions as marking a definite separation of the Republic into two parts. With a few exceptions this attitude is not to be attributed to *Schadenfreude*, but rather to the wish and the conviction that separation could be achieved without war. That wish, in fact, is the key to the situation. Englishmen, whether on sentimental or selfish grounds, were above all anxious that there should be no armed conflict, for war would do neither the Americans nor the slaves any good and would be disturbing and harmful to the rest of the world. Most newspaper writers, at least, were unable to understand either why the North was not glad to be rid of the South or why the South should be so anxious to leave the Union. If war was coming at all, it was plain that it was not coming on the clear issue of slavery. Englishmen knew perfectly well that war would seriously disturb the commercial world of which they were the center, besides interrupting existing business relations with the United States. By the time that Lincoln's inaugural address was being read in England, it was evident that if the Americans drifted into civil conflict, they would be regarded in England as criminal fools.

Lincoln's inaugural was received as doubtingly and variously in England as in America. If it conceded too much to the South to satisfy the abolitionists, it did not give the hope of peace for which the majority of Englishmen were listening. The period of waiting that followed was so long that the firing on Fort Sumter finally came as a surprise. This event was quickly succeeded by Lincoln's call for seventy-five thousand soldiers, by President Davis's call for privateers, and by the proclamation of blockade of Southern coasts.

Thus civil war was fairly started. The fact that the South had opened hostilities had some effect in England, but was of less strategic importance than in America, for it had long been recognized that the Southern States were forcing the issue. The fact that in the Fort Sumter episode no one of the combatants had been either killed or wounded was amazing to men who had been long entertained with tales of American ferocity and bloodshed; and there was a tendency, confirmed by the continuing delay of the armies in coming together, to wonder whether the whole affair might be a farce, or even a put-up job. It was all very strange and abnormal, and there was nothing for England to do but to await developments and to act correctly.

Indifference and perplexity were now succeeded by absorbing interest, as attested by English news and editorial columns alike. American affairs, said the London correspondent of a provincial paper, were almost the only subject on which men talked seriously in the metropolis; and certainly the press discussed all aspects of the situation without ceasing. Most of the questioning was general: whether the North would really fight if the South persisted firmly; how emancipation of the slaves might be expected to be eventually attained; whether or no 'the republican bubble had burst'; how free the free trade of the Confederacy would turn out to be; whether a blockade could possibly be effectual; and the possible dangers from Confederate privateers. Those who felt some responsibility for the course of British policy at once took the stand that their country should steer a neutral course and that recognition of the South or any sort of official interference should not be considered. There soon appeared, to be sure, a motion in the House of Commons proposing recognition of the Confederacy, but discussion of it was very distasteful to the Ministry and, after a series of postponements, its proponent was induced to put it off *sine die*. Though the Houses of Parliament, even in April and May, 1861, contained ardent vindicators of both the American causes, the number on either side which would have been willing to bring on a debate on American affairs was very small. Unquestionably 'The Times' expressed the sentiment of all public men of importance when it congratulated England on the adjournment of such a delicate matter.

Interference by England was, indeed, quite out of the question until the cotton deficiency should raise the issue in a different form. For one thing, England's practice, ever since the days of the Holy Alliance, had been one of non-intervention in the affairs of other states except when her own honor or interest was concerned; and there was some belief that this policy might actually be considered a principle of international law. Lord Palmerston, indeed, had in 1834 asserted that civil war formed an exception to this rule, but as recently as on the occasion of the freeing of Italy, England had ostensibly observed it. As a standard of policy, non-intervention was almost unquestioningly accepted. Recognition of *de facto* revolutionary governments must await incontrovertible proofs that their independence was actually established. Expediency required a criterion the application of which would create as little ill-feeling as possible: that of recognizing the *status quo* until it was perfectly clear that it had gone forever. In the case of America, the obvious impolicy of further irritating the already overexcited Americans was quite enough to defer any active movement.

Hence the matter-of-fact way in which Her Majesty's proclamation of neutrality (May 13) was received. It was so natural and obvious a procedure at this juncture that many journals hardly found it worthy of editorial comment. Some of them, self-styled 'organs' of important segments of the country, had already issued their own declarations of neutrality; and nearly all comments were merely quietly approving. The latent difficulties of enforcing neutrality were recognized, particularly by the commercial community, which vividly apprehended the possibilities of Southern privateers.

If expediency were not enough to prevent immediate recognition of the Confederacy, anti-slavery influence would alone have sufficed. In May, 1861, the first Southern commissioners in England reported to the Confederate Secretary of State: 'We are ... satisfied that the public mind here is entirely opposed to the Government of the Confederate States of America on the question of slavery, and that the sincerity and universality of this feeling embarrass the Government in dealing with the question of our recognition.... We are of opinion that neither England nor France will recognize the independence of the Confederate States at present....' All the influence of the anti-slavery movement was thrown against the South, but there was no compensating movement toward a vindication of the Union. There were public meetings in a number of important towns in the North of England and Scotland, from which memorials were sent to the Foreign Secretary, Lord John Russell. Letters from the secretaries of obscure anti-slavery and Negroes' Friend Societies spurred the local press elsewhere to editorial activity; and after some delay the British and Foreign Anti-Slavery Society, the only nationally active body, petitioned the House of Commons against recognition.

By early June, when the secession of Virginia and several Border States had completed the alignment of the opposing sections, and when the organization of the opposing armies was proceeding apace, English opinion showed certain definite features. There was a rather acute realization that England was more closely tied in interest and feeling to her rowdy relatives than she had appreciated before the crisis. The thought of civil war in the United States was probably a more formidable prospect for Englishmen than could be any other disaster outside their own realm, and they were very loath to admit that it was inevitable or in any sense desirable. Since it was quite plain that the South could not be brought to reason, English batteries of argument were turned on the North, to persuade it of the wisdom of their wish that there might be no war. Such a man as Thackeray, whose predilections disposed him to sympathize with the North, asked how it could benefit the free States to be recoupled to the South. In the second place, the events in America aroused hopes that emancipation of the slaves might be expected in the near future, and there was a disposition to throw a high light on anything that seemed to point to this consummation. But as Lincoln was trying to keep the Border States by avoiding positive declarations against slavery, the only large fact hostile to that institution which could be observed was the separation of the slave regions from the confederation and the prospect of their political isolation. Anti-slavery sentiment and the desire to avoid war both led the English to counsel letting the wayward sisters go in peace.

These facts and opinions explain in large part why there was no appreciation of the fact that the cause of the Union was that of national integrity. Abolitionists did not care about nationality where the slaves' cause was concerned, while the continuance of a federation formed by a number of States did not seem worth such a war as that of the liberation of classic Italy. The English-speaking peoples were already divided politically, and divided as the result of revolution. As 'The Times' phrased it, it was a strange spectacle to see 'a Sovereign Democracy of Federal Republics punishing and conquering a Rebel Democracy of Federal Republics.' That the bases of nationality, traditional and psychological, existed in

America, as in Italy, Poland, and Hungary, the English were unable to understand. They sympathized in a patronizing elder-brother fashion with the tribulations of the Americans, while suspecting those tribulations to be quite unnecessary. Americans may compare their own sentiments about events in Ireland between 1916 and 1923, or at the outbreak of the World War.

Events were still too few, and issues too confusing, to produce a clean-cut division of public opinion or even a distinct formulation. A striking and instructive international exchange of ideas took place in the early summer of 1861. As the tone of the English press became known through extracts and editorials in the newspapers of the North, Unionists in the great surge of war enthusiasm which preceded the battle of Bull Run realized that they had been mistaken in taking English sympathy for granted. They were surprised by English coolness in regard to the prospects of the Union and said very flatly that they neither liked nor understood it. In a generation that knew nothing of what a national war was like, a bellicose mood was easily induced; Secretary Seward was not alone in turning from the repellent prospect of coercing the South to thoughts of uniting all Americans against a foreign power and possibly securing Canada into the bargain. Many irresponsible persons in the North, and much of its not very responsible press, felt no fear of England and a great deal of irritation. The result was a large amount of hasty diatribe against the unfeeling country which thought only of her own purse. Declarations of neutrality, official or otherwise, looked to the Northerners like declarations of sympathy with rebels, and they lost no time in protesting in terms more vigorous than tactful.

The 'New York Herald,' reckless and inconsistent, but enjoying an amazing prestige in England, charged that abolitionism was a devilish contrivance of the British ruling classes to break down American institutions, and that English emissaries and money had been sent to organize and execute John Brown's raid on Harper's Ferry. The more moderate 'New York Times' averred that nothing could remove from American minds the conviction of the base selfishness and canting hypocrisy of the British governing class; while 'The World' believed that France had been able to judge the American case from a point of view above the low material considerations controlling English sentiments.

All this and much more was reprinted in the English press and commented on editorially, with results that may be imagined. Meanwhile, in Europe there were attempts by Americans to remonstrate with those who seemed too willing to see an independent South. The ablest effort of this sort was made by the historian and diplomatist J. L. Motley, whose pamphlet,[1] first printed in 'The Times' on two successive days, was frequently republished in both England and the United States. Coming from one whose literary reputation was at its height, this essay on the causes of the Civil War was given wide publicity as a reasoned and authoritative statement of the case for the North; but it came too late to have much effect on the prevalent diagnosis of the situation. The comment frequently made was that the North had a good cause — surprisingly like that of Great Britain in 1775!

More influential still were the pronouncements of

[1] *Causes of the Civil War in America*, London, 1861.

another American diplomatist. Cassius Marcellus Clay, a Kentucky abolitionist with a reputation for courage, was on his way through western Europe to his new post as United States Minister to Russia. In passing through London and Paris, he could not resist the temptation to say a few words in defense of the misunderstood cause of his country. On May 20, with the advice and concurrence of Motley and other Americans, Clay sent a letter to the London 'Times' in which he appealed to the spirits of liberty and nationality to justify the cause of the North, and mentioned that fifty years thence America would probably have twice the population of the British Isles. The letter attracted a good deal of attention and caustic comments to the effect that England was able to take care of her own interests without advice. A little later, Clay capped the climax in a speech to a meeting of Americans in Paris, which deserves permanent record as a warning to those who would meddle with other people's patriotism. He declared that, although England might not improbably decide to 'mingle the red crosses of the Union Jack with the piratical black flag of the "Confederate States of America,"' France would certainly unite her Tricolor with the Stars and Stripes; nor would France forget what power it was that had checked her advance at every turn, had 'hedged in all the fields of her glory,' and had confined an earlier Napoleon on St. Helena. An incredible blunder to menace England, already over-suspicious of Napoleon III, with French hostility! Everywhere in England men discussed this latest example of American arrogance and brutality. It confirmed the feeling that the Americans were unreasonable to the point of insanity, and that there was no dealing with them on a normal basis. Richard Cobden, well-informed and disposed to favor the North, indicated the situation when he remarked that 'The Times' and the 'New York Herald' might be paired against each other, but that England had nothing bad enough to offset the speeches of Cassius M. Clay.

A very effective process, to which both sides contributed, was thus alienating each country from the other. The British middle classes, conscious of their own rectitude, could hardly view with complacency this criticism of their conduct by their blustering cousins, and the violent expressions of American disappointment which came by every mail were intensely irritating to persons who had no previous motive for being anything but benevolent spectators. That the whole of the North was in a towering passion against England and that, perhaps, Seward and his following were but waiting for an opportunity to embroil her in war, became commonplaces of English thought for the rest of the year 1861. The reaction was universal after the end of May. The 'Saturday Review' started articles on five successive weeks with animadversions on American vituperation, while everywhere 'honourable exceptions' to the torrent of abuse of England were noted with surprise, as were even 'moderate and gentlemanly' assaults. A very sober commentator summarized English feeling accurately when he said that American malignity over the neutrality proclamation, and the violence and barbarity of Americans among themselves, 'induce the looker-on to reconsider the bearings of the altercation, to question the righteousness of the cause which banishes reason from its counsels, extols rowdyism, and revels in slaughterous intents.'

Thus old sores were opened and old grudges revived. The memory of the Crimean War and of the diplomatic friction which it had involved was recalled, and American neutrality in that struggle, seemingly friendly to Russia, was remembered. It is surprising to read in 'The Times' that in England's European disputes her statesmen, when called upon to face hostile despotisms, had 'always been haunted by the fear of having the American Government on their backs.... Neutrality — strict neutrality — is all that the United States' Government can claim; and, as we maintained neutrality in the Italian war, where all our sympathies were awakened, much more shall we maintain it when we look on a struggle where our judgment still waits for further information, and where assuredly we shall not rejoice at the military success of either party.'

This posture of affairs was not appreciably changed by the traditional and widespread hostility of Great Britain to slavery. It is possible, as Bright and others claimed with too much confidence, that an out-and-out war against slavery at the outset would have won the approval of English educated opinion at once, as well as that of the masses; but the necessities of the Union did not permit this. Periodically and explicitly the Union Government denied that any attack was intended on the 'domestic institutions' of the slave States. As these disclaimers often arrived in the same mail with the passionate pro-slavery and Anglophobe diatribes of the 'New York Herald' and with bitter complaints of the honest free-soil folk of the North, it is not to be wondered at that English opinion, by and large, grew increasingly chilly.

Moreover, the belief was growing ever firmer that the North could not conquer the South, and that, if she could, it would be impossible to rule a subject population of ten millions. At first it had been thought, owing to the enthusiastic declarations of the Northern press, that there was a strong Unionist party in every State of the Confederacy except South Carolina. When events showed that everywhere the Unionist minority was swept along in the seceding current, there was a complete swing to a belief in the unanimity and firmness of the South. The more the North talked about the unbreakable and unbroken Union, the more that Union seemed unmistakably in pieces. Kentucky's endeavor to maintain an officially neutral position fostered a conviction that the United States had never been other than a *federal* government, and 'federal' to the educated Englishman had Greek connotations rather than those national ones which had accrued to the word in America. The South was already furnished with many of the attributes of an independent state, even though only another 'confederate' one: all that seemed necessary to an end of the war was that it should prove that it could not be subdued.

This proof, to men who were above all anxious to see a settlement of any kind, was not long in coming; it consisted simply in the fact that the Federal States did not at once conquer the Confederacy. 'Well,' said Lord Robert Cecil [1] to a Northern acquaintance, 'there is one way to convert us all — Win the battles, and we shall come round at once.' Unfortunately, instead of winning battles, the North lost a great one very early in the war. The first meeting of the hostile armies on a large scale had been looked forward to for many weeks as promising either a decision of the war itself or an indication of its outcome,

[1] The later Marquess of Salisbury.

so that the battle of Bull Run was used in support of many preconceived theories.

The spectacular defeat suffered by the Union on July 21 greatly strengthened the position of those writers in England who had 'constantly held' that the subjugation of the South was impossible. The disgraceful panic of the Federal army was hailed with somewhat crude delight by those who were only too glad to jeer at every consequence of democratic institutions; and the determination and pluck of the less numerous Southerners were brought into sharply contrasted relief. The largest body of the English public, who had not yet definitely taken sides in the struggle, was most affected by the results of Bull Run.

Americans have sometimes been led to believe that the reports of the panic of the Federal army were received with smiles of satisfaction by all but an heroic minority of the English people, but this was not the case. Rejoicing — the word itself was used in England — over the disgrace and defeat of the North was confined exclusively to those who had reason to wish ill to American institutions. The mass of Englishmen were more surprised than anything else. They were surprised that the North had so dishonored the common heritage of England, and their first impulse was to disown her as an heir to British stamina and character. 'Punch,' which had seen in Sumter only a farce, now reported that he would be unable to consider numerous applications to be his war correspondent until there should be a war, and pictured Brother Jonathan rushing from the battle-field in long-legged haste, on his way 'jist to take Canada'; yet 'Punch' gave no favor whatever to the South. Bull Run lent a fictitious appearance to some of the English prints of failing to take the war seriously, but this was partly the inevitable recoil from the nature of the defeat itself and from the frank and eloquently descriptive narratives of 'The Times' correspondent, W. H. Russell, and to some extent a bit of bravado on the part of persons who were precisely being forced to take the war seriously.

Of course the outcome of the fight was variously explained. With a good deal of justice, the American newspapers were made to shoulder a large part of the blame for forcing the armies to advance too soon; but there was a strong tendency to draw conclusions unfavorable to American character, and the tone of many leading articles leaves no doubt that American language toward England contributed to this. The rout was often viewed as a sort of judgment on the bragging and boasting of the North, even as showing that Northerners were all cowards. Justin M'Carthy wrote of this affair in retrospect that the English people 'have a perfect mania for discovering cowardice all over the world. Napoleon was a coward to a past generation; the French were for a long time cowards; the Italians were cowards.... In 1861 the Yankees were the typical cowards of the earth. A very flame of enthusiasm leaped up for the brave South, which though so small in numbers had contrived with such spirit and ease to defeat the Yankees.'

But the resolute spirit evinced in the Union after Bull Run soon helped Englishmen to read its true lesson — that the war would be neither short nor unreal. The preponderance in strength and numbers of the North was partially realized. The South had not taken Washington, so an indefinite prolongation of the contest was easy to foresee. At the same time the onus of the prolongation was laid squarely on the back of the North, and the burden of opinion in England for the rest of the year was that the war would be long and exacerbated, but that the North must be coming to realize that the reunion of the sections was an impossibility.

This conviction did not render Englishmen more desirous of recognizing the Southern Confederacy, and it was only Americans who apprehended such a measure. It was openly wished that the North would make peace with the South on the basis of independence, but this was quite different from a desire to force the North to desist from its efforts. Only a few journals thought it necessary to reassert that England would continue to be scrupulously impartial, and there was little or no belief that the South had definitely won its independence. Many persons and interests were affected by American troubles, but so far as the mass of the general public is concerned, the governing motive was the wish to keep out of hot water. That is probably the fundamental reason why the mirage of recognition so continuously receded from the Southern Commissioners. Sympathy, even enthusiasm, for the South might wax and wane; disgust and disappointment with the North might increase or be diminished; but always it was kept in mind that England would eventually have to live in peace and amity with America divided or America whole, and there was no wish to sow by hasty action seeds of future hostility with either party. Neutrality of word was not kept by any one in England; but neutrality of deed, as the course of highest expediency for her prosperity and tranquillity of mind, was not to be departed from unless in case of great need.

2

ENGLAND AS A NEUTRAL
THE TRENT AFFAIR

I

MEANWHILE, as the autumn progressed, events were imperceptibly moving toward a crisis in Anglo-American relations. English opinion slowly drifted in the direction of greater hostility to the North. 'Every post,' wrote Henry Adams from London in October, 'has taken away on one hand what it brought of good on the other.... How do you suppose we can overcome the effects of the New York press? How do you suppose we can conciliate men whom our tariff is ruining? How do you suppose we can shut people's eyes to the incompetence of Lincoln and the disgusting behavior of many of our volunteers and officers?' Mismanagement, vacillation as to the high command, the violence of American language, all seemed to point toward a breakdown of the character and institutions of the North. One of the most conspicuous features presented to English eyes was the growth of despotic government in the Union. A great outcry was raised among all classes of Englishmen over the system of arbitrary arrests and coercion of the press by which the Government was trying to suppress the more outspoken dissenters of the North. The 'Newcastle Guardian,' for example, which was trying to be friendly to the Union cause and not succeeding very well, admitted frankly that it could not defend such acts and regretted that they were costing the Union valuable sympathy. Another Liberal journal considered the use of the 'American Bastile' (Fort Lafayette) as a 'forerunner of that great military despotism which it was foreseen long ago would result from the policy pursued by Mr. Lincoln and his advisers'; and innumerable writers compared Milan under Austrian and Naples under Bourbon rule with America under Lincoln — parallels of very definite meaning in those years. There was apparently no recollection of the anti-Jacobin measures of Pitt in 1794 and 1795. The establishment of a passport system in America, always annoying to travelers, as the present generation knows, was also objectionable to people who had recently and with relief seen the lifting of this restriction 'even in despotic France.' 'Punch' announced 'A New Sovereign for the United States. — Martial Law, *vice* King Mob, put Under Restraint'; and there was a good deal of honest fear lest the formless and unchastened American democracy be headed toward a real military despotism which would make it a menace to European peace. These sentiments were brought more close to the British by the fact that some Englishmen had been imprisoned and denied the writ of *habeas corpus* by the Federal Government; the fact that Foreign Secretary Seward had the better of the British Minister in their correspondence on the subject did not suffice to erase the added count in the indictment of the North.

In spite of all the growing antipathy toward the North, sympathy did not go out in full measure to the Confederates. 'Punch,' a pretty faithful expositor of the commonest views, shows this plainly. If it derided the North after Bull Run for continuing the war, it did not hesitate to call

PUNCH, OR THE LONDON CHARIVARI.—JULY 6, 1861.

NAUGHTY JONATHAN.

"YOU **SHAN'T** INTERFERE, MOTHER—AND YOU OUGHT TO BE ON MY SIDE—AND IT'S A GREAT SHAME—AND I DON'T CARE—AND YOU **SHALL** INTERFERE—AND I WON'T HAVE IT."

A 'PUNCH' CARTOON OF 1861

the Confederacy a kettle as black as the pot; and when Yancey, one of the Southern Commissioners, referred at the Fishmongers' banquet to 'the land of the free and the home of the oppressed,' Mr. Punch opined that he meant the South in particular, where the whites were the free and the blacks were the oppressed.

One argument there was, however, which served the South well. The Confederacy was fighting for independence, and it had chosen a day in the nineteenth century which was most favorable for the utilization of all the prestige which this fact could bring. In the very earliest stage of secession 'Punch' had called attention to the contrast afforded by the United States and Italy, suggesting that Columbia would soon have to hand over to Italy her motto of *E Pluribus Unum*; but English sympathy for oppressed nationalities was called into play often thereafter in the cause of this new 'people' who wished to live by themselves. Poles, Hungarians, Italians fought for independence while the liberals of France and England applauded; why should not Southern Americans do likewise? If, it was asked, any government 'derives its just powers from the consent of the governed,' who might choose their government if nine millions might not? There was a disposition to quote Burke on indictments against a whole people, nor was it possible to avoid proceeding further to the instance of Lord North and his royal master, who eighty years before had tried vainly to resist the secession of a people related to them in blood and language but determined to become independent. Even Garibaldi's public declaration of his sympathy for the North failed to shake the sentimental feeling of those who believed in secession for every one but Ireland.

President Lincoln's putative offer to Garibaldi of the commandership-in-chief of the Federal forces occasioned not only abuse and insult in London, but a good deal of amusingly ponderous advice to Garibaldi to remember that his life was consecrated to Italy.

In the middle of October, 1861, Earl Russell, Foreign Secretary and co-chief of the Palmerston Ministry, was received at a great public dinner at the city of Newcastle-on-Tyne. There, full of years and esteem, he made to the Liberals of England an address which summarized and defended his long political career and outlined the principles on which he was at the moment conducting the foreign relations of the country. In the course of his speech Lord Russell took occasion to consider at some length the problems of Italy and America as they affected British policy; and in describing the American revolution, he hit on a most happy phrase. It would be a great misfortune, said the noble Lord, if anything should happen to shake or peril the great experiment of the new continent in free institutions. 'I am sorry to say,' he continued, 'that such events have happened, and we now see the two parties contending together, not upon the question of slavery, though I believe that was probably the original cause of the quarrel — not contending with respect to Free Trade and Protection, but contending, as so many states in the Old World have contended, the one side for empire and the other for independence.' This final phrase suddenly lit up a complex and confusing situation. That the war in America was a more commonplace affair than at first thought was a conviction that had been growing for some time; that none of its alleged explanations were satisfactory was only too clear. Here was the key that opened the lock, and Lord Russell said only what many of his countrymen had for some months been trying to say. For once Palmerston was certainly beaten at his own game of reading the thoughts of the public before they were formulated.

While slavery had been pushed almost out of the picture and the North was believed to be fighting in the cause of an almost hopeless imperialism, the Union navy was slowly rendering the blockade effective, and Union diplomacy was still arguing with those who could not be convinced. American secretaries of state had not prepared for a crisis like that of the year 1861. The diplomacy of the United States in the preceding generation had been self-conscious and self-confident and had taken little account of the traditional amenities of Old-World discussion. Many of the governing class in England felt that they had grievances against the American Government which had been hitherto dismissed with too much *bonhomie*. British susceptibilities had been frequently irritated by bluster in the American press and intransigence on the part of American statesmen. Englishmen never quite understood the spirit in which their cousins issued the claim that the British could lick the rest of the world and they could lick the British. Manifest destiny likewise was startling doctrine to the possessors of Canada, and persons were never lacking to point out that the chief causes of Anglo-American friction even during the period when Southern statesmen were in power were Northern ones — the Canadian Rebellion of 1837, Oregon, Maine, the San Juan Island dispute, the tariff, and shipping. Even the African slave trade was conducted largely by vessels from Northern ports. Rightly or wrongly, many Englishmen felt that their country had been too forbearing toward the United States, and that a strong line must be taken against future aggression.

It must be admitted that Secretary Seward did everything possible to foster English doubts as to the peacefulness of American intentions in 1861. The precise terms of the famous 'Thoughts for the President's Consideration,' written on the theory that the imminence of foreign war might be the means of reuniting the severed sections of his country, were not contemporaneously known; but it soon became common knowledge that the Secretary of State was not very averse from a war with England. His notion was not one of sudden growth. Sitting next to the Duke of Newcastle at an official dinner to the Prince of Wales in 1860, Seward made some half-serious remark about the probability that he would soon hold high office in the United States, in which case it would become his duty to insult Great Britain; and the Duke, though not at all understanding that Seward wanted war, naturally spread the conversation abroad. From officialdom and society it soon reached the press, of course in a more lurid version than that started by His Grace. Later, when actually 'the American Prime Minister,' Seward made no secret of those pugnacious dispatches which caused Charles Francis Adams so much embarrassment in his capacity of Minister to England, and Seward's instructions to Dayton at Paris were published in London and aroused unfavorable comment there. Adams noted as early as June 'how very general the dislike of the Governor [1] is in society here. The English express fears of his

[1] Seward was known to his friends and associates by this title, as he had been a conspicuous Governor of New York.

intentions towards them and intimate suspicions of his duplicity....' These suspicions were enhanced by belligerent articles in the Boston and New York press during the early months of the war, particularly by their tendency to fawn upon Louis Napoleon as a balance to 'hostile' England.

There was fear, too, for the safety of Canada, and again a reported conversation of Seward was put in evidence. Lord Palmerston's Under-Secretary for War (later well known as Lord Ripon) had already been concerned, as far back as 1859, about the Yankee menace to Canada, and these fears, though publicly denied, had evidently been back of the decision to send additional troops to Canada in June, 1861. Yet, to judge from the way in which this dispatch of troops was received by the British press, the menace to Canada was not a general subject of anxiety.

'The towering passion of the whole North with England' in the summer and autumn did a good deal, in the absence of more exact provocation, to keep British scaremongers on the alert. Then, with all the fitness of coincidence, Seward himself, in October, determined to issue a circular to the State officials of the loyal regions, calling on them to bring the maritime and Great Lakes front defenses of the country into a state of greater readiness than the Federal Government, in its absorption elsewhere, was able to do. In England this letter, published at the same time as the correspondence with Lord Lyons about arrests of British subjects in America, seemed to indicate anticipations of war on the long peaceful Canadian frontier. A writer in 'The Times' thought that Seward's insinuations lowered the credit of the United States equally with those who considered a war of England and

America possible — the New York money market — and with those who considered it impossible — England. A later writer believed that Seward was trying to store up a plausible ground of quarrel with Great Britain, in order to use the American army at the end of the Civil War to indemnify America by conquering Canada. Everything, said another journal, points to the desire of the 'rash and unprincipled rulers' of the United States to force a war with England: insults to Lord Lyons, arrests of British subjects, the raising of defenses on the Atlantic Coast and the Great Lakes.

English statesmen and a part of the press were distinctly nervous about American intentions. The people of the 'dis-United States' seemed positively mad, preposterous megalomaniacs like James Gordon Bennett, reckless of their own welfare as of their place among civilized nations, in need of a cold-water ducking which only England was in a position to administer.

II

The inflammable material so conspicuously heaped up only wanted the striking of a spark. On November 8, 1861, Captain Charles Wilkes, of the United States Navy, acting on his own responsibility, stopped the British mail steamer Trent on the high seas, and removed from her the Confederate States Commissioners to England and France, Messrs. Mason and Slidell, with their secretaries and baggage. He then suffered the Trent to go on her way, and himself steamed for the United States with his prisoners. On November 27, the news of this affair reached England in the shape of accounts from the purser and passengers of the Trent.

The general indignation with which this 'outrage' was received in England has been often described. The excitement was tremendous — greater, men said, than at any time in their generation. Spontaneous public meetings were held in various towns to urge the Government to take strong measures; on the streets men talked of almost nothing else; and everywhere it was assumed that this meant war. Hardly any one stopped to ask whether the American commander had by any chance been within his legal rights; hardly any one doubted that the act of Captain Wilkes had been ordered by his Government and that it was the consequence of a direct purpose to insult and defy England. The public feeling was very righteous. England had done nothing to provoke a war, but on the contrary it was being deliberately forced on her. She was assailed at two of her dearest points: freedom of the seas and the right of asylum. Both were infringed by the same deed, and reparation, ample and prompt, was required.

'Of course,' said Henry Sidgwick, who in the main favored the cause of the Union, 'if Seward wants a war with England, he must have it.' Matthew Arnold thought the time had come when it was necessary to give the Americans a lesson. Sir George Cornewall Lewis, a member of the Cabinet and the coolest of all public men, could hardly believe that Seward really wanted war; Sir John Acton [1] took the same point of view; and scarcely a well-known man is to be found on record who did not think that Seward desired a conflict.

If this conviction was all but universal at first, there were some who welcomed the Trent incident more heartily than others. 'The Times,' comparatively calm for a day or

[1] Better known as Lord Acton, the historian.

two, grew more and more belligerent as it grasped the popular trend. Its editorials called Seward a reckless adventurer who could evoke at will all the wild passions of a sovereign mob, and remarked that it was very seldom possible in a polite and decorous age to 'accumulate so much evidence of a deliberate and long-cherished intention to do us an injury as we are able to bring against Mr. Seward, the present Prime Minister of the Northern States of America.' The 'Bucks Herald,' a Tory journal in Disraeli's region, rejoiced in the unanimity of English opinion, which it felt was only the proper consequence of a hostility to the North which had been of long and steady growth. 'The cause is simple.... With the North is to be associated insolence and defiance of almost every diplomatic conventuality.... For years the Cabinet of Washington has left not a stone unturned to lower us in the opinion of Europe. Our forbearance has been called cowardice.... Now the most plausible defence cannot screen the American ministers from the charge of aiming at a rupture between our country and their own. The curtain has been drawn aside, the machinery is exposed, and we, without hesitation, pronounce that President Lincoln and his colleagues are doing their utmost to compel us to relinquish our neutrality, and by that means to bring on a European war.'

Other editors were more violent still. The 'Wakefield Journal and Examiner,' in its only leading article of the week, said that 'whatever the law of nations may be, we are certain that the law of English feeling will be that Lord Palmerston will ill sustain his ancient reputation for courage if he allow us to submit tamely to such indignity. ...Ever since the Union of the States we have allowed the Americans to provoke, insult, and bully us. They have with impunity robbed us of our trade, our territory, and our good name. There is, however, a limit even to an Englishman's patience, and our own opinion is, that had we shown a little more determination in years gone by the present indignity would not have been offered to us. The feeling of the people of England before this happened was decidedly in favor of the Southern States, in spite of the fact that those States are mainly supported by slavery, which we have spent millions of money and oceans of blood to put down. We hope that that feeling will now be allowed to have vent, and that we shall show those Northerners that we are no longer disposed to cripple our commerce and ruin our cotton manufacture for the sake of keeping up what they are pleased to call a blockade. If France and England break the blockade, and protect our merchant ships, there will very soon be an end of the American war, for the Southerners will be able to carry it on as they have hitherto done, vigorously and effectively, and in spite of all their boast and bluster the Northerners must submit. We shall then be fully avenged for the insults they have heaped upon us.'

These quotations are worthy of scrutiny because the evidence is very clear that neither the action of the Government nor the more responsible organs of the press went so far in indignation as did the mass of the public. Yet by no means every one was disposed to subordinate international law and anti-slavery sentiment to the desire of England to avenge an insult. At the very first, indeed, the metropolitan newspapers showed a calmness which was due only to a feeling that the anger of laymen must not be suffered to put England legally in the wrong. Of all the sixty-odd leading articles of 'The Times' during the difficulty, the least vehement and objectionable to Americans were those of the first two or three days; and other papers show equally the desire to make sure that the law was on England's side before plunging into unrestrained expressions of feeling. Many of the weekly papers went to press without the opinion of the law officers of the Crown, and so had either to play safe by avoiding consideration of the law, or to chance their reputations on statements which would appear before the public at the same time as the official decision. The result is naturally unsatisfactory, but there is enough evidence to show that, indignant as Englishmen were, many of them were not at all sure that the American captain had not been within his rights. They knew that English precedent in general was not likely to be very favorable to neutrals. The majority of journalists, however, solved their problem of tactics by saying, in effect, that international law was a thorny matter for ordinary people, and that so long as there was doubt of its decision, Englishmen, outraged as they were, should avoid committing themselves too far. More than one editorial writer explained that it was the duty of journalists to appease and subdue public feeling in cases like the existing one, and many acted accordingly, to the honor of the profession be it said.

The opinion of the lawyers of the Ministry that the seizure of the Confederate envoys had been illegal was based on the narrow but safe ground that if the American captain had suspected the presence of contraband on the Trent, it was his duty to have taken her to a prize court, and that he was wrong in taking off her anything but dispatches. The technicality of the decision and the knowledge that a messenger had been promptly sent to the United States to demand reparation tended to restrain the more careless of the war-mongers. But it may be confidently stated that any failure to act quickly, or the existence of a Ministry less popular than Lord Palmerston's, would have rendered it next to impossible to avoid handing Minister Adams his passports — an action which would probably have prevented a peaceful issue.

When the Government had acted, there was nothing to do but wait; the period of delay was one in which every one was free to say what he wanted without fear that he could affect the result. Before long the storm intensified and led by 'The Times,' the 'Morning Post,' and the 'Daily Telegraph,' the spirit of belligerency on the whole grew until about the third week of December. Conversation and writing on all sides served to increase British ire. Every story unfriendly to the United States and its people was dug out from memory and repeated; every Anglophobe expression of American orators was quoted; Seward, James Gordon Bennett, and Wilkes became the most talked-of persons in England. It was pointed out that never before had England been so well prepared for war. The alarms of 1859 and 1860 had caused her navy to be brought to a high state of readiness; the Volunteer Movement had provided her with a body of partly trained troops which would defend her when the regular army should be sent away; her prospective opponent was distracted and weak. 'The great bond of cotton had ceased to bind the two countries to peace': it was believed on the contrary that a war would secure cotton. The other chief reason for avoiding war with America, fear of her privateers, was minimized by the war-mongers, as it was thought there would be no difficulty in blockading the ports of the United States; nor was the invasion of Canada thought a very serious danger. All the British pugnacity which had been kept warm since 1856 — and there was very much of it, due to suspicions of Napoleon III — flared up. At agricultural dinners a few patriotic remarks were always called for in response to the customary toast of 'the Army, Navy, and Volunteers,' and retired colonels sometimes spoke with a frankness worthy to match the perorations of Irish-American orators about England. On one of these occasions a rector of the Established Church ventured the pungent hope 'that there would be no more of that maudlin sentimentality of which we have heard so much, about the Americans being our blood relations and that a war with them would be as bad as a civil war at home. It was all nonsense.... He was very much of the opinion of the writer who said that a Yankee was as great a parody on an Englishman as a monkey was upon the human race.'

The excitement was not entirely self-sustained. The account of the purser of the Trent, a not unbiased eye-witness, was at first the chief source for knowledge of details of the episode, but it was supplanted by a more vivid narrative. More than two weeks after the first news, Commander Williams, the retired naval officer in charge of the mails on the Trent, told his story at a dinner of the Royal Western Yacht Club in Plymouth, and it was generally reported in the press. The account was particularly lurid. The brutal American marines sent to seize the prisoners advanced with their bayonets pointed at the undefended breast of Slidell's daughter, while Commander Williams bravely thrust himself between, crying, 'Back, you damned cowardly poltroons!' The sentiments of the English gentry as they heard of this occurrence on the deck of a British ship may be imagined.

Worse, of course, was the rejoicing over Mason and Slidell in America, which had the effect that was to be expected. Englishmen were perhaps beginning to grow a little less vulnerable to the pointed shafts of the New York papers, but when the correspondent 'Manhattan,' in the London 'Herald' and 'Standard' and the famed and trusted Russell in 'The Times,' described the exultation, when the most respected and highly placed individuals in Boston, the Athens of America, met to applaud and defend Captain Wilkes, men were at least hardened in their original impression that America was reckless to the point of wishing to force a war. What, indeed, could be expected of the American populace? Even should the Government see the error of its ways and wish to disavow the act, it was so mob-ridden that it would be impossible for it to do so. 'The real difficulty,' said friendly Monckton Milnes, the poet and politician, 'will be to get Mason and Slidell away alive.'

It seemed very unlikely that war could be avoided. The earnestness of the Government's preparations, the actual sailing of troops for Canada, the great activity known to exist in naval dockyards, the calling in of officers on leave, all tended to keep tension at a high pitch. 'Punch's' cartoon of Britannia leaning on an Armstrong cannon and looking forth at the unquiet Atlantic precisely denoted the situation, thought many. There was more talk of what the war would be like than of whether it would come. Projects for a kind and moderate conflict were aired. 'Break the blockade of the Southern ports, and blockade the harbours of the North to prevent privateering; that is all we ought to do. In every other respect, if the Northerners let us alone, we must let them alone.' Many other remarks show less explicitly a belief that the war would be mostly naval, very short, and though humiliating for the Americans, not doing them much real harm. The elder brother is truly surprisingly in evidence.

III

Meanwhile several forces tending toward more peaceful counsels were coming into operation. Inevitable, probably, was a certain let-down in attention as the weeks passed by without any definite answer to the demands of the British Government, but its extent cannot be analyzed. Americans resident in Europe, moreover, impressed and alarmed by the intensity of English feeling, hastened to do what they could to dispel the notion that their countrymen were straining at the leash to jump at the British lion. Plaintive arguments appeared in 'The Times' and the 'Daily News' from the pens of J. Randolph Clay, Thurlow Weed, and William Wetmore Story, the sculptor, which may have done some good, although the leading articles brushed them impatiently aside. More effective, probably, were the tactful talk of Thurlow Weed, who dined out assiduously, and the indefatigable conversation and letter-writing of his colleague from New York, Bishop McIlvaine. The most successful single bit of propaganda of the whole war, however, was the letter sent by General Winfield Scott to the Paris newspapers. It was the product of much consultation and was actually written by John Bigelow. The promptness with which the name of the veteran general, fresh from America and from the command of the Union armies, was used to express the conviction that Wilkes's act was not by order of his Government, was a very wise thing.

In the course of time peace-loving elements in England began to come into action. A few of the extremer Tories were by no means anxious to see Palmerston's lease of power extended by a war, while the leaders of the Manchester School, the only open defenders of the United States in public circles, fought the idea of war as well as they were able. As might be expected, John Bright was first in the field with peaceful counsels. In a very fine speech at Rochdale on December 4, Bright devoted all his powers to the American question, and reviewed the whole case for the Union with high and earnest eloquence. Attempting to throw the Trent affair into perspective by reserving it as only the last quarter of his broad but partisan appeal, he castigated 'The Times' and Earl Russell, denied that the American Government could possibly be so infatuated as to desire a war, and pleaded for moderation and a peaceful spirit on the part of England. Bright's position in English public life at this time was a peculiar one and must be discussed in a later place. But he was one of the limited number of men who always got a hearing, and 'The Times' expressed the exact reverse of the truth when it described his voice as without an echo and fit only to amuse a sixth-rate provincial town. In the intransigent mood of the moment he was indeed in a small minority, and there was always a large number of writers ready to refute whatever Bright said on whatever subject; but no reader of any newspaper could well fail to know something about his utterances, which were taken as the texts for leading articles with surprising unanimity by journals of all opinions. On this particular occasion men could not but think of the fact that Bright had been in a manner right about the Crimean War, so that it was not entirely easy to dismiss his words as insignificant 'twaddle and treason.'

Richard Cobden joined his argumentative powers to the fervency of Bright. At the latter's Rochdale meeting the speech of the evening was preceded by the reading of a letter in which Cobden remarked that the opinion of English law officers on international law was not conclusive. Later, in a letter declining for personal reasons to take part in a meeting at Brighton, Cobden elaborated the idea of arbitration, and was honored by 'The Times' with two leading articles in refutation.

Bright and Cobden stood almost alone among public men of the first rank, yet they received support in relatively obscure though not unimportant quarters. Before long the Peace Society and the Quakers — who were almost identical — entered the field with pleas for arbitration. The Friends, who were the only body in the Kingdom that could preach anything but national honor without drawing down floods of contumelious abuse, memorialized Lord Palmerston suggesting arbitration, while the Peace Society addressed two successive letters to the representatives of the Christian churches, stating that the occasion neither required nor justified war, which would be a reproach to Christianity, and urging concentration of 'the distinctively Christian element in both' Great Britain and America on the effort to pour oil 'on that public opinion which, more than the communications of diplomatists, or the councils of cabinets, must ultimately decide the question of peace or war.'

In fact the influence of the churches, especially of the Nonconformists, was brought to bear in the direction of arbitration. The Evangelical Alliance, a non-political organization composed of Dissenters and Churchmen, convened a meeting at Exeter Hall of something like four thousand persons to pray for peace; though Lord Shaftesbury refused to attend, the assemblage was presided over by Sir Culling Eardley, one of the chief laymen of the Nonconformists. Lord Ebury, equally conspicuous as leader of one wing in the Establishment, wrote 'The Times' in favor of arbitration. On December 17, a general meeting of ministers of the three chief Dissenting denominations in London was held to consider the Trent affair and adopted unanimously resolutions deprecating war and calling for arbitration; while the Congregational Union by itself took similar action and adopted an address to its American co-religionists. Later a joint deputation of Baptists and Independents interviewed Lord Russell in order to urge him to do everything possible for peace.

It appears likewise that the working classes came to be peacefully inclined. There was, of course, a good deal of truth in the claim of the Conservative 'Press' that 'the Demos' felt the national indignation most sharply at first, and probably the incident of Miss Slidell and the bayonets was duly appreciated in thousands of public-houses. Great wrath is also shown in the speeches to their constituents of members of Parliament sitting for the large London boroughs and in the columns of the ribald 'Weekly Despatch.' At Birmingham early in January — even after the probabilities of a peaceful outcome seemed overwhelming — an audience of six thousand persons decisively rejected arbitration in favor of an amendment proposed by a working man expressing complete confidence in Russell and Palmerston. Nevertheless, it is fair to say that labor was not as completely carried away by the excitement of the moment as most other groups of the people. It was of the working men in the towns that Bright was thinking when he put forth the claim, adopted by Cobden, that there was no town in which a public meeting would not vote for arbitration; and though Birmingham (an arms manufacturing center) gave him the lie in the literal sense, there is other evidence besides Bright's own prestige and knowledge of the manufacturing districts to show that he was speaking of something real. Newman Hall, a popular Independent minister, convened a large and enthusiastic meeting of laboring men in London to listen to a fervent argument against alliance with slaveholders, and early in January a committee of working men called a public meeting in Brighton which passed resolutions calling for arbitration by an independent power. 'A Working Man' who sounds genuine wrote to the 'Huddersfield Examiner' that, without palliating foreign bravadoism, he wished to protest against the persons who seemed gladly to seize on every pretext to invoke the spirit of war. 'Some of the carpet heroes in this locality even go so far as to wish the Americans not to make the *amende honorable* lest we should be prevented thereby from giving them a good thrashing. Were some of these compelled to maintain a family of five or six children with fifteen or twenty shillings a week of their own earning, their valour, like that of Bob Acres, would soon ooze out.'

The gradual marshaling of the forces of peace was an interesting process, and if it could be fully seen, would be a curious study in leadership. The more men thought about war with America, the more distasteful the prospect became. The swing — it must be remembered that it was a swing of certain elements only — was quite slow. The 'Birmingham Daily Post,' usually very sympathetic with Bright and most of the time pretty friendly to the North, went off into spasms of belligerency at first, and it was only after nearly two weeks that it began to come around to Manchester views again. The 'Leeds Mercury,' property of the energetic Edward Baines and the chief lay organ of the Nonconformists, passed from a phase of extreme hostility through perfect confidence in Palmerston to an inclination toward arbitration; for lack of complete analysis we may attribute this evolution to a combination of Cobdenite pressure on it with realization of the waxing opinion of its constituents against war. A very few other newspapers, after the first shock, failed to fall in with the prevalent excitement — the doctrinaire 'Morning Star' and the more important 'Manchester Examiner'; the 'Daily News' (though it could not advise the Government to be other than 'firm'); the 'Liverpool Chronicle'; the 'Sunderland Times'; but the majority of the press reflected rather than led the changing course of public opinion.

In the midst of the confusion of hopes, guesses, fears, there occurred one of the few events which could have served to divert attention from the international crisis. This was the sudden death of the Prince Consort on December 14, which aroused nation-wide sentiments quite different from the speculations which for over two weeks had engrossed the public mind. All the nation's loyalty to a queen who had already ruled for nearly a quarter of a century was aroused by this loss of a prince who, if he had enjoyed little popularity, had yet come to be respected and was known to be infinitely close to the affections of Her Majesty. America could be partly forgotten in the preparations for national mourning, while knowledge of the prostration of the Queen rendered doubly abhorrent the notion of warring with the power to which she had recently been sending thanks for its reception of her son, and conflict with which would mean bereavement for not a few less illustrious English families. Feelings were not so much changed as softened and attenuated at this time.

Shortly came further mails from America, containing the President's annual message to Congress, the vote of thanks of the House of Representatives to Captain Wilkes, and the congratulations of the Secretary of the Navy. Lincoln's failure to mention the capture of the Southern Commissioners was rather chilling to those who were bound to see in every act of the Northern Government an intention to insult England, and was a cause of real hopefulness to the greater number who were anxious only for signs of conciliation. What the President gave, the House of Representatives and Secretary Welles, to be sure, tried to take away; but in the balance the President's word had the greater weight, and, with General Scott's letter, was one of the major calming factors of those intense six weeks. A little later still was published the note of the French Foreign Minister to the American Government advising that Mason and Slidell be given up and quite emphatically supporting the law and justice of England's demand. This 'manful support of us' (the phrase, amusingly enough, is that of the Francophobe Lord Malmesbury) could not much change opinion, but it greatly improved hopes of peace, in spite of those who would have preferred to have France keep her hands off England's affairs.

It is remarkable that during the whole crisis so little was said about the Confederacy. Reading closely, however, one may see that there was in most Englishmen a very decided aversion to adopt a position of open alliance with slaveholders. Intervention by Great Britain to stop a hopeless and fratricidal civil war would be a move defensible by many arguments; but intervention in the character of an angry belligerent suddenly siding with the slave States presented moral objections to which nine men out of ten were sensitive.

It is also true that economic motives were at this time preponderantly discouraging to the war fever. The business community of Liverpool, the center for cotton importation, appeared to pass into spasms of belligerency, yet when scrutinized the degree of unanimity of this feeling proves to have been grossly exaggerated and it is likely that a good deal of it was due to the desire of speculators to raise cotton prices for a moment. On the other side operated fear of American privateers, which was acute and genuine, and, after a little delay, the aversion of holders of cotton to a sudden opening of the ports of the South. Liverpool did not want war so much as the Independent success of the Confederacy. Manchester, where the greater part of cloth made was still going into stock rather than being sold, was even less warlike, and the strong party desirous of building up cotton cultivation outside of America was naturally anxious that a war should not remove the motives for planting cotton in

India and elsewhere.[1] Furthermore, heavy investments in American railway and other securities were held in the Manchester region, and a prolonged war would destroy their value.

If the influence of cotton was not enough to create a strong willingness to break the blockade by means of war, one might look to shipping as possibly not averse. A portion of the shipowners, particularly on the Tyne and the Clyde, were frankly jubilant at the prospect of war, which would give the final blow to American competition and enable England eventually to extort the privileges of the American coasting trade. On the other hand, the important 'Shipping Gazette,' though often pessimistic, was not anxious for war, and the fact which was continually present to all shipowners was that however low war insurance might be in consequence of English naval supremacy, some risks a belligerent must undergo, which could not but inure to the advantage of neutral competitors. Even during the period of waiting, the war premium demanded by underwriters was hurtful to British shipping engaged in the Far East. It seems safe to say that shipping men, though not unwilling to accept war, did not see enough prospect of gain in it to make them in any wise eager.

The truth is that estimates differed very widely as to what the effects of hostility with the United States would really be, and commercial views varied accordingly. Birmingham, Sheffield, and the South Staffordshire iron trade stood to gain by war and expressed their views accordingly. On the other hand, it was realized that

[1] As a matter of fact the price of cotton did go down enough to cause the cancellation of some large orders for the Indian staple.

England had in 1861 been importing far more largely of American grain, flour, and provisions than ever before, and that the cutting-off of this supply was not to be lightly envisaged. Undoubtedly a strong deterring factor also was the prevalent belief that the Civil War would not in any event last many months longer. The financial management of the North was striking horror into the breasts of English business men and was expected by many to result in imminent exhaustion; or, it was thought, the South might succumb from similar pressure or from failure to produce enough foodstuffs to support itself; or Napoleon III might intervene and pull British chestnuts out of the fire; or, improbable but not unthinkable, the North might even come to its senses and realize that it could not conquer the South.

The near approach to unanimity with which Englishmen accepted the gage of battle they assumed to have been thrown down itself served to induce satisfaction and to relax tension. Commercial cupidity, jealousy, spite, fear, and resentment all played their parts in this episode, but the dominant motive, without any question, was simply national pride, and if it could be satisfied, little else would be necessary.

On January 8, 1862, the American reply, consenting to give up the prisoners, though without formal apology, reached England. The worst was over well before this date. Although 'the most painful anxiety' was felt in some quarters up to the last moment, Thurlow Weed in London was largely freed from his worries by the end of December, the price of consols had risen a point and a half in the first four days of January, and the price of cotton had surpassed its previous high point by the third of the month. Certainty of peace was generally welcomed, for the most part sincerely and with enthusiasm. The myth that the Washington Cabinet wanted a war with England was dispelled, though some persons professed to be alarmed by the very argumentative tone of Seward's dispatch. The long six weeks of discussion had enabled the press and public speakers to indulge in a deal of patting of backs, and when all turned out happily, men were disposed to consider everything done as exactly right. A few of the extremer Tories were sorry and exulting in the same breath. 'There is a general feeling of regret that they [the Yankees] did not persist in holding the prisoners, but it is giving way to the opinion that the Northerners have humiliated themselves in the eyes of Europe, and have thoroughly exposed their bad qualities. The victory is as great as though we had sunk their fleet.' 'It is unmistakable,' we read in another place, 'that the firm, though temperate proceedings of the British Government — backed by the universal indignation of the British people — have had their due effect, and have at last convinced the Government and people of the United States that we are not to be trifled with for even a moment, when the honour of our country is at stake. So far from being offended with us for the attitude we have taken, they ought to be proud of coming from such a stock.' In short, this was one of those agreeable occasions when every one had been victorious — England over America, Lincoln over his supposed mob, peace over war.

The reaction was decidedly in favor of the North. People had been forced to consider the meaning of alliance with the Confederacy and had not been attracted; Manchester, pressure from which had been expected, had held off from the war fever and continued to speculate on a rising market; Englishmen were disposed to feel kindly toward an antagonist who had provided them with a comparatively costless victory. They were a little impressed, too, with the relatively small place which the Trent business had occupied in American attention, and some were surprised at the vigor with which the anti-slavery people were now issuing from their holes and corners. The general feeling was, naturally if not very logically, that if the North did after all have sense enough to avoid plunging into new complications, it should be given an opportunity to labor yet a little further at its impossible self-appointed task. 'Show us that you can win and we shall have nothing more to say; but we do not see any likelihood that you will do so.' Such was the tone of British comment, and the trend was thus diagnosed by competent observers.

3

THE GENTLEMEN AND THE MASSES
THE KEYNOTE OF BRITISH OPINION

THE winning side in America would undoubtedly be treated with great courtesy by English opinion, which after all was chiefly anxious for the unreasonable war to stop. But so long as the struggle continued and neither party was victorious, practical questions of policy and events worthy of remark were constantly arising. The attention of Parliament and the press was thus sustained for a long period, while the struggle as a whole was a complex fact which claimed a high degree of interest from Englishmen of all classes. In order to understand the series of American questions which came before the Cabinet and Parliament, it is necessary to examine the relations of America to English political questions.

The general election of 1859, which seated Lord Palmerston in power for six years and the rest of his life, turned on foreign affairs and on parliamentary reform. Although its result was the substitution of a 'Liberal' Ministry for that of Lord Derby, the victory was less a party one than might be imagined. Not only was the nominal majority of the veteran leaders, Palmerston and Russell, a small one, but it was a majority representing a coalition of shifting and uncertain elements. While the new Chancellor of the Exchequer, Gladstone, did not resign his membership in the Carlton Club until 1860, Cobden, chief of the Manchester School, had been offered a place in the Cabinet and his associate Milner Gibson had taken one. The Ministry, as Gladstone said, was not Burke's famous mosaic, but a mosaic in solution, that is to say, a kaleidoscope — composed of men for the most part of aristocratic tastes, strong and able personalities, and doubtful party discipline. The Liberal Party was almost impossible of definition at this period.

The problem of Lord Palmerston — for he, far more than Lord John Russell, was the political head of the Ministry — was twofold. He had to preserve working harmony within a Cabinet where differences of temper and outlook were marked; and he had, at the same time, to handle all unavoidable parliamentary questions in such a way as not to drive into the opposition ranks at one time any considerable part of the rather large floating population of the House of Commons. One of the chief reasons for his success in this task was the predominant place which foreign affairs took in public attention between 1859 and 1865, for this not only diverted the demand for domestic reform, but was a field in which Palmerston enjoyed a high degree of popular confidence. It is also true that Gladstone, the powerfully growing colleague who caused most Cabinet difficulty, was himself attracting reformers' confidence which might otherwise have turned against the aged Premier.

However we may view the delicate balance of political forces, it is clear that this Ministry was to an unusual degree a national one, opposed perfunctorily and half-heartedly by Conservatives who were as good as supporting it. Yet many of them did, in the course of a few years, grow somewhat hungry for the sweets of office. In this situation, when no groups in the country seemed to want anything very badly, the Government was left to work out for itself lines of conduct consonant with the national welfare and public opinion. And it paid particular attention to public opinion and was, at least so far as concerns England's foreign relations, on the whole successful in pursuing a popular policy.

II

Under the party truce, however, under even the discussion of all foreign matters, was fermenting the significant question of the ultimate location of political power. This problem, known in nineteenth-century England as that of parliamentary reform, had a persistence and an insistence all its own. It kept bobbing up in all sorts of discussions, insinuating itself into all kinds of problems. Every one who wanted any institutional change was tempted by the democratic ideal; every one who was satisfied with things as they were tended to dread an extension of the franchise. Since 1832 the notion that the reform of that year was 'final' had been gradually abandoned, yet very little progress had been made in the development of a theory of the franchise. There were many Tories who were quite certain that the British constitution would never be improved, but who were equally unwilling to provoke revolution by resisting its degradation; there were many old Whigs who rather wanted to be able to pose as Liberals, but who thought that tinkering with the franchise and the boroughs had gone far enough; while the upper layers of the middle class, who were told that they were ruling

England, were quite satisfied if that was the case. On the other hand, all those persons who desired particular reforms — regarding the game laws, trade unions, 'financial reform,' Dissenters' grievances, and so forth — could see no other path to their goals than a great extension of the right to vote.

To a very high degree the United States belonged to the debate on these matters. That country had embarked on a governmental experiment, the theory of which was closely allied to French Jacobinism, and that experiment, social as well as political, was felt to have great significance. Jacobinism, to be sure, had gone more or less to smash, but American democracy had not. If 'liberty' of the English variety was anywhere subject to serious criticism, it was not in the politically backward countries of the Continent, but in the universal suffrage system, based as it was on English law, of the United States. Americans themselves saw this and somewhat truculently urged the advantages of their free country on the attention of Englishmen. Even more to the point was the fact that certain groups of Englishmen were already converts — and, furthermore, many who did not believe in American principles nevertheless subscribed reluctantly to De Tocqueville's thesis that democracy, desirable or not, possessed the future and could not be escaped. It was about the middle of the century that the danger of an Americanized England began to be stressed as imminent — an alarming peril which has truly increased with the passage of time.

Sir John Acton, speaking soon after the close of the Civil War, summed up the situation in measured and emphatic terms: 'Now the experience of the Americans is necessarily an impressive lesson to England. Our institutions as well as our national character spring from the same roots, and the fortunes they encounter must serve as a beacon to guide us, or as a warning to repel. Now the world had never yet beheld a Democracy combining a very advanced civilisation with a very extensive territory.... It had almost become an axiom in political science that... Democracy, to be consistent with liberty, must subsist in solution and combination with other qualifying principles, and that complete equality is the ruin of liberty, and very prejudicial to the most valued interests of society, civilisation, and religion. That was, until a generation ago, the verdict of history; whose decision the Americans have undertaken to reverse. [If America under pure Democracy could give a refutation of this view], then I believe that the venerable institutions of European polity would go down before that invincible argument.'

It was this belief that in large part explains the subacidly controversial tone of so large a proportion of British writing on America, that explains, indeed, the 'conspiracy' of denigration which has so annoyed certain Americans. America was for Englishmen but a part of an endless political campaign within England itself, and was used as a stick with which to belabor domestic opponents. If democracy was the inevitable fate of Europe in the near or distant future, it remained to ask what democracy would be and how it would affect English life. As most persons judged democracy by a combined view of France, England, and the United States, their opinions of it were very often unfavorable. Universal suffrage had led in France, as was infinitely repeated, to the despotisms of the First and Second Empires; it had led in the United

States to a society of tobacco-chewers, political duelists, and border ruffians — in a word, to anarchy; while British limited monarchy with a governing class or classes had secured the blessings of liberty, prosperity, and high intellectual culture. 'By men of all parties,' wrote a reviewer, 'democracy is condemned.... But what is strange and very sad is, that to men of all parties, with a few individual exceptions... democracy nevertheless, the absolute dominion of mere numbers, seems to be inevitable. It is the dark destiny of England at a future day....'

Conservatives in the wider rather than in the party sense were in fact retiring on their last defenses about 1860 and did not know but that any day they might find themselves fighting in the last ditch. Change had gnawed steadily at the old order since about 1820 and was stealthily sapping the foundations of the social order which had seen the days of English greatness. The opening of the franchise and creation of equal electoral districts would be only the crowning folly in a process that had already gone perhaps fatally far. Compulsory church rates were tottering in annual peril; the removal of the taxes on knowledge was providing the multitude with a cheap, licentious, and potentially revolutionary press; members of the House of Lords had been heard advocating the secret ballot; and, what was most disquieting of all, the very men who ought to have been the ministers of stability, men such as Gladstone and Disraeli, were themselves dallying with reforms.

Nevertheless, the two or three years beginning with 1860 witnessed what was called a 'Conservative reaction.' Two reform bills in succession, sponsored respectively by Disraeli and Lord John Russell, had failed of passage, while the Commons' majority for the abolition of church rates fell steadily. Bye-elections in 1860 and 1861 seemed to show a steady drift away from advanced views, and Conservatives even gained a few seats which had long been held by the other party. On the whole, apathy in political matters marked the electorate, and this itself, being the absence of popular agitation, was part of the Conservative reaction — a reaction, be it repeated, which was by no means a threat to Palmerston.

It was in this situation, when a people politically minded to an extraordinary degree was relatively indifferent to politics, that the American crisis came to hand. For decades the affairs of the United States had been used in England especially by two classes of publicists, the more advanced Radicals and the more active Conservatives. John Bright in particular had decidedly overdone the appeal to the example of America, to which he had pointed constantly as an instance of the benefits of popular government, a country ruled by and for the people, peaceful and without a national debt, where there was no selfish aristocracy with its game laws and monopoly of public office, no standing army to menace world peace, where government was cheap and the people lightly taxed, where there was small need of poor laws and workhouses, where the absence of social barriers opened the way to talent and abilities from whatever source they sprang. The chief weakness in this case, aside from its not too serious inaccuracies, was its ignoring of the non-political conditions which were the real cause of the advantages of which he spoke. But in this period when governmental institutions were commonly viewed as the determinant of the ways in which civilization developed, few of Bright's opponents tried to force him off his own ground. They accused him, it is true, of talking about a country where conditions were not the same as those of England; but with surprising consistency the trend of their refutations was simply an examination of American facts to show that he and his like had misapprehended them. In this they were not entirely successful. However much British travelers might say about the disagreeable 'domestic manners' of the Americans, about the discomfort of their railway trains and hotels, the sensationalism of their press, and the Elijah Pogramism of their public men, every one knew that ordinary workaday Englishmen were constantly settling in America and there becoming prosperous and satisfied, though Americanized; every one knew that material welfare and social freedom were there more widely spread than in the old world. The Tory reply that America was anarchical and headed for the rocks of disunion, or that practically all Americans connived at slavery out of dollar-hunting materialism and megalomaniac nationalism, was too vague and insincere to be effective.

III

Thus the arrival of the long-predicted crisis in the United States found partisans in England waiting and eager. Almost a sigh of relief went up to the effect that 'now Mr. Bright will be forced to stop wearying us with his blessings of universal suffrage and of government by numbers.'

'Democratic institutions,' said 'The Times' after Lincoln's election, 'are now on their trial in America' — and for once it seems to have been right. A Scotch Whig wrote in January, 1861: 'Liberals like ourselves who had long looked with pride and hope to the splendid fabric of free government and national and commercial greatness, built up by our kinsmen across the sea... feel as if their own principles had exhibited a failure, and as if the capacity of mankind for self-government had been half refuted.' 'John Bull,' the weekly of perfect Toryism, hastened to precede the less partisan press in leading articles on 'Uncle Sam in Pieces' and 'The Untied States,' and the 'Liverpool Courier' could hardly restrain its delight over the blow American events were dealing to the doctrines of the Manchester School. The earliest stage of the 'Saturday Review,' when it was still cautiously friendly to the Union, shows clearly the motive which was to make of it one of the most savage opponents of the North. In spite of their appeals to English self-interest, said this journal, 'the seceders have not seduced a dozen Englishmen into sympathy with their revolt, or impaired in the slightest degree the universal wish that their ambition may be disappointed. And if the country deserves credit for having withstood the bribe of cheap cotton, still more does the greatest part of it merit praise for not having exulted at events which are, morally speaking, a sounding slap in the face to Mr. Bright. We cannot, indeed, prevent this passage in American history from carrying its own moral. ... But blood is thicker than water, and the confutation of an English demagogue is felt to be less important than the maintenance of the sister-State which is yoked with us to the chariot of freedom.' Two weeks later, the same review said that one of the first thoughts of Englishmen on the American rupture must be 'that the quarrel has a material bearing on the question of parliamentary reform.... The shallow demagogues of Birmingham[1] and

[1] Bright was member of Parliament for Birmingham.

other kindred platforms must bear the blame of the inference, drawn nearly universally at the present moment, that, if the United States become involved in hopeless difficulties, it would be madness to lower the qualification for the suffrage in England.' The degradation of the Americans, said another writer, is a most painful sight, but full of instruction to Englishmen — 'what they are, we may become, unless we study their career and avoid their mistakes; it is impossible for our statesmen and political philosophers to delve in any richer mine.'

It is, in fact, quite fair to say that the most considerable portion of the English press and of English public men fell into line on American subjects according to their already settled attitude on the democratic doctrines of the Manchester School. On May 27, 1861, Sir John Ramsden in the House of Commons said that the republican bubble had burst, on which the American Secretary of Legation commented: 'His remark was very warmly cheered by the Tory side, and not much disapproved by the Liberal. I was a little surprised, but only a little, at this.' Very many of the lucubrations of 'The Times' were plainly inspired by a willingness to agree that democracy had broken down; the 'Saturday Review,' most brilliant of all the weeklies, was frankly governed by the same feeling; and the Tory press without exception showed the political prepossession in fullest bloom. Public men likewise pointed with horror to the United States. Major Beresford — who, said 'The Times,' was as significant in Essex as Cobden in Lancashire — refuted democratic theories with gusto by the lamentable condition of America: 'these were the blessed effects of Republican institutions, and this was the position to which Radicalism would bring

England.' No more accurate, concise statement could be made of the Tory attitude, which, however, was sometimes embellished, as by the former Cabinet Minister who phrased the curious belief 'that the real instigation for this terrible war was the shame they [the Americans] felt that the world should witness the disruption of that great experiment.'

Two considerations became commonplaces in the summer of 1861. For one thing the United States was ruled by a mob: the executive was helpless, the legislature powerless, before it, and matters in controversy must be determined not by 'justice or expediency, but in accordance with the will of an inflamed and exasperated population.' In the second place, Americans were almost simultaneously, in a sort of Platonic progression, giving themselves up to the most arbitrary and cruel of executive despotisms — a despotism which was occasionally likened to that of King Bomba at Naples.

To the charges against America, all reducible to the claim that democratic institutions had proved their unfitness, reformers found it hard to reply. Harriet Martineau, favoring both democracy and the North, wrote that 'the despair of the American case is in the vices of democratic government'; while John Stuart Mill, equally staunch in his beliefs, admitted that the crisis had exhibited all the defects of the American social system. Though Bright and his colleagues on radical platforms were not immediately silenced by American events, as their opponents said they should be, the blow was truly a hard one, and reformers admitted it to be such. 'The Examiner,' commenting on 'English Feeling Towards America,' said that the predominant sentiment was sorrow over the existence of civil war. 'It is certainly impossible for any right-thinking man to look on such a spectacle with supercilious indifference or speak of it with any kind of satisfaction. Bad men and mad men there are, we are sorry to say, amongst us, who not merely do so in private, but who are not ashamed even in public to give vent to a selfish and sinister glee at what they mistake for the break down of popular government on the other side of the Atlantic. Before a campaign has been begun or a battle fought, these birds of ill omen raise their exultant cry... over the ruin of the vast home of republican liberty, which has always been to them a cause of spite and spleen.' William Howard Russell, the war correspondent, wrote to Charles Sumner: 'I do not approve of the tone of many papers in Great Britain in reference to American matters, but do not forget I pray you that in reality it is Brightism and republicanism at home which most of these remarks are meant to smite — America is the shield under which the blow is dealt....'

The gentle art of journalistic curvature was brought into play in the first year of the war by very many Liberal editors, and not a few men who had seen good in the reform proposals of 1860 now admitted, without apparent inconsistency, that it was perhaps well that the constitution had not been tampered with. A Northumberland Conservative was not far from the truth when he asserted that only the more infatuated of the English Radicals had persisted long in the belief that the existence of free institutions was involved in the American struggle, while 'the most respectable' of the Liberal press had completely given up the laudation of democracy.

Those who had previously been accustomed to looking

toward America for one of the main buttresses of their arguments were now, in fact, sadly encumbered. Reform associations in provincial towns languished and in some cases went out of existence, and platform speakers, who could not ignore America, were forced into an attitude of rather lame defense. Northern policy and the pronouncements of Northern leaders had discouraged the anti-slavery people, whose quandary was rather pathetic, and their absence made it more difficult for those who were interested only secondarily in slavery to use that shield to ward off the storm of political attacks. Little more could be said than that democratic institutions were *not* responsible for the disruption of the United States, and that slavery, in spite of the disclaimers of President Lincoln, was the real cause of disunion. The fact seems obvious enough to a subsequent generation, but in that time when political institutions were seen as the cause of social phenomena, and when such great importance was habitually given to questions of free trade and protection, there was a good deal of excuse for those who did not see beneath the surface. Yet it is curious that of those who in 1861 were clear that the issue between North and South was one of slavery, practically all were convinced reformers in British politics.

Democracy was not the only dilemma of the Liberals. Even should they forbear to turn away their faces from the Union in sorrow or in anger at the blow to Liberal principles, how could they give their sympathy to a Government fighting to reduce to obedience a numerous and resolved people who declared only that they wanted independence? Acton, the very apostle of liberty among politicians and scholars, saw in the assertion of State rights the essential qualities of liberty, while in the North he discerned the principle of imperial domination, the omnipotence of a majority just as tyrannical as any oligarchy or despotism. More frivolously, 'The Times' defined the difference between a 'nation' and a 'nationality' as lying in the fact that 'the latter is conventionally regarded as a proper object of foreign sympathy. No one ever heard of a nationality that was not an "oppressed nationality."' The South was fighting to get free of the North, and asked only its independence; was it not, then, just as much oppressed as had been the Continental Colonies in 1775, and would it not be a reversal of recent British policy — as instanced in the cases of Greece, Belgium, Hungary, and Italy — to refuse her moral aid and sympathy? The 'Daily News' put the matter succinctly: 'It is the misfortune of liberals in the Old World that they have been accustomed to associate the triumph of "law and order" over revolution with defeat of liberty and the slaughter of a people.' Revolutions were by no means always right — but attempts to put revolution down were almost invariably wrong. The recent half-analogies on the Continent were too strong for many Liberals — though with the real Mazzinian republicans it was quite another matter.

It is not, unfortunately, possible to study in a general election the degree to which the trans-Atlantic catastrophe formed subject-matter for English politics. Two bye-elections, occurring in the interval after the parliamentary session of 1861, are, however, worth looking at in this connection. The first was the election of a representative for a new, third seat in the division of South Lancashire. The opposing candidates were Charles Turner, chairman of the Liverpool Dock Board, a 'Liberal Conservative,'[1] and John Cheetham, former member for the division, president of the Cotton Supply Association, and a member of the Cobden-Bright political group. America figured very largely in the contest. John Bright brought his aid to Cheetham, accused Turner of having been a protectionist, and argued that Cheetham's efforts to secure an independent cotton supply deserved recognition, for interference or sympathy on the side of the slave confederacy would not ensure the safety of English manufacturers' interests. Turner in reply gladly identified Cheetham with Bright, whom he quizzed about his praise of France and the United States, saying that if Bright exercised the right of free speech in America as he did in England, he would be strung up to a tree or at least tarred and feathered. At the nominations, where each candidate presented himself before an open-air audience, Turner concluded his speech by asking the electors 'whether you prefer the principles of the Conservative party, the principles of attachment to our Constitution, with such amendments as may be found necessary to improve our institutions, or whether you prefer those revolutionary doctrines of the separation of Church and State, vote by ballot, triennial Parliaments, and American democracy, which are advocated by Mr. Cheetham.' Cheetham's reply dodged the American issue, and he obviously tried to avoid the impression that the reforms which he advocated were American at all in their nature. At a large Conservative meeting in Liverpool the same charge was repeated by almost every speaker: Cheetham wants to Americanize the English Constitution; Turner is truly British. In the editorial columns of the

[1] Liberal Conservatives were Conservatives willing to support Palmerston.

press the situation was the same: Cheetham is 'a sort of *half-bred American*... a wild *Americanizer*... an un-English politician'; while the Liberals, though maintaining their specific reform demands, avoided, so far as possible, the mention of the United States.

The Conservatives won the seat by a vote of 9714 to 8898, nearly ninety per cent of the electors voting. It is impossible to say what was the decisive factor in the result, but the vote of the Catholics was commonly held to have turned the election. 'The Times' remarked that 'the only issue fairly raised' between the candidates was 'on the present posture of affairs in America, the one pointing to the disruption of the Union as a warning to Democrats, and the other identifying the two sources of that disruption — Slavery and Protection — with the abuses under those names once patronized by the English Tories.' 'South Lancashire' wrote to the same paper to supplement this editorial, saying that Turner's victory was one of moderate Conservatism and moderate Liberalism over 'advanced Liberalism,' which 'is essentially anti-English; its disciples are one year Russians, the next Chinamen, Americans they are always, true-hearted Britons never.' A Liverpool journal, lamenting the failure of the Liberals, threw all the blame on the support given by Bright, 'at present the most unpopular man in England.' 'It is vain to disguise the reaction in the minds of the English people at this time, not that they have a distaste for progressive amendments, even in our representation, but a feeling of uneasiness has got abroad that we were drifting into a current... the end of which no prudent politician could see. Now, it is well to consider the causes which have given rise to this change, and no doubt it originated in the arbitrary demands of the Trades' Unions and the hopeless stand which the more sensible of the working classes made against the socialistic principles of their leaders. To these were added the wild and anarchical proceedings of the Legislatures in Australia, where universal suffrage and vote by ballot had become the rule; and lastly, and probably above all, the complete failure of Republican institutions in America, where a supposed popular form of Government had degenerated into a mob despotism.'

Another bye-election shows a different facet of the situation. The borough of Carlisle had been usually Liberal, but had returned a protectionist as one of its members in 1847 and 1848, and the same gentleman, W. T. Hodgson, merely as a Conservative in 1857. On the death of Sir James Graham in 1861, the same candidate, a local figure, promptly issued his address, and the Liberals as quickly started the rival candidacy of Edmund Potter of Manchester. Potter was a large calico printer, president of the Manchester Chamber of Commerce, and a Unitarian. The issue was so clearly one between Tory and Radical that constructive argument, definitions, and interpretations were hardly necessary. What happened was that both candidates said that, in general, they stood for peace and non-intervention — which meant that neither was prepared to make difficulties for Palmerston — and then proceeded to abuse each other. Potter declared positively (in November, 1861) against breaking the blockade of the Southern ports, and advised the development of India as a source of cotton and a market for British goods; while Hodgson did not commit himself on this point. The Liberal was accused of belonging to a sect of people no better than atheists, and, on the strength of his advocacy of the secret ballot, of wishing to extend the suffrage to an American length. This Potter denied: Mr. Hodgson spoke of the warning from America. 'I think the warning is to America. If America had abolished slavery and encouraged free trade she would never have exhibited the melancholy spectacle she does at present.... It is not her democracy that is causing her troubles, though I have not the slightest wish to imitate her institutions — far from it.' The outcome of the election was not in any way significant. The electors voting were fewer than eleven hundred, and Potter was successful by a majority of three, attributed in the local press to the fact that the twenty-five Catholic electors had failed to plump unanimously for the Conservative! However that may be, the occasion throws a little further light on the function of America in English politics.

IV

As a matter of fact, the political currents cannot with any reality be separated from more general social considerations. Political thought has in all times been but the main branch of social philosophy, and never is this more true than when the position of an aristocracy is in question. Politically speaking, England in the nineteenth and twentieth centuries overtook and possibly passed America in the development of what may be called democratic control; on the other hand, democratic manners and social customs have failed there to keep logical pace with the universalization of the suffrage franchise. Some observers are inclined to the belief that even after the Great War the most conspicuous mark of difference between Great Britain and the United States is the presence of a much greater degree of social stratification in the older country, the existence of *classes* more clearly defined than those across the Atlantic, and much more adequately supplied with conventions of intercourse between them as such. The career open to talents is a ladder of separate rungs in England, not an inclined plane.

It was the social and political implications of democracy — seen as one general phenomenon — that were in large part responsible for the hostility of the upper classes to constitutional 'reform' — or, if you please, to America — in the mid-Victorian period. That is the thought underlying the unpleasant connotations of the word 'Americanization.' The boisterous, formless, *vulgar* American democracy could not be sympathetic to a society in which every one knew his place and acted accordingly, a society in which the best elements were recognized and given their due. The most durable and effective of British criticisms of the American form of government has always been that under it the type of citizen most valuable to the community was in the main excluded from participation in its government, thus leaving to the demagogue and the grafter an all too important rôle. In England the gentleman as a gentleman was given much, and much was expected of him; and if the upper class was sometimes selfish and narrow, it had nevertheless a good deal of justification for thinking itself a most useful and desirable part of society. If democracy added to expatriate Englishmen meant America, there was no telling what might be the result of democracy plus domestic Englishmen: should it be the loss of the wise and propertied classes, the development of a wooden nutmeg code of commercial honor, and the growth of a metropolitan press like the 'New

York Herald,' then it was certainly to be hoped that the Americanizing process might be early arrested.

The point must be emphasized that much of English antipathy was not to persons or causes, but to types. The English had no objection to a gentleman whencesoever he came, and while Richard Cobden could breakfast in close conversation with James M. Mason, Seward's partner Thurlow Weed could dine freely in the company of Southern sympathizers. J. L. Motley, who was at home in just the society in London that was most predominantly Southern, does not seem to have found that his ardent Unionism seriously chilled the atmosphere. On the other hand, the upper class English saw the majority of Americans as vulgarians and their ways of doing things as objectionable. J. S. Mill himself commented on the way in which 'the very best people' were disappointed by the low tone of American politics — 'and all the more so because it is the likeness of what we may be coming to ourselves....' Leslie Stephen, another friend of the North, wrote in the United States that he found it difficult to explain to his hosts the true nature of English misunderstanding: 'I really don't know how to translate into civil language what I have heard a thousand times over in England: that both sides are such a set of snobs and blackguards that we wish they could both be licked, or that their armies are the scum of the earth and the war got up by contractors, or that the race is altogether degenerate and demoralized, and it is pleasant to see such a set of bullies have a fall. I really can't tell them all these little compliments, which I have heard in private conversations word for word, and which are a free translation of "Times" and "Saturday Review."...'

Between Bright, who never concealed his opinion of the British aristocracy, and Northern apologists who constantly asserted that the Civil War was being fought against an oligarchy, it is no wonder that the natural selfishness of class was aroused in England. Radicals never failed to remember that parliamentary reform was only a means to an end, and that end a social one. If Bright and his cohorts had their way, would not the House of Commons cease to be the best club in the land? Would it not become impossible to obtain servants who knew their place? Would not the game laws be entirely swept away? What even would be the fate of landed property? A member of the old governing class said in 1866: 'I no more believe that political democracy in England will be compatible with social aristocracy than I do that Colenso is compatible with Christianity. Perhaps an American England may produce a larger average of happiness than the existing system, but it would not be a country for gentlemen, and I for one would be quite strange in it.' There is an order of government intended by nature, wrote the historian Sir Archibald Alison during the American struggle, and it is the rule of the richer and more educated classes over the working classes; England is already becoming Americanized, with destructive effects horrible to behold. Or, as Archdeacon Denison wrote in the eighteen-nineties, 'if a man wants Democracy in England, he wants the biggest Revolution the country has ever seen, or thought of.'

As has been seen, it has been an axiom of British critics of the United States that the best men in that country are not called to the duties for which they are fitted, but are left to literature or money-making. It was not so in the South, where the leaders of the people really led. Aristocratic sympathy for the South was the sympathy of like for like. 'You know,' said the Duke in Disraeli's novel 'Lothair,' this Southern Colonel Campian 'is a gentleman; he is not a Yankee. People make the greatest mistakes about these things. He is a gentleman of the South; they have no property but land; and I am told his territory was immense. He always lived at Paris and in the highest style, disgusted of course with his own country. It is not unlikely he may have lost his estates now; but that makes no difference to me. I shall treat him and all Southern gentlemen, as our fathers treated the emigrant nobility of France.' R. H. Hutton, a keen observer also writing shortly after the close of the Civil War, said that it was sympathy with an aristocracy *qua* aristocracy which governed 'a large part of the country party, and of the House of Lords' in their pro-Southern sentiments. And it is interesting to note that James M. Mason — who is credibly reported to have chewed tobacco in the best society — returned English compliments with interest. In London he 'found far the larger portion of the élite but the type of our best Virginia circles.'

The critics of aristocracy, *mutatis mutandis*, point to the same facts. The essence of the American struggle, we learn from a pamphleteer, is Aristocracy against Democracy. 'It is to this forecast of the possible uprising of the popular political influence in the State, here at home, that we must ascribe the habitual abuse of the Americans of the North, and apologies for those of the South — the one section being simply Democratic Republics, the other governed by their slave-holding oligarchies! Our lords don't fear the latter, but do hate and fear the former.'

When I referred in conversation with an English gentleman to the preference of the working classes for the North, he promptly answered that the lower classes automatically took any views which were in opposition to the upper. Young Henry Adams, writing near the middle of the war, said: 'The old revolutionary leaven is working steadily in England. You can find millions of people who look up to our [American] institutions as their model and who talk with utter contempt of their own system of Government.' Of this attitude of the working men more will be said in later chapters.

The American question, as it was called, interlocked with the existing party divisions in England, yet was not exactly part of them. Potentially it was a party question of force, while actually it never became the matter for a crucial division in Parliament, for reasons to be indicated. Over many months of two sessions there were recurring expectations that it would soon become an issue; but so long as the party councils of the Opposition failed to make it an integral part of their strategy, individuals were free to indulge in their particular opinions. The trend toward one side or the other in the American conflict was thus left to be decided by current impressions and by the broad political and social views of the individual, so that for the greater part of the war expressions of sympathy or hostility for the contending parties did not denote a positive attitude in the problem of intervention. This fact, of course, was not often realized in America and explains a little of the mutual hatred that was aroused between the countries. Meanwhile the English judged the Americans from the point of view of a nation which was closely connected with them by fate as well as by blood, and made free use of their events and 'institutions' as illustrations in matters of domestic concern. America was to very important sections of English opinion interesting chiefly as characteristic of things which were to be desired or dreaded in the future of English society, and the Civil War provided a kaleidoscopic scene which greatly stimulated discussion.

4

PERSONAL INFLUENCES

AMONG the influences which serve to mould public opinion, not the least is that of the intellectual leaders of a generation. It will be interesting to see a little of the views on America of some of the men who were important in their day — men whose social philosophy was not quite as simple as that of abstract Tory and Radical. It should be pointed out, however, that the ultimate victory of the North gave justification to the friends of the Union, so that British biographical material, taken in the mass, does not furnish an adequate idea of the strength of sympathies with the Confederacy. The biographer, as well as the writer of reminiscences, tends to slur over the instances in which his subject was, judged by results, in the wrong. The consequence is that friendship for the North shows conspicuously in their books, while unsympathetic and hostile criticism has too often been forgotten or ignored.

I

The most influential thinkers in England in 1860 were probably Thomas Carlyle and John Stuart Mill, who toward the end of their lives came to typify and lead opposing conceptions of human society. Carlyle during the American Civil War was struggling to finish his 'Frederick the Great' and had little thought to give to passing events. He even admitted after the war that perhaps he had not seen into the bottom of the matter. His contemptuous opinion of the 'nigger emancipation' agitation had, however, been known since the notorious controversy with Mill in 1849–50, and in his conversation now he did not conceal his impatience with people who were 'cutting each other's throats, because one half of them prefer hiring their servants for life, and the other by the hour.' (August 30, 1862.) Carlyle's only published statement on the war appeared in 'Macmillan's Magazine' and is simply a Carlyleian elaboration of this impatience. Yet according to Moncure Conway, Carlyle 'respected the desire of the Americans to preserve their Union.' He was rather friendly than hostile to Americans; but he scorned the tendencies of uneducated democracy and feared the crash which would come from putting government into the hands of 'collective ignorance and folly.' Carlyle belonged to the number of Britons who believed that their country could follow America on the path of democracy only to its own destruction.

John Stuart Mill, on the other hand, the utilitarian, the individualist, the apostle of liberty unconsciously turning toward socialism, was not so greatly alarmed by the spectacle of American democracy and saw slavery only as an evil to be scotched. Thoroughly well informed on American history and politics, he could, in his own words, correct Englishmen 'of high principle and unquestionable liberality of opinion, who thought [the American quarrel] a dispute about tariffs, or assimilated it to the cases... of a people struggling for independence.' His first open discussion of the question was in an article in 'Fraser's

Magazine,' written immediately after the resolution of the Trent difficulty. In this brief paper Mill agreed that in regard to the Trent, England could not have acted otherwise than she did; but he thought that the manly and straightforward nature of the American reply ought to demonstrate 'even unlimited democracy to be a better thing than many Englishmen have lately been in the habit of considering it.' His main point was that the American contest owed its origin and continuance entirely to slavery, and that even an unwilling alliance of England with the slaveholding South would be an act she would heartily regret. A second article, published later in 1862 in the 'Westminster Review,' reaffirmed the thesis that no right-thinking Englishman could give any countenance to the oligarchic and barbarous slave power. These pronouncements undoubtedly had a certain influence, though Mill's public position had not yet reached its apogee. Having, as he said himself, performed his duty, Mill turned his attention to other things, though he later allowed his name to be used in connection with the pro-Northern agitation of 1863.

The book taken as the text of Mill's second article was John Elliot Cairnes's 'The Slave Power,' one of the best bits of pleading of the war. Cairnes was an Irish economist, later the intimate friend of Mill and Fawcett and one of the most eminent of the orthodox school. His work was first published in May, 1862, and was a lucid review of American history and a formidable indictment of the South. The indictment was the more effective because the author, though not without an underlying passion for righteousness, was scientific rather than sentimental. Cairnes desired England to give all her moral weight to the

North, but he did not foresee the possibility of a peaceful reunion between the sections and hoped that Northern military success would prepare the way for a territorial compromise which should isolate the South until its plague spot had festered away. Unlike Mill, Cairnes remained throughout the war an active worker in the Northern cause, and his lectures and letters to the newspapers were able and important.

Comparable on the other side to the work of Cairnes was James Spence's 'The American Union.' Spence was a youngish business man of Liverpool, who had been engaged, according to his own account, in a number of large commercial enterprises, including a contract for iron for the Illinois Central Railway, but who had been hard hit by the panic of 1857 and was not very prosperous in 1861. 'I am of those whom difficulties stimulate to mental exertion,' he said; in fact, he must have been one of the class of capable drifters, who inspire more confidence at first contact than in the long run. At any rate, and whatever his ultimate ideas of usefulness to the Confederacy, 'The American Union' was written to please himself and proved a most successful and influential book. The first edition appeared in November, 1861, and a fourth four months later. It had the honor of a long double notice in 'The Times' and was an arsenal of arguments for every one who wished reasons why the North should be blackened and why reunion was undesirable. According to Spence's thesis, federal government of all types is inherently unstable, and especially that of the American Constitution; while it is manifestly ridiculous to attempt to bind into one whole such a large and diverse territory as that of the former Union. The North has not even adhered to its own Constitution, which is conservative, but by adopting Jefferson's imported notions of ultra-democracy, has done much to create the intolerable situation of 1860. The Union has fostered and exaggerated all the vices and weaknesses of an untutored pioneer people, and by giving place in the national councils to abolitionists and protectionists has driven the South into its entirely legal secession. Slavery is of course bad, but the compulsory commercial alliance of the South with the North has helped more than anything else to perpetuate it, and the South when free will gradually work out emancipation. This book became the manual of Southern sympathizers in England, and in the eyes of Confederates did immense good to their cause.

Carlyle, Mill, Cairnes, and Spence were among the most potent personal influences which bore on the war — always excepting the journalists and politicians. But others than publicists had their views. Of men whose memory is mainly literary or scholarly, Lord Acton, the opponent of all tyranny, saw in the South the essential qualities of liberty, much as he sympathized with the Boers a generation later. Matthew Arnold was disgusted by all things American, and saw possibilities of a richer development of American civilization if political subdivision could be achieved. T. H. Green, the philosopher, was a young Oxford Fellow at the time of the Civil War, with an admiration of Bright and distrust of Palmerston which ensured pro-Northern feelings; and Henry Sidgwick, of about the same age, indulged similar leanings at Cambridge, though with an occasional revulsion from 'sentimental politics.' George Grote, on the contrary, philosophical Radical as he was, thought Mill one-sidedly abolitionist and 'never expected to have lived to think of' the Americans as unfavorably as he did. Froude and E. A. Freeman, historians, did not take sides during the war, and only the most common opinion of its outcome is evinced in the often cited title of the latter's unfinished work, 'History of Federal Government from the Foundation of the Achaian League to the Disruption of the United States.' Herbert Spencer thought separation of the sections desirable; but he did not seem to dislike Americans in general and had no friendship for the South as such. Benjamin Jowett, who contributed to the Anti-Slavery Society in 1861, favored the North at Oxford, where he was still the center of a famous controversy, and so did old William Whewell at Cambridge, whom Mill reported as feeling so strongly as to exclude 'The Times' from his house.

Monckton Milnes, poet, politician, and man of society, stood staunchly by the North, though he, like others, had moments of depression when he could 'see no gleam of good in anything American.' His biographer tells us that his position on this matter brought him the plaudits of the populace in Yorkshire and Lancashire, where he shared the popularity of Bright and Forster. Sir Edward Bulwer Lytton, who was an active Conservative politician as well as a man of letters, saw no adequate reason for the war and thought that the Americans would be the better for a monarch and a few hereditary gentlemen. Swinburne, Allingham, and the Rossettis are reported to have espoused the Union cause. Tennyson did not, being hurt by Northern denunciations of England, but he was fond of humming the 'Battle Hymn of the Republic.' Browning was decidedly 'Northern' and as a great talker must have been interesting in society. Dickens treated belief in the triumph of the North as a 'harmless hallucination'; while Thackeray, I believe, is not on record, though his kindly spirit must have been depressed at the slaughter going on; he had friends in the Union. Trollope traveled in America and published a book during the war; his views were 'Northern,' but he did not expect reunion. Ruskin, whose expressions are particularly full, was simply distressed by the spectacle of a bitter war in a thoroughly unjustifiable cause and said so in 'Fraser's Magazine.' Of less familiar lights, Joseph Parkes, the learned and garrulous biographer of Junius, objected to the violence of the North, with which side his wife was more sympathetic; and Martin Farquhar Tupper, author of a now forgotten best-seller called 'Proverbial Philosophy,' held pro-Northern views.

Some of the eminent men of science have left traces of their opinions on the war. Charles Darwin, with strong anti-slavery sentiments, lost sympathy with the North as the war progressed, complained like so many others of its 'bullying' tone toward the rest of the world, and, with his wife, came to wish for peace at any price. He agreed that American affairs were having 'a very Torifying influence on us all.' Huxley said of himself that, like most thoughtful Englishmen, his heart went with the South and his head with the North. While he had no love for Yankees, he believed the South to be struggling to uphold an ultimately impossible system which was bad for the whites. Sir J. D. Hooker, the intimate friend of Darwin and Huxley, read De Tocqueville while the American conflict was in progress. His opinions were anti-Northern rather than pro-Southern, and he believed, on biological grounds, that America and England could never be expected to be thoroughly friendly to one another. Some of the early devotees of the principle of natural selection found that it strengthened in their minds the idea of a natural aristocracy, in which sense it had some effect derogatory to the democracy of the Northern States. Adam Sedgwick, the geologist, felt the current fear of a powerful and aggressive United States and found the Civil War cruel and savage almost beyond precedent. Sir Charles Lyell, on the other hand, who had traveled extensively in America, took active part on the side of the North, joined the London Emancipation Society, and even went with a deputation to congratulate the American Minister on Lincoln's reelection in 1864.

II

The power of journalism in the mid-Victorian age was far greater than it is now and in forming public opinion journalists were more important than private persons or than the writers of books. Until about 1880, British journalism was largely covered by the decent veil of nominal anonymity. While the curtain was often lifted even to contemporaries, the fact that important articles, in the monthly and quarterly as in the daily press, always appeared unsigned and were as a rule truly anonymous to all but a few initiated readers, lent a degree of magisterial weight to the pronouncements thus made and greatly increased the power of journals and reviews which could be criticized only as 'organs' of schools of thought or shadowy groups of proprietors representing particular interests. The 'Saturday Review,' for example, could not possibly have been what it was but under conditions of complete reserve as to its contributors; nor, *a fortiori*, could 'The Times.'

Very little information has ever been divulged concerning the editorial writers of 'The Times' under Delane's editorship, but in regard to its special correspondents there has been less taciturnity. William Howard Russell, who is best described as a man with a genius for friendship and a talent for observation and vivacious writing, was sent to America by Delane just in time to witness the United States in the first half of April, 1861. He stayed there until the spring of 1862, when Secretary Stanton refused him permission to accompany McClellan to the Peninsula. During this period his letters to the leading journal formed by far the most influential source of knowledge on American affairs that was presented to British readers. His letters were reproduced everywhere that English was read, and in England his reports and generalizations were accepted as the most authoritative of all accounts from the seat of war. They penetrated to many persons who hardly ever saw a 'Times' leading article. Russell — known to Americans chiefly as the maligner of their army at Bull Run — saw much to condemn and much to admire in the uprising of the Northern people; and he broadcast his sometimes contradictory impressions frankly and without malice. Circumstances outside of the control of individuals, were they war correspondents or ministers, explain the British reaction against the North in the first summer of the war, and no personal peculiarities of Russell, for all his prestige, contributed to this. If he had not reported the rout of Bull Run, some one else would have; American accounts alone were sufficient to create the views which were held in

England on that affair. But Russell also made a longish tour of the seceded States before the mailing of his correspondence became too difficult — a journey which enhanced and crystallized his hatred of slavery and made him positively unable to act as a defender of the Confederacy. At the same time, as a journalist, he wrote fully of the determination of the South to secure its independence, and in that way helped not a little in the formation of English opinion of the inexpediency of the quarrel, though not himself one to call it wicked and senseless. He was convinced, however, that the Union could never be restored as it had been — a judgment for which he is hardly to be condemned.

Secretary Stanton made a great blunder in keeping 'The Times' correspondent away from the army and thus forcing him home. Russell was a better correspondent than any of his rivals or successors, less likely to lose himself in cliques or to take umbrage at the incidents of war-time; and he was quite acceptable to the Federal army officers under whose immediate countenance he would have to work. Not only that, but his return to England, of which every one knew, strongly confirmed beliefs of the tyranny and illiberality of the Northern Government, and did a good deal to render Englishmen suspicious of the official reports from Northern armies. Back in England, Russell late in 1862 published extracts from his diary in America. The book had an excellent sale and was reviewed with almost unanimous praise. In its equally stringent criticisms on both South and North, the effect was distinctly unfavorable to the South: the North could no longer be injured by anything said of it, while Russell's experiences served as a check to current admiration of the Confederates. Russell's biographer insists that after his return from America he preached far and wide the doctrine that the North was in the right and deserved to win; and Russell himself, at the close of the war, noted in his diary his conviction that 'The Times' had been all wrong and had gone counter to his advice in its abuse of the Americans. But he was also editor of the 'Army and Navy Gazette,' which existed for a vigorously pro-Southern constituency, and the columns of that journal are eloquent of anything rather than support of the Union or belief that it could win.

Charles Mackay was sent out as successor to Russell and remained in the United States until the end of 1865. Mackay was a journalist and *littérateur* who was convinced against the Unionist cause before he sailed, a fact which Delane knew when he sent him. Most of his time was spent in New York, where he consorted largely with Copperheads, as he did not choose to make himself welcome to Republicans. Mackay's correspondence did not have half the prestige of Russell's, but it fitted in splendidly with prevalent upper-class conceptions, and of course it was necessary for 'The Times' to have some one who could report on America as an Englishman. In the Confederacy also 'The Times' maintained a special writer for a while, though the arrival of his letters was too desultory to give satisfaction. This was a gentleman who had been a Liberal member of Parliament and private secretary to Gladstone, but who had spoiled his career by overindulgence in horse-racing and gambling. It is needless to say that he sympathized warmly with the Confederates.

The course of 'The Times' on the Civil War was natural, probably inevitable, and thoroughly bad. Leslie

Stephen as a young man exposed its inconsistencies and immoralities at that time with much warmth. But though its editor, Delane, 'ran' the leading journal in the amplest sense of the word, seeing that the leader writers carried out his instructions, the only measure of the judgment which can be passed upon 'The Times' is its success with its own public. Delane believed that the indefinite attrition of American power by the Americans themselves was a good thing for England, and 'The Times' acted accordingly. The leading journal and its most serious rival the 'Daily Telegraph' took the same line on American affairs, and both prospered.

Besides the writers of 'The Times,' a number of other Englishmen represented British journals in the country of civil conflict. The most widely read of these was George Augustus Sala, a literary figure turned journalist. Though he has lived longer in some pages of Matthew Arnold's than in his own writings, he was very successful and popular, with an incredible ease and verbosity in the art of expressing very small ideas embedded in a mass of personal anecdote. Sala was editor of the light monthly 'Temple Bar,' but he spent thirteen months in the United States as correspondent of the 'Daily Telegraph.' His contributions were immensely long and not very serious letters on the Americans and their war, letters not at all calculated to edify English readers on the subject of Northern morality and earnestness, and imbued with the one conviction that the genus *gentleman* was hardly represented in the Federal States. Sala tells us that his editors knew before asking him to go that his sympathies were Southern.

Another sort of traveler was Edward Dicey, a young

man known in 1861 as the author of a timely life of Cavour. Dicey, who was a grandnephew of Wilberforce and the brother of A. V. Dicey, wrote for 'The Spectator' and 'Macmillan's Magazine' in 1862, and had been known before his departure from England to take a 'Northern view' of the causes and ends of the war. He published a book on his experience, but it was not a success. A somewhat similar journalist was F. M. Edge, who had been several years in the United States and who undertook of his own motion a defense of the North. He left the 'Morning Herald' staff about the middle of 1861 and went to America for something like two years as special correspondent of the 'Morning Star.' The 'Star's' correspondence was earnest rather than brilliant.

The 'Morning Herald' and the evening 'Standard' — Mrs. Gamp and Mrs. 'Arris, as they were often called — did very well without sending out any English correspondent. Their writer was 'Manhattan,' a New-Yorker of Copperhead leanings, whose very strong American flavor, compounded of anti-Republican and Anglophobe sentiments in the vernacular of Jefferson Brick, was infinitely entertaining to British Conservatives. With never a kind word for the Washington Government or for the Negro, but with a rabid Unionism, this Joseph A. Scoville, a former private secretary of Calhoun, was a decided asset to the great Conservative dailies. It has been said that his communications 'often sent up the circulation of "The Standard" as much as 20,000 a day.' Manhattan's letters were quoted even by pro-Northern sheets and did incalculable harm to the cause of the Unionists. He was to the journalism of the Civil War what Cassius Clay was to its diplomacy. The prevalent ignorance of all things American lent much weight to the writings of individuals at the seat of war, even if they were composed in a New York hotel.

Two of the most effective opponents of the North were men for whom writing was only an avocation. In the 'Quarterly Review' in this period Lord Robert Cecil wrote the great majority of the American articles, which were very able. His mind was thoroughly clear and he was able without abusiveness to be pretty devastating at the expense of the sentimental democrats of England. In the other great Tory magazine, 'Blackwood's,' the chief contributor on America was E. B. Hamley, a soldier of scholarly tastes and, like most of his profession, a 'red-hot Southerner.' Garnet Wolseley, later at the head of the British military establishment, also wrote an article for 'Blackwood's' — an enthusiastic account of a visit to Confederate headquarters.

The attitude of British newspapers toward America was of course mainly determined by their proprietors and editors, of whom the latter held the whip hand. In general the defenders of the North in the better papers were pulling against the current, and so we find that such editors were always moved by conviction and gathered around them contributors actuated by moral enthusiasms. Walker and Robinson, of the 'Daily News,' with E. L. Godkin as New York correspondent and Harriet Martineau as chief leader writer, nearly ran the paper on the rocks with their pro-Northernism, to which they held in spite of great pressure from their anti-Yankee proprietors. R. H. Hutton and Meredith Townsend, of 'The Spectator,' were likewise controlled by hostility to slavery, and 'The Spectator' also lost ground in these years. William Blanchard Jerrold, the editor of the penny 'Lloyd's Weekly,' was a strenuous advocate of the interests of the working classes and warmly supported the North. General T. P. Thompson, an old Radical and Anti-Corn-Law Leaguer, contributed to this paper. The staff of the 'Morning Star,' led by Samuel Lucas, a Quaker of militant politics, was tolerably homogeneous and included such philanthropists as Washington Wilks and F. W. Chesson. Justin M'Carthy tells an amusing story of its difficulty in securing first-hand knowledge of America for the use of its leader writers. The Sunday 'Observer,' then far from having risen to its present greatness, grew quite friendly to the North in the course of the war, but lacked the usual crusading tone. An American described Joseph Snow, its editor, as 'a clever sandy-haired snub-nosed Irishman, who talks well and is in the main sincere; but who has a good supply of flattery for his friends.'

Friends of the Union formed a very fair proportion of the men who were making English journalism in that generation. R. H. Hutton; J. R. Robinson; Michael Whitty, of the 'Liverpool Daily Post,' and E. R. Russell, who later completed its success; Charles Cooper, subsequently editor of the powerful 'Scotsman'; Dunckley, of the 'Manchester Examiner and Times'; Frank Harrison Hill; Justin M'Carthy; John Morley — probably a good half of the editors who were really important in the development of British newspapers from 1860 to 1880 — were writing against the South in the early sixties. Even curious old James Grant, editor of the ''Tiser' and anthologist of British journalism, was a member of one of the pro-Northern societies. The majority, however, went with 'The Times.' Borthwick, of the 'Morning Post' (later the first 'newspaper peer'), and Hamber, of 'The Standard,' enjoyed intimate relations with Confederate agents. Walter Bagehot, of 'The Economist,' was thoroughly independent, but dominated by commercial considerations and by a steady distrust of democracy of the American variety. Alexander Russel, of 'The Scotsman,' was an old Whig who could not see anything good in America. Most of the professional leader writers could not afford to have convictions of their own and probably not all were above the suspicion of venality. The greater part of editorial lucubrations on America, however, were in their own manner similar to those of the politicians.

III

A study of the position of individuals in these years, incomplete though it must be, reveals with particular clarity that the prevalent current among the English upper classes was far more definitely anti-Northern than pro-Southern. The Confederate cause had weaknesses which made its frank defense difficult and for this reason there were fewer active and aggressive apologists of the South than of the Union. Yet among the real aristocracy those who pressed against the social tide as open champions of the North were few. Such were the Duke of Argyll, a natural political idealist and a member of Palmerston's Cabinet; Sir George Cornewall Lewis, Secretary for War, aloof and scholarly; Earl de Grey, also a member of the Ministry and later, as Lord Ripon, a memorable Viceroy of India; Lord Dufferin, still young in 1861 and with a distinguished career ahead of him; Lord Frederick Cavendish, the tragic victim of the Phœnix Park murders; Lord Teynham, an obscure and very Radical peer; and C. P.

Villiers, of anti-corn-law fame, a brother of Lord Clarendon.

The active party leaders usually avoided public statements which might be misconstrued, but they were not much constrained in their expressions of feeling. There are remarkably few cases of neutral-mindedness among prominent politicians outside of the Cabinet. Lord Derby and almost all the lesser leaders of the Conservatives made no concealment of their Southern sympathies; while most of the 'old Whigs,' from Edward Ellice to the young Marquess of Hartington, allow the same sentiments to be perceived. Lord Stanley and Sir Stafford Northcote were conspicuous exceptions in that they positively urged neutrality. But the most striking exception, it is not surprising to find, was the cleverest man of his day, Benjamin Disraeli. Disraeli had neither especial knowledge of American conditions nor interest in them, yet for real intelligence his course of action in reference to the Civil War was not surpassed by any man in England. Though in private he went with the majority in believing the reunion of the sections to be impossible, his public attitude was consistently one of distantly sympathetic neutrality. In Parliament he always insisted that the right part for Englishmen was to respect the efforts of the North; he never lent his countenance openly to recognition; and his prophecies of the future in America were specific and sensible. Yet Dizzy, of course, was not the man to place all his cards on the table: on several occasions he was consulted by the Confederates and encouraged them in the desire to get the French Emperor to repudiate the blockade. Nevertheless, there was real justification for John Bright's encomium near the end of the war, when he told the House of Commons that its members might profitably have imitated Disraeli in the use of their tongues on America.

The active apologists of the South whose names have any meaning for a later generation were relatively few. In the House of Commons the spokesmen of the Confederacy were W. H. Gregory, William Schaw Lindsay, and John Arthur Roebuck. Of Gregory, an Irish landlord and former Peelite who voted with the Cave of Adullam in 1866, there is very little to learn, though his autobiography has been published. He later became Governor of Ceylon. Roebuck, an anti-Whig Radical whose political career went back to 1832, probably did the South more harm than help by his advocacy. He always pushed independence to the point of eccentricity, and though maintaining his hold on his constituents until 1868, he was frequently squabbling with them and with the public on one account or another. Lindsay, the chief promoter of recognition in 1862, was an interesting man. Starting at the bottom of the ladder, he saw active service at sea in his younger days, and in due course became the largest shipowner of London and a Liberal member of Parliament. As a self-made man and a shipowner, it is not surprising that he espoused the cause of the Confederacy. It was his boldness and enterprise that had made the fortunes of his firm after the repeal of the Navigation Acts in 1849, when older shipping men were predicting utter disaster, and he was enough of a pioneer to see much more reality in the vision of future trade with the Confederacy than could many of his less progressive contemporaries. Perhaps imitating Cobden's French activities in 1860, Lindsay had undertaken a journey to the United States in the hope of obtaining for British ships a greater share in the trade of the Pacific Coast. But he had returned disgruntled and irritated by the obstinacy with which the Americans clung to their exclusive coasting trade. Slavery did not interest him; and, furthermore, he became involved in blockade-running.

Other members of Parliament to whom a definite amount of pro-Southern activity may be ascribed were Lord Robert Cecil, former Justice Haliburton (the creator of Sam Slick), Sir E. C. Kerrison, J. T. Hopwood, G. M. W. Peacocke, W. Vansittart, W. E. Duncombe, Sir James Fergusson, and James Whiteside, all Conservatives; and Frederick Peel, Secretary to the Treasury. In the House of Lords, Lord Stratheden (Lord Campbell), Lord Wharncliffe (the great mine-owner), the Earl of Donoughmore, and the Marquess of Lothian were the most eager Confederate supporters. A. J. Beresford Hope, chief proprietor of the 'Saturday Review,' High-Churchman, and brother-in-law of Lord Robert Cecil, was one of the most conspicuous advocates of this side. Many Confederates were received at his estate, Bedgebury, and he kept up a sentimental correspondence with Jefferson Davis after the war.

On the other hand, the Federal cause was relatively weak in Parliament, at least in numbers. William Ernest Forster, of Quaker antecedents and training, a nephew of T. F. Buxton and brother-in-law to Matthew Arnold, was without question the most active pro-Northerner in the Commons. Still in the very early stages of his career, his position during the Civil War was governed by deep-laid hatred of slavery; and he had no past extolling of American democracy to be cast in his teeth when he defended what he regarded as the anti-slavery side. Matthew Arnold remarked in this connection that no public man in England 'would be damaged by having even "fanaticism" in his hatred of slavery imputed to him.' It is certain, at any rate, that Forster's course was popular with his constituents of Bradford, and that in this period he laid the foundations of an important position in the Liberal Party. Necessarily he kept in tolerably close touch with the American Legation, and he declined giving his name as a vice-president of the Union and Emancipation Society on the ground that he could serve the cause better if it were withheld. But there is nowhere any hint that he was moved by motives other than profound conviction.

Another man who was not quite a follower of Bright and Cobden was Peter Alfred Taylor, M.P. for Leicester. He was a theoretic republican of considerable wealth and culture, and a close friend of Mazzini. His wife, who made of their house in Notting Hill a veritable salon, organized a 'Ladies' London Emancipation Society,' which held occasional soirées and issued a series of anti-Southern tracts.

John Bright during the American conflict did not take part in movements except from behind the scenes, but retained his unique position in public life. Within Parliament he was not especially active, and indeed in the current reaction against his 'model Republic' he could have done little good there. But in many speeches in the country he set forth the rights of the problem as they appeared to him — speeches which for force and feeling would be hard to match. Bright's part in upholding the cause of the Union has been exaggerated by his biographers and by historians because he was such a conspicuous figure and because he was made the target of so much of the anti-

American feeling. It is not unduly minimizing the importance of his work to say that the most important feature of his course in those years was the process, accelerated by his attitude on American affairs, by which the Bright group of reformers at last secured the confidence of important sections of the working classes which had until then viewed them with suspicion.

Cobden followed in Bright's wake. At first he was unfavorably influenced by the Northern tariff and did not escape some disgust at the conduct of the Federal Government; but his antipathy to slavery was very real; he did not fear American power; and he was resolutely against anything which might bring England and the United States into conflict. Cobden's real interests were economic rather than political, and his greatest activity during the war period was in a campaign against belligerent rights at sea, in which he won very little success. With Cobden and Bright went George Wilson, last of the big three of the Anti-Corn-Law League, but no longer engaged in politics, as well as various leaders of local Radicalism, such as Joseph Cowen at Newcastle, the two Baineses at Leeds, and Handel Cossham at Bristol.

Perhaps the most ardent English worker for the North was Thomas Bayley Potter, a Manchester magnate who in 1865 succeeded, rather as of right, to Cobden's seat in Parliament. He was a Unitarian and a friend of Garibaldi; a large man, 'with a happy optimistic countenance.' Potter was the president and chief financial support of the Union and Emancipation Society of Manchester, formed in 1863; and Bright wrote of him long after the end of the war, 'I believe he spent more money, and I may almost say that he worked harder, than any other Englishman, to give sound opinions to our people on the subject of your war.' Potter himself stated to Charles Sumner that his motives were 'to uphold the great principles of liberty involved in your present struggle, to aim unceasingly to elevate the DIGNITY OF LABOR in America and *here too* as the best foundation and security for the prosperity and progress of mankind.'

But it is not possible to commemorate all those men who were conspicuous in the philo-Northern movement which started after emancipation had been proclaimed in America. There was William Evans, of London, 'deeply interested in American stocks,' and generally known as 'Little Evans.' There was George Thompson, probably the greatest anti-slavery orator in England, though one fears that by Civil War days old age had made him somewhat tedious. His son-in-law, Frederick William Chesson, was an indefatigable worker who combined philanthropy and journalism into a real profession. He was on the staff of the 'Morning Star,' and editor of its offshoot 'The Dial'; an attractive figure, quite without cant.

Less identified with locality than the Manchester and London groups were Goldwin Smith, Thomas Hughes, J. M. Ludlow, and a number of Nonconformist clergymen. Goldwin Smith, brilliant, learned, and pugnacious, was too 'otherwise-minded' to fill a professorship at Oxford with content, and his activity in regard to the Civil War and the attack of 1865 on Governor Eyre of Jamaica marked him out for a political career on which he deliberately declined to embark. Newman Hall, one of the most popular preachers of the day, rendered effective public service to the North and, according to his own very plausible account, was able to exert some influence on Gladstone and other members of Parliament. Baptist Noel and J. W. Massie were other important members of this group.

By and large the friends of the North drew the intellectual radicals to their ranks. A galaxy of economists — Mill, Fawcett, Cairnes, J. E. T. Rogers — is found on this side. So, too, were the Positivists E. S. Beesly and Frederic Harrison, who were especially interested in the advancement of labor. Pro-Northern likewise were the middle-class friends of Mazzini and Garibaldi in England; many temperance advocates; the majority of the Unitarians [1] and Quakers; the advocates of secularism like G. J. Holyoake; of atheism like the later notorious Charles Bradlaugh; of women's rights, anti-vivisection, and new thought in religion and ethics like Frances Power Cobbe and F. W. Newman. In short, in other fields as well as in politics, those persons opposed to the forces of vested contentment were drawn into defense of American democracy.

[1] James Martineau seems to be an exception.

5

THE DANGEROUS YEAR: 1862

As the excitement of the Trent incident died down, it became clear that the next thing on the calendar was the matter of intervention. The increasing pressure of unemployment in the textile districts assured the raising of the question. But the problem could not be made a party one. Every one knew that the Conservatives as a body were more favorable to the South than the Liberals, but this very fact tended to arouse the party spirit of the latter and to dispose them to listen to the inquiry why they of all people should wish success to an insurrection which began in rejection of a popular vote and which was based on the principle of human slavery. Furthermore, the Trent affair itself precluded the prompt use of America as a party issue, for the Conservatives had applauded the firm action of the Ministry and had to give its course their formal approval at the opening of Parliament in February, 1862. In view of the extreme tension at once manifest in the United States over any suggestion of interference by European powers, the Conservatives could not at once attack the Government for maintaining neutrality. Even had they wished to do so, Palmerston's position in the country was so strong that the chances of a general election were all in his favor. There was, too, the condition of the Queen to be considered, and if a persistently repeated story be true, Lord Derby, after the Prince Consort's death, pledged his party not to precipitate a political crisis in the near future.

The crucial point was the attitude of Lancashire. In the months after the Trent affair, English attention was largely concentrated on the blockade of the South, and there was a general expectation, especially in the Conservative press, that Lancashire was about to demand the raising of the blockade. Two days after the final Trent news, it was reported from Manchester that the question, 'What are we to do for cotton?' had become prominent. Bright and Cobden united in the opinion that the blockade was likely to produce a perilous situation for the Union, and the press of the manufacturing districts at once began to show unusual restlessness. 'The matter now ripe for consideration,' said 'The Economist' late in January, 'which is much discussed in political and manufacturing circles, which is known to be pressing strongly on the mind of the French Emperor, and which some believe to be also occupying the mind of our own Cabinet — is, whether, *the blockade being notoriously ineffective and therefore illegal*, we ought not at once to notify to the Federal Government our determination to disregard it, and to our own merchants that they are at liberty to trade with the Southern ports, just as if no blockade had been proclaimed; and that they will be protected in so doing?' The price-current circular of a firm of Manchester cotton brokers anticipated a great increase of distress in the manufacturing districts: 'The policy of non-intervention, however right and high-minded for the nation at large, may be pushed to a Quixotic extent.... Parliament may look forward, at no distant day, to a loud and imperative cry for relief....' And 'The Times,' commenting on a popular political meeting at Salford, professed to 'hear the whistling of the rising wind' of a demand for intervention, while another journal reminded men of English intervention in Greece in 1827 and suggested 'if need be, another Navarino.'

Had such expectations been fulfilled and had a real movement to raise the blockade arisen in Lancashire, it is impossible to say what would have happened. But Lancashire did not move, either masters or men, and there was no echo to an attempt to identify the operatives with the demand for interference. The reasons for this were twofold. In the first place, the working men were already dominated by anti-slavery and democratic sentiments and by old and deep-seated feelings of friendship for the Union; and secondly, the manufacturers, many of whom shared the same sympathies, were not being forced by economic pressure to feel as strongly about the blockade as London journalists had expected. Bright, though in a somewhat combative and fearsome mood, appears to have been near the truth when he expressed the belief that '...he spoke the sentiments of the merchants, manufacturers, and work people of Lancashire when he said that any of those extremes of interference and war which certain politicians and newspapers advanced, would not only be perilous but absolutely fatal to the interests of that county.'

Various considerations seem to explain the prevalence of this opinion. For one thing, many persons thought intervention to be unnecessary because the North was likely soon to give up its impossible task and was at any rate headed straight for the rocks of bankruptcy. Then, as 'The Economist' said, the majority of Englishmen still believed, however mistakenly, that the victory of the Union would be a blow to slavery, and this belief prevented a move to break the blockade from having the support of a sufficiently unanimous opinion. Other evidence shows more concretely that an unusually mild winter was mitigating the sufferings of the unemployed operatives, while some of the wealthier manufacturers found 'consolation for their losses in the downfall of weaker competitors, whose rapid multiplication of late years was endangering the profits of cotton manufacture.' Hostile critics, such as the good old Tory Sir Archibald Alison, pointed out that speculators in cotton who were holding for a rise were averse to breaking the blockade, as were the holders of large stocks of cotton goods, who had 'completely glutted every civilised market,' and the holders of American railway and other securities, who might lose their property in case of war.

Manchester, in so far as Manchester was composed of manufacturers, spoke out clearly enough at this time. The yearly meeting of the Chamber of Commerce took place about a week before the opening of Parliament, and concurred without any difficulty in the opinion that strict neutrality was alone to be desired. A few days later, a large public meeting, convened on the requisition of between five and six hundred individuals and firms, was held to agitate the repeal of the duties on manufactured cotton imported into India, and made it clear that the Indian market and Indian cotton-growing were regarded as of greater importance than America. Lancashire, opined 'The Economist,' spoke 'with one consentaneous voice' against any present interference with the blockade;

and there is no reason to question the statement of 'The Spectator' that these meetings had a considerable influence on Parliament.

The situation was not favorable to the Confederates nor did it become better. With Lancashire quiescent and the Conservative Party muzzled, there was no one of importance to criticize the Ministry's policy of abstention. 'The Times' forgot the whistling of the rising wind and, after summarizing the arguments for leaving the blockade and America alone, remarked: 'We have waited so long that we can well afford to wait a little longer.' Yet the effectiveness of the blockade of the South was constantly increasing, and it should be impugned at once if a legal argument against its validity was to be made. The Confederates and their parliamentary advisers decided to make the attempt.

Although Lord Derby, in the debate on the Address, hinted broadly at an attack on the Federal blockade, there was no party protest against Earl Russell's plea for continued neutrality on the ground that within a few months the conflict would be over. In the House of Commons, Disraeli was almost cordial to the Unionists and, 'in words which would have been a direct reply to Lord Derby if they had been delivered in the same House,' pleaded for a friendly construction of the American dispatches. The attack, however, was persisted in, and the night of March 7 was secured for the discussion.

It was, necessarily, an independent member who charged himself with the duty of proving the ineffectiveness of the blockade, the same W. H. Gregory who had been the first to move for recognition of the South in the preceding year. Before the day for the debate arrived, however, came the news of Federal victories in Tennessee, and the task of the Ministry and of the friends of the North was made easier. Though the general attitude of the country was such as to make it no surprise that the press showed comparatively little interest in the blockade debate, the occasion seemed an important one to Americans, and its significance was exaggerated by partisans of both sides. The American Secretaries of Legation were both present in the House, as well as Thurlow Weed and Henry Adams, and from the other camp James M. Mason and his secretary, and Dudley Mann. Gregory opened his speech with a brief discussion of the recognition of the South. Had he been allowed by the House to speak freely last June, he said, he would have affirmed 'that secession is a right, that separation is a fact, and that reconstruction is an impossibility. I should have additionally stated that all my heart and sympathies were with one portion of the American people — not that portion that is fighting for empire, but with that portion which is struggling for independence. If I rejoiced to acknowledge these sentiments on the occasion of Bull's Run, I am not going to slink from them now, on the occasion of Donelson.' The bulk of the following argument was designed to prove that the blockade of the Southern coasts was ineffective and hence illegal; more particularly, that it was to the vital interest of England to secure cotton and the friendship of the free-trade South. Eight speakers succeeded, ringing the changes of all arguments on both sides in a manner that must have been a relief to the House that had so resolutely curbed itself in the previous year. An example of the points made was the statement of W. S. Lindsay that the Confederacy was evidently not the aggressor because her troops had not entered Washington on the day after Bull Run! Gregory's speech, the mainstay of which was proofs of successful blockade-running furnished by Commissioner Mason, was answered by W. E. Forster with proofs (from Minister Adams) that the blockade *was* effective. The Government's Solicitor-General, Roundell Palmer, contributed an exceedingly able argument on behalf of the Ministry's hands-off policy. Lord Russell had already issued a parliamentary paper giving data on the blockade which did not strengthen the charge that it was ineffective. The honors of the day went very clearly to the opponents of interference, and 'Punch' concluded that 'the English Commons evidently mean to wait, but not to be dumb waiters.' Lord Palmerston, said 'The Spectator,' slept through the evening 'with a tranquillity known to him only when he is going to win.' The first great American debate of the war was rather anti-climactically over.

II

During the spring and early summer of 1862, the prospects of the North seemed excellent. Victory followed victory, and European opinion reflected the roseate hues painted in the New York and Washington press. Southerners in England became lugubrious and began to harp on a plaintive note that was heard again and again as the war progressed. One disgusted Confederate wrote from London shortly after the blockade debate: 'We need not expect this Government to do anything for us; on the contrary they would be charmed to see us destroy each other like Kilkenny cats. In fact no one can judge of the opinion here without he is on the very spot. They care nothing for us except as far as cotton and dollars and cents are concerned. On the subject of slavery they are a nation of fanatics.'

After the first military successes in the West came President Lincoln's proposal for compensated emancipation of the slaves, and the signing of a treaty with Great Britain on the slave trade. These moves were of real help in Europe as an indication of the future. The battle of the ironclads Merrimac and Monitor in Hampton Roads, occurring less than two days after the American debate at Westminster, aroused enormous interest in England. Though it enhanced the respect of the English for the Federal blockade, and was a factor increasing the reluctance to being drawn into war with the United States, the discussion aroused had no direct bearing on the question of intervention or on public sympathy for the American combatants. This event was followed by reports of the battle of Shiloh and of the success of Federal gunboats at Island Number Ten, while the coincidence of the capture of New Orleans with the opening of the drive on Richmond doubled the great effect which these events would have had separately. The taking of the queen city of the Gulf was particularly calculated to impress English opinion. New Orleans was second only to Charleston in the eyes of the world, and was commercially more important. Coming with the gunboat victories on the mid-Mississippi, this triumph made it seem that the great valley was about to be unlocked, and visions of a peaceful cotton supply appeared quickly before English eyes. The alarm of Liverpool speculators, who by this time had become very numerous, is a measure of this. At the same time the imminent peril of Richmond, in the early stages of the Peninsula campaign, made the actual termination of the war seem very near. Journalistic turncoats began to hail 'each success of the Federal arms as a conquest made in the interest of humanity'; and those papers too deeply committed to the Southern cause talked feebly of guerilla warfare which might be maintained for years in Southern fastnesses. The Confederates began to take the place which the Unionists had held after Bull Run, and in June the same journal which in January had suggested another Navarino was calling the Southerners 'a lot of cowards, who will not fight behind stone walls or before them.' 'The Times' and many of its followers lent color to the charge of the working men's 'Lloyd's Weekly Newspaper' that Englishmen were proving themselves clumsy time-servers.

But the transmutation of the Southerners from heroes to cowards did not have time to become complete. Though there can be no question that at the end of May and in the first part of June the belief was quite general that the end of the war was approaching, and though the earlier conviction of the inevitability of the separation of the sections was in partial abeyance, there was no great shift of sympathy, but only a quite natural interest and wonder as to the outcome in America. Even talk of intervention did not entirely die down. Gladstone, whose opinions on America were strangely ill-fated, had spoken to the Manchester Chamber of Commerce in April without showing any reflection of the Northern victories already made public: separation he considered, as he had in January, to be unavoidable, and he reminded the Union that the revolt of the American Colonies, so strenuously resisted eighty-five years before, was no longer regretted in England. Persons were not lacking to take these personal opinions of a prominent Minister as significant of the future, and when it became known that the French Minister to the United States was visiting Richmond, rumors of impending action grew frequent. The pressure of cotton famine was much more seriously felt in the late spring than it had been, and the friends of the South, together with many newspaper writers, could not believe that this did not mean a popular demand for interference.

Meanwhile the situation in Virginia was gradually being unraveled. First came the news of Stonewall Jackson's campaign in the Valley, which put some heart in the friends of the South. The 'Bucks Herald' announced that it would not be surprised at another Bull Run rout (from Yorktown to Washington!), and as mail after mail reported that McClellan's advance on Richmond was not succeeding, Southerners and Liverpool speculators were able to breathe more freely. General Butler's 'women proclamation' at New Orleans intensified feeling against the North, and Conservative journals of the 'Morning Herald' creed began to grow more violent against the Federals and against the stolidity of Lord Palmerston's official attitude. The Liberals were silent, but there was a clear divergence between official and unofficial Conservative opinion, for the responsible party heads never wavered in their determination not to embarrass the Government.

Yet the cotton famine was growing steadily more acute, and a new movement for intervention awaited only the defeat of Northern arms. 'The Times' admitted to its columns a series of long and strong interventionist letters from 'A Lancashire Lad,' and Cobden, who always overrated the cotton factor, expressed grave apprehensions: 'Merchants, manufacturers, spinners and operatives are all on the same footing, and they are all anxious to obtain new cotton, and they will be all equally pressing on our Government the necessity of "doing something."...' In spite of the fact that the Manchester cotton market itself showed no desire for governmental action, the situation was in some respects serious. Although only avowed friends of the South were willing to agitate for intervention, large numbers of good people would approve of any plausible measures for 'stopping this terrible war.' As McClellan's lack of success in Virginia grew patent, the general public, rather than Lancashire, did wonder if something might not be done about stopping the conflict. 'One word,' said that shining mirror of opinion, 'The Times,' 'one word has been in the hearts of men of reason and feeling for some time past, though the passions of the hour in America have prevented it from rising to their lips. That word is "Mediation." That North and South must now choose between separation and ruin, material and political, is the opinion of nearly everyone who, looking impartially and from a distance on the conflict, sees what is hidden from the frenzied eyes of the Northern politicians.' Let us then, the article continued, offer friendly mediation by way of anticipating the inevitable recognition of the South. The next day, to be sure, Lord Russell declared himself firmly against mediation, and 'The Times,' a little grudgingly, had to support him; but for many weeks following it continued an intervention campaign of the most thinly veiled hints. At the same time it was becoming well known that Louis Napoleon was entirely ready to interfere in America as soon as he could be assured of some sort of British coöperation. Most Englishmen would undoubtedly have preferred to see him pull the chestnuts out of the fire alone, not realizing that his international position required him to follow a British lead. But it happened that at this particular time there was no European crisis in progress: the Roman question was quiescent, Poland had not yet revolted, the Mexican situation was not far developed; and so joint action with the redoubtable Emperor of the French was regarded with less disfavor than usual.

In Parliament the second American night of the year was more carefully prepared than had been the blockade debate of March. W. H. Gregory had now lost the lead to W. S. Lindsay, who in April and May had conducted an abortive intrigue with Napoleon III in the hope of pushing Palmerston and Russell into an Anglo-French interference in America. The Emperor had apparently used Lindsay as a stalking horse to ascertain whether the British Government was subject to stimulation; finding that they were not, he had quickly retired behind the façade of normal diplomatic intermediaries. Lindsay, piqued but hopeful, now persisted against the advice of some friends of the South in trying an attack in Parliament. As early as May, 1861, he had affirmed his conviction that England and France should intervene when the proper time arrived. Apparently that time was the early summer of 1862.

The motion in the House of Commons was at first to be for mediation; then it was put on the notice paper for June 20 and called for recognition of the Confederate States. But by that time it was not certain that the advance on Richmond was checked, and Lindsay was persuaded to postpone his motion, which was set for July 11 and changed to a form implying both recognition and mediation. A second time the debate was postponed, and when, on July 18, the protagonist of the South finally insisted, the motion appeared in 'very much diluted terms,' which in consultation with the Southern envoys had been decided on as least subject to attack and yet strong enough to mould the policy of the Government. The revised terms asserted that in view of the practical independence of the seceded States, the British Government ought to offer mediation with a view of terminating hostilities.

The debate which followed was unsatisfactory. 'The Times' — on the same page on which it so forcibly announced to the English people the epoch-making determination of Prussia to enter the Zollverein — prepared for it by a curious leading article that in an ambiguous and highly characteristic manner egged on the interventionists while advising the Government to avoid interference except in company with other European powers, apparently because independent intervention would mean war with the United States. The immediate moment, as it chanced, was not propitious for a full-dress debate on America, for a universally reported telegraphic canard earlier in the day had alleged that the Federal army in Virginia was annihilated and that McClellan was a fugitive on a gunboat. The stopping of the Federal offensive was well known, but the new rumor gave every one pause, and it was expected that further news might show a definite military result which would lead to voluntary negotiations on the part of the North.

The argument of the cotton famine showed its weakness plainly in the whole debate. No representative from the cotton districts stood up to describe in moving words the sufferings of the unemployed and the stagnation of all business; no speaker was able to refer with confidence to the superlative desire of the workers for cotton; and Lindsay's documentary evidence of a demand for intervention consisted only of a letter from a working man at Ashton-under-Lyne, who said that in his part of the country 'we are very anxious' to see the recognition of the South. The other side at once retorted by referring to an open-air meeting at Blackburn at which a vote of no confidence in pro-Southern agitators had been passed.

The debate went on without the participation of front-benchers until near its close. Lindsay, who was a poor speaker, lost a good share of his audience, but was applauded by the Tories. He was answered by P. A. Taylor and W. E. Forster, who filled the House again, but whose remarks friendly to the North were received with jeers and hisses. Both these speakers made as their main points that interference by England would be interference on the side of slavery and would involve England in a disgraceful and wasteful war. We had, said Forster, a cotton famine; did we want a corn famine too? James Whiteside, a former Conservative office-holder and an eminent member of the Irish bar, delivered a lawyer's plea that recognition, on the basis of the precedents since 1820, was quite compatible with neutrality, while W. H. Gregory joined in with a very long speech gathering up all the fragments of Southern partisanship and attempting, with some force, to make use of Lord Russell's prophecy in March that the war would be over in three months. The Tories' attitude was stressed by the appearance of Lord Derby in the gallery to hear Whiteside's speech, and by brief support of the motion from Seymour Fitzgerald (C. F. Adams's landlord!), the Conservative spokesman in the Commons on foreign matters. But before this last speaker, Palmerston had concisely settled the affair: he regretted that such a weighty and delicate matter had been thus brought up in a place where any discussion was certain to irritate the Americans, defended the ministerial policy of non-intervention, and begged the House to leave the question to the decision of the Government. The only motive for non-interference that could be deduced from the Premier's speech was the feeling that any false move on England's part would precipitate war with America. The motion was withdrawn without a division.

The outcome of this intervention movement did not in any way shake the confidence of the country in the cautiously maintained neutrality of the Government. The policy of the Ministry 'is applauded by the almost universal voice of the country,' said 'The Observer'; and 'The Times' suddenly lost interest in the matter, remarking on the morning after the debate that, although recognition would undoubtedly come before long, the best course for the press and the public was to leave matters to Palmerston. The 'Manchester Guardian' congratulated the country on the quietness and ability which marked the debate — a debate which, it added, should not be thought to have anything to do with the sentiments and sympathies of the English people, for these were entirely with the South — and applauded the actual decision not to interfere. Harriet Martineau took the occasion to deny the existence of a *war* party in England, though admitting the presence of one hostile to the North, and other friends of the North took heart and attacked the pro-Southerners of the House of Commons for having rendered peaceful mediation more difficult by the tone of their speeches. The advanced section of the Liberals claimed great credit for the working classes, and 'Lloyd's Weekly,' speaking for laboring men, insisted confidently that their high-minded and unselfish attitude would in future deprive even 'the rankest conservatives' of their main ground for refusing the franchise.

Disgust at the ministerial policy was expressed only by the 'Morning Herald' type of opinion. That journal chose to attack Lindsay for climbing down rather than embarrass the Government — which he *had* embarrassed — and even intimated that he had been 'got at'; and it accused the Ministry of being responsible for all the suffering, present and prospective, in the manufacturing regions on account of its acquiescence in the illegal blockade and its refusal to join with France in an offer of mediation. The debate had one good effect in causing this organ and its followers to state outright that recognition of the South would be more than worth the cost of a war with the North; but it may be doubted that this belief was sincere, for every one knew that for the present there was no risk of war with the Union. The business of the Conservatives at this time was to oppose the Ministry, not to undertake any responsibility. When Palmerston, Bright, and Disraeli were agreed; when 'The Times' and 'Saturday Review' had no bone to pick with the 'Daily News' or the 'Anti-Slavery Reporter,' it mattered little that the 'Morning Heralds' and 'John Bulls' declared English policy to be the pusillanimous caution of a minority.

III

The remainder of the year is characterized mainly by what the American Minister called 'progressive consolidation of the popular prejudice against America.' The public gradually, as the statesmen promptly, had come to realize that an offer of mediation would be contumeliously refused by the North and that any other interference would involve war, for which no one was prepared; and yet the Union, losing campaign after campaign, did not inspire much respect. It had lost caste also, if that were possible, by certain incidents in the conduct of the war. Some of the barbarities of American life had long before 1860 struck English observers very forcibly, to such an extent that when war broke out there were many expectations that it would be particularly inhumane. Six or seven months later, during the splendid opportunity for invective provided by the Trent affair, these sentiments got a thorough airing, and a responsible politician was quite typical when he assured his constituents that the conduct of the war by the Americans was 'so ferocious and savage, so ruthless, so inhuman, that it possesses more the character of the Red Indians they have displaced than of the Saxons and Christians from whom they are descended.' It became necessary to call in the parallels of Louis XIV in the Palatinate and Alva in the Netherlands to express the horror with which the civilized world regarded the fratricidal struggle.

It is somewhat difficult to ascertain what precise atrocities were had in mind by alarmed commentators in England, but two at least stand out conspicuously. The first was the project of the Federal Navy to assist the active blockade by sinking vessels laden with stone in the channels leading to the harbors of certain Southern ports. The Foreign Office, ignoring excellent British precedents, remonstrated with Seward about this, apparently thinking that the damage done would be irreparable; and the Liverpool Shipowners' Association and the Liverpool Chamber of Commerce were vastly excited. Even Cobden denounced the act as barbarous, and other writers described it as 'a deed without a name,' 'an act of hostility to the whole human race,' and utterly unworthy of a civilized state. It was soon understood that a port could not be destroyed by these means and that they had been abandoned as unsatisfactory, and yet the 'stone fleet' for many months constantly returned to plague the Unionists.

Far more lasting in its effects and far more damaging to the Federal cause was the atrocity known as 'Butler's woman order.' The affair is too well known to need much explanation. General Butler, after the capture of New Orleans, was so thoroughly exasperated by the ingenious tortures devised by female Confederates for the occupying troops, that he finally issued an order that any such persons grossly insulting the soldiers of the United States army should be 'treated as women of the town'; i.e., locked up overnight by the police. The implications of this most unfortunate incident were too much for English equanimity, and the torrent of obloquy which the Federal general drew down overflowed on the whole Northern cause, bespattering it with a disgrace more harmful than another Bull Run. Palmerston was so aroused as to write a quite unjustifiable and undiplomatic note of protest to the American Minister, and public opinion was expressed in terms of unmeasured opprobrium. Nothing since Cassius Clay and the episode of Miss Slidell and the bayonets had done so much to nourish hatred of the Yankees. The army, the nation, which could give high command to such a fiend in human form as Butler, must, it was thought, be worthy of the worst that had been said of it. Then indeed must it be true that large portions of the Federal States' population were composed of 'the worst "rowdies," the best-trained scoundrels in all the world'; then must there be some wisdom in the words of the emphatic Roebuck that the Northerners were 'the scum and refuse of Europe.' Butler became a rod in pickle ready at all times for the chastisement and confusion of any Englishman who dared to suggest that the North was fighting for liberty and decency against slave-drivers.

With the victory of the South at the second battle of Manassas in August, there was even a slight recrudescence of intervention sentiment coincident with admiration for the gallantry of the Confederates. Though it was in October that the issue of slavery began to be felt with increased pressure on British opinion, the current against the North continued to flow in the inlets after the ebb had begun from the shore. It was, curiously enough, only a single day after the news of Lincoln's preliminary emancipation proclamation had reached England, that a pronouncement was made in that country which seemed to mark the nadir of the Northern cause. While Lee's retirement into Virginia after the battle of Antietam had done a little to bring the partisans of the Union into the light again, and had been even more potent in raising hesitations in the Cabinet about Russell's mooted plan for interference, it had no considerable effect on public opinion. On Gladstone, an increasingly popular Minister and one who had long thought that the South should be recognized, it had no effect at all. In a speech at Newcastle on October 7, Gladstone committed perhaps the most notorious blunder of his entire career and struck a stunning blow at the hopes of the North in England. In the course of his address on various matters of public interest he had, as had all politicians of those years in addressing popular audiences, to touch on American affairs, and in this instance the obligation was accepted with gusto. Expressing undoubtedly sincere sentiments of good will toward the people of the Northern States, and pride in England's 'perfect neutrality,' he concluded with a striking passage which obliterated from men's minds almost everything else he had said. 'There is no doubt,' he declared, 'that Jefferson Davis and other leaders of the South have made an army; they are making, it appears, a navy; and they have made, what is more than either — they have made a nation.... We may anticipate with certainty the success of the Southern States so far as their separation from the North is concerned.'

The sensation created by this pronouncement was enormous. It could not but seem a promise of recognizing the Confederacy. Said the reluctant 'Spectator': 'We cannot, bitterly as we lament the decision, honestly blame the Cabinet.' On the Liverpool 'Change it was reported that Gladstone's speech had convinced nearly everybody of the imminence of recognition, though in this community where blockade-running was now become a large business, 'many gentlemen of every shade of opinion' said that a more foolish and mischievous speech was never made by any minister of state. The Manchester market for cotton goods was depressed and fluctuating, and it was necessary for spokesmen for the South to reassure the apprehensive by pointing out that recognition would not at once bring great supplies of cotton to England. The protagonists of intervention were of course greatly cheered. The Southern Association of Liverpool decided that the time was ripe to memorialize the Government for recognition of the South. Sir John Pakington, who according to Louis Blanc personified better than any one else the general tendencies of the Conservative Party, spoke at Worcester the day after the Newcastle banquet and showed an evident desire to make the most of Gladstone's opinion, expressing his earnest wish for a joint intervention of European powers in America.

In general, however, the response of the country to the suggestion of recognition was unenthusiastic. The majority was entirely agreed with Gladstone's personal opinion of the situation, but still not at all sure that it wanted intervention or even recognition. 'The public,' to tell the truth, was quite willing to take the lead either way from the decision of the Cabinet. 'The Times' and the 'Morning Post,' with ears always close to ministerial lips, showed quite extraordinary reserve and discretion, while the bulk of the independent and Liberal press awaited patiently whatever might come from the oracle of Downing Street. Commercial interests as a whole were opposed to governmental action, and this seems to have been as true at Liverpool, the hotbed of Southern sympathies, as at Manchester and London.

There was no long suspense over the matter. Lord Palmerston, who was at his best when handling situations of this sort, refused to allow his fire to be drawn, though Russell's proposal for initiating a general European move on America was not yet abandoned. Exactly a week after

Gladstone's outburst, Cornewall Lewis, another Cabinet member speaking on his own responsibility, coolly destroyed any belief that the policy of the Government was settled. His Hereford speech was as cold and impartial as possible, and entirely in line with the speaker's character as a man who frequently pricked hastily blown bubbles. The Government might choose, he said, between recognition of the South and sympathy or alliance with the North; but it had avoided both extremes and had acted with the perfect neutrality which, since the issue of the war was still undecided, was the only course in accordance with international law. Lewis's speech, the curb, as Louis Blanc said, corresponding to Gladstone's spur, was accepted without grumbling, and the public side of the intervention movement was again painlessly suspended.

Only a short time later it seemed that it might be renewed, and this time the stimulus came from France. Napoleon III had been thoroughly occupied during the British discussions of October with a ministerial crisis of his own, but by the end of October he had a new foreign minister through whom he at once made a somewhat carelessly considered overture at London and St. Petersburg. This proposal was for a joint move of France, England, and Russia to secure a six months' armistice — including a cessation of the blockade — in America in the hope that by that means the Civil War might be ended. Had Gladstone's speech not already precipitated things in Great Britain, it is quite possible that this suggestion would have been the basis of a not unpopular movement of some scope in that country; as it was, the vast majority of interested people stood aside in perfect willingness to allow the Cabinet to come to an untrammeled decision.

The Tory papers, which looked to the 'Morning Herald' and 'Standard' for leadership, played up the French proposal for all it was worth, but they were not followed by any of the Whigs, and the ministerial and independent journals of all shades withheld their comment with entire unanimity until the answer of the Cabinet had been prepared. That answer, which was published to the world with unusual alacrity, politely declined to accede to the French Emperor's request, on the ground that Russia had already refused, and because 'there is no ground at the present moment to hope that the Federal Government would accept the proposal suggested, and a refusal from Washington at the present time would prevent any speedy renewal of the offer.'

The continuation of the policy of 'not yet' surprised no one and was unsatisfactory to very few. 'The arguments of Lord Russell's note,' said 'The Times,' 'have been anticipated by the public, and this is the best proof of their soundness.' Hammond, Under-Secretary for Foreign Affairs, described public opinion as 'almost universal in this country against interference.' A strong reason for this attitude was the recent success of the Democratic Party in the autumn elections in the United States, which seemed to English observers to presage the downfall of the war party in the North and voluntary negotiations for peace and Southern independence.

A very interesting question occurs at this time in connection with the appearance in 'The Times' of two letters by 'Historicus.' 'Historicus' had made his first communications to the public on international law at the time of the Trent affair, when he had shown himself a learned, positive, and peppery antagonist to the arguments of the

Americans and the Bright school. Since then his voice had not been often lifted, and it was something of an event when, on November 7, 1862, and before the leading journal had printed a word about the French dispatch, a long letter signed 'Historicus' appeared again. This unusually able document was entitled 'The International Doctrine of "Recognition,"' and its effective purpose was to destroy nearly all of the current arguments in favor of recognizing the South — a purpose which it achieved with devastating and impartial learning and candor. This letter and its successor 'Neutrality or Intervention?' made a very considerable impression on the opinion of the time and did much to suppress loose talk of interference. It was not universally known that 'Historicus' was William Vernon Harcourt, a man very close indeed to Cornewall Lewis and Clarendon, nor that on this same day Lewis was circulating a long memorandum — concocted with Harcourt — to Ministers against recognition. But it was entirely clear that at last some one had spoken who knew thoroughly the law of which he wrote and whose view of policy was not tinctured with any of the jaundice of partisanship. The writing of 'Historicus' had an accent of authority; and if Harcourt was not yet, in the words of his biographer, 'the spokesman of English policy to the unofficial world,' his argument was yet so energetic and lucid, so different from the usual *ex parte* briefs and from the time-serving of the writers of leading articles, that it enjoyed great weight. It is not possible to explain completely this powerful support to the anti-interventionists, but certain facts are interesting. 'Historicus's' letter of November 7 was printed four days before the Cabinet meeting on the French proposal and three days *after* the last of a long series of interventionist pleas by 'S.' — James Spence of Liverpool. 'The Times' refused to print Confederate answers to 'Historicus.' Furthermore, while London Tory organs were noticing the inspired rumors of the French 'Patrie' about the Emperor's proposal, 'The Times' noticed nothing, and it was only in its second edition of November 11, the day of the British Cabinet meeting, that its news columns reported the matter. At the Cabinet meeting Palmerston gave only lukewarm support to Russell's desire to accept the French offer, and capitulated easily. Had he gone over to non-intervention earlier, and does the course of 'The Times' reflect this? Otherwise why did 'The Times' go out of its way to support Lewis?

In any event, the policy of watchful waiting was again vindicated. 'England may be said to be unanimous,' wrote 'The Spectator,' and even the anti-Northern 'Manchester Guardian' took pains to reply in the name of Lancashire to the Tories who were attacking Russell for being cruel to the unemployed by his refusal. Once again Southern protagonists were forced to avow that they desired interference even at the price of war with America.

IV

In summarizing the ten or eleven months following the Trent affair, certain assertions may be made with confidence. In the first place, the issue of slavery played no greater part in moulding the opinion of 1862 than it had in 1861. To a certain degree by the beginning of the second winter of the war sympathies with North or South had hardened on account of or despite slavery, but the North had made very few converts and the South lost few supporters on this score, while the impatience of American abolitionists with Lincoln's dilatory policy had a very audible echo on the European side of the Atlantic.

In the second place, it may be noted that the direct play of economic interest was much slighter than Americans believed at the time to be the case, or than later writers have often been led to assume. Anticipation had been more fearsome than experience, and in the very months when the cotton famine was at its worst we find that the masses suffering from unemployment were doing nothing to influence public policy beyond that quiet sympathy with the North which they had manifested from the outbreak of the war. Merchants and manufacturers of cotton goods were being saved from the consequences of overproduction by the very scarcity of cotton, while the other manufacturing trades were all, or nearly all, prosperous and infinitely less interested in American affairs than they had been in 1861. Undoubtedly English business interests desired to see the war brought to an early end, and merchants and traders showed a good deal of temporary animosity toward the party that seemed to be responsible for its perpetuation. Yet when a manufacturing neutral becomes adjusted to war conditions, there are many profits to be had, as the United States found between 1914 and 1917. Between war contracts which were many, the French commercial treaty of 1860 which opened new markets, and a new freedom from competition for the carrying trade of the seven seas, there was not much need for English industry, aside from cotton, to concern itself with other considerations than a desire to stand well with both North and South for the future.

The most conspicuous fact concerning the English view

of the American war in 1862 was that practically no one considered the recementing of the Union as a probability. The questions of interest were as to the date of termination of the war and the boundaries which would result — not as to the outcome. Even Cobden doubted that the North and the South could ever lie in the same bed again; and Gladstone's personal recognition of the South was not prompted in the least by hostility to the United States, but was due entirely to the same conviction. It should be repeated that much of what Americans considered hostility to their cause and their Union was merely the expression of the belief that the South could not be conquered, or that, if conquered, it could not be ruled with any more success than if it were another Poland or Venetia.

Much of the talk against the Yankees, however, was not a matter of foreign relations at all. 'The American question' had become a party one in Great Britain to almost as great an extent, in this period of political stagnation, as any other of the openly discussed problems of the time. Its actively divisive force was not very potent, nor was that of any of the political issues of the early sixties; but, as has been shown, it formed part and parcel of the fundamental reform question which lay never very far below the surface of consciousness. America was the field of many a light skirmish between the party of progress and the party of resistance.

So far as British intervention is concerned, the events of 1862 illuminate brightly certain features of the Palmerstonian régime. A close study of English opinion must lead to the conclusion that Secretary Seward's policy of carrying a chip on his shoulder was entirely successful.

At no time, naturally, did Englishmen say in so many words that they were afraid of risking war with America. What was true was that throughout all discussions of policy ran a constant thread of reluctance to embark on any course which might result in conflict. It was because the American Government and press made it clear to the world that proffers of mediation would be instantly rejected that there was so little pressure put upon the British Ministry to mediate; it was partly because of the hair-trigger attitude of the American people that so many elements in England showed a desire to let Napoleon III pull their chestnuts out of the fire; in short, it was largely broad considerations of expediency that kept England neutral. Fear for the security of Canada undoubtedly played its part, but there is no evidence that this greatly influenced more than the active politicians, for only they knew how hard Canada would be to defend. In the summer and autumn of 1862, interference would have been popular in England, but only interference which could be peaceful. Slavery, general prosperity, the bonds of kinship, the influence of the non-voting masses, and the indecisive military situation in America — all these influences worked on the politicians to avert parliamentary or Cabinet action which would mean either a humiliating rebuff or war. Lord Granville, opposing Russell's scheme for mediation, noted with emphasis the complete approval which the policy of non-intervention had met in the country as a whole, while Palmerston, a better diagnostician than Russell if less friendly to the Union, abandoned the plan of intervention before his colleague, remarking a little sourly, 'The French Government are more free from the shackles of principle and of right and wrong on these matters, as on all others, than we are.'[1] In this year 1862, the only time when intervention was seriously possible, the British Cabinet is to be praised not for resisting public opinion but for understanding it correctly. In determining foreign policy Downing Street weighed factors unknown to the man in the street and gave a different value to those which were known to him. Nevertheless, taking the situation as a whole, public opinion and ministerial policy were in close correspondence.

It is impossible here to give an accurate impression of the place of British interest in America in the life of the time. But there is no question of the magnitude of that interest which ensured that literally every one outside the ranks of agricultural labor had opinions of some sort on trans-Atlantic affairs. To judge by the press, from the penny weekly of the working man to the half-crown quarterly, the Civil War occupied a place which for a year and a half had not even temporary rivals. English opinion was in a real sense the opinion of the public, not sporadic or factitious, but continuous, real, and forming a part of the thought and conversation of all orders and sorts of persons.

During the military campaigns of 1862, then, British opinion had developed along the lines earlier laid down. Peace with the United States had remained the convinced attitude of the mass of the people, while increasing impatience with the duration of a war in which most of them saw no prospect of a satisfactory issue was countered by economic adjustment and mental habituation. On the whole, the failure of the North to achieve successes in the

[1] Russell Papers, quoted in E. D. Adams, *Great Britain and the American Civil War*, II, 61.

field had strengthened the sentiment that the South should be allowed to go its own way in not entirely blessed tranquillity, and such occurrences as Butler's proclamation, suspension of the writ of *habeas corpus*, the war tariffs, and the violence of the press, had contributed to an exacerbation of anti-Northern feelings. On the other hand, the South had gained by its gallant resistance and by the silence and apparent unanimity of its ranks which contrasted with the wrangling and Anglophobe North. The slavery question alone was not yet settled as a factor in England, and a few days after the first of October news came which, though few realized it at the time, marked the turn of the tide.

6

SLAVERY, EMANCIPATION, AND THE REACTION TO THE NORTH

On September 26, 1862, Henry Hotze, the most well-informed and the shrewdest of Southerners in England, expressed confidence that the opinion of the 'intelligent' classes in England was so strongly in favor of the South that the battle of Antietam and Lee's retreat into Virginia would do no harm to his cause. Though the tone of the British press and knowledge of the Cabinet discussions of October show that the Confederate agent's view was not without justification, he overlooked one factor — slavery. What the British Ministry in its procrastination dimly realized, what English friends of the North had often tried to say, and what ardent Conservatives and Southern emissaries failed utterly to see, appears to the historian as an undoubted fact: the ultimate diplomatic weapon was in the hands of President Lincoln.

I

American slavery as a factor influencing English opinion during the Civil War can be in part understood by examining the group in England which cared most about the question — which formed, in fact, the so-called anti-slavery party. There is no need here to describe the activities of the band of devoted men who were finally successful in obtaining the emancipation of British Negro slaves in the West Indies. That achieved, within the decade following 1833, the older generation of laborers speedily passed away, leaving largely in other hands a movement which was hardly so much a movement as a creed, and which was sustained especially by the continued existence of slavery in America. The only persons sufficiently philanthropic and leisured to maintain a constant concern over conditions so remote were the more religiously minded of the upper middle classes. And so it came about that the British and Foreign Anti-Slavery Society between 1840 and 1860 was largely composed of and supported by a comparatively small group of Quakers, who formed also the mainstay of the Peace Society and whose strongest members were highly respected and prosperous business men of the City of London. To these, who were actuated by a staunch idealism not very comprehensible to most people, were added an also limited number of 'religious' people — a large scattering of the ministers of the various Nonconformist churches, an occasional rector of the Establishment, and a few prominent laymen of the Evangelical persuasion.

This mild body was the anti-slavery party of 1860. It published a monthly newspaper, the 'Anti-Slavery Reporter,' and included, outside of the main Society in the metropolis, a number of smaller organizations — Ladies' or Young Men's Negroes' Friend or Anti-Slavery Societies in towns of the provinces and Scotland. It formed, naturally, the chief link between the British public and the American abolitionist movement, to whose tenets of immediatism and no compromise the British anti-slavery people usually subscribed. The influence of their views on the generality of the population of the British Isles was not strong; but they were listened to with respect by the members of successive British ministries, and served at least to keep official activity in regard to the slave trade up to the mark.

On the outbreak of the war in America, the Anti-Slavery Society did not find its line of action entirely clear. It solved the initial question by throwing its weight, not in favor of the North, but against all dealings with the South. But after the month of June, 1861, in the midst of the general reaction from all things American, with the failure of the Federal Government either to win military or political success or to place itself even half-heartedly on the side of the Negro, the Anti-Slavery Society abstained from taking a public position. As by midsummer the conviction had been forced on England that the North was not, whatever might be the ultimate explanation of the conflict, fighting to destroy slavery, there was no point on which sentiments primarily anti-slavery could focus.

The friends of the slave in England were in a quandary, as their expressions plainly show. The Reverend George B. Cheever, who was perhaps the American abolitionist most familiar to Englishmen, represented a considerable fraction in Great Britain and the United States who could see matter only for condemnation in Lincoln's policy, and these extremists did not hesitate to call his administration a pro-slavery one. Not only that, but the libertarians who alone were interested in the welfare of the Negro were profoundly shocked by reports of high-handed actions by the Northern authorities, and many of them would have been much pleased had they been able to wash their hands of the whole business. Only a small group led by George Thompson followed Garrison in the policy of supporting the war. The difficulty of anti-slavery Englishmen, even when they were not pacifists, is well instanced by an extract from the diary of one of the most earnest of the workers in the cause. F. W. Chesson wrote after a committee meeting in the autumn of 1861: 'A little argument took place between Mr. Thompson and Mr. J. S[t]ella Martin [a Negro minister] of Boston. Struck very forcibly with the really slender grounds of hope upon which the Abolitionists base their expectations that Emancipation will result from the war. The strongest fact that Mr. Martin appeared to be able to adduce was some remark which Mr. Lincoln had made to some member of the Seward family who had told it to somebody else, that somebody else repeating it to Mr. Martin! For the present, however, one cannot help putting an unfavourable construction upon Lincoln's letter to Fremont modifying the latter's proclamation emancipating the slaves of rebels.'

In the long run, however, the trend of the anti-slavery movement was bound to be in favor of the North, since it could not possibly say a good word for the South. The opinion of American abolitionists, though they were not able to present satisfactory arguments to the reason of their British interlocutors, was necessarily of some effect, and they encouraged their friends in England to recur to the habit of urging the Federal Government to act against the iniquitous institution. The crisis over the Trent was a sharp reminder of the meaning of an alliance of England with the Confederate States, and near the end of the suspense before the American answer, the Anti-Slavery Society broke its silence by an address to Lord Palmerston in the interests of peace. Next to doubts about the slavery issue itself, in the ranks of the Society, was the fact that a large proportion of its membership consisted of Friends and members of the Peace Society and that its constitution pledged it to use and countenance only peaceful methods against slavery. The war waged by the North, whatever its purpose, was a war.

Nevertheless, with the opening of 1862 the attitude of the movement toward the Washington Administration warmed perceptibly. 'The Reporter,' which was edited by the Secretary of the Society, Chamerovzow, was in advance of the official position of the Committee, but the annual report of June, which had to satisfy severe scrutiny, elaborated a refutation of all the arguments which had appeared in England in support of the South and explained in some detail the progress which the Republican Administration had already made in behalf of the slave. Even as early as April, stimulated by Lincoln's suggestion of compensated emancipation for the Border States, the Society had ventured on a first overt act, and a deputation which included three members of Parliament was sent to Charles Francis Adams to welcome him as an ambassador whose antecedents proved his principles to coincide with their own. Until emancipation was proclaimed in America, the Anti-Slavery Society took no further public measures.

II

While the abolitionists of Great Britain were undergoing the evolution which might be expected, the generality of the great English middle classes had been subjected to influences inclining them to temporize with slavery. It is quite accurate to say that in the first eighteen months of the war there was a widespread tendency to view the peculiar institution with increasing complaisance. Many factors combine to explain this trend. As the English became persuaded that the war was not being fought against slavery, and as the press, people, and even clergymen of the North succeeded in rendering themselves distrusted and disliked, their diatribes against the 'slaveholding oligarchy' recoiled strongly. The arguments of Southern emissaries gained in force as the Northern case weakened. Admiration for a united and homogeneous people fighting gallantly and successfully for independence against a larger antagonist was not consistent with the would-be Northern conception of the Southerners as a nation of Simon Legrees; and the ill-treatment of free Negroes in Northern States was brought out as an offset to abolitionist attacks on the South. While it was plausibly stated that the Union was fighting not to destroy slavery, but to retain its profits, extenuations of that institution could be made with some effect. It was a system of patriarchal simplicity, in which the cultured and civilized white man ruled over his family with a large humanity strongly contrasting with the race fanaticism of Northern mobs; the Negro was not yet fit to take his place in the ranks of self-governing peoples and was being led by slow and skillful steps toward the achievement of his best potentialities, whatever they might be. Slavery was not all bad by any means, though of course Britons could have nothing to do with it, and the North at any rate was not in a position to throw stones. It was a matter of some importance in England that the American apostles of the slave who were there known in person or by reputation — men like Garrison, Phillips, Cheever, Neal Dow — were prophets without honor in their own country: in this comfortable, smug Victorian England the burden of proof was always laid very heavily on those who sought change of any kind.

All this must be largely deduced from a reading of the popular periodical literature of the time. One particular example seems remarkable enough to deserve full description. It is told by Dion Boucicault, playwright and theatrical manager, in a letter to 'The Times' in November, 1861. It appears that in the last act of Boucicault's new drama, 'The Octoroon,' the beautiful slave girl, purchased by a ruffianly overseer to become his paramour, committed suicide. This tragic dénouement was very badly received by the public — so badly that the act was changed to provide a happy ending. Boucicault expressed puzzlement and some distress. Long residence in the South, he said, had convinced him that Uncle Tom was exaggerated and not a true picture of slave life, and accordingly in the first four acts he had shown the sunny side of Negro life, while the audience applauded. 'Yet, a few years ago, the same public, in the same theatre, witnessed with deep emotion the death of Uncle Tom under the lash, and accepted the tableau of the poor old negro, his shirt stained with the blood from his lacerated back, crawling across the stage, and dying in slow torture.... Has public sentiment in this country,' the author concluded, 'veered so diametrically on this subject, and is it possible that this straw indicates that the feeling of the English people is taking another course?'

The great middle opinion in England, the attitude rather than the thoughts of the half-educated mass which lacks convictions outside of home, business, and country, certainly wavered during the first third of the war. It had recovered, with that stolid elasticity which is the despair of all reformers, from such shocks as Uncle Tom and bleeding Kansas, and was now subjected to new influences — the Northern Butlers and M'Neils,[1] copperhead newspaper correspondents in New York, even the very fact that the slaves had failed to rise in insurrection against their masters. This is shown in the tone and arguments of the 'Daily Telegraph,' cheaper and more popular though less influential than 'The Times,' in the pages of the unpartisan weekly press in the provinces, and in the articles of the less ponderous of the magazines, such as 'Temple Bar,' 'The Athenæum,' the 'Illustrated London News,' and in 'Punch' and its two rivals. But perhaps most interesting of all in illustrating the failure of slavery to alienate the British public from the South is the timid and ambiguous attitude of most of the religious denominations.

The voice of the Church of England was neither hesitating nor uncertain. There is no avoiding the conclusion that the clergy of the Establishment were with very few exceptions far more sympathetic to the South than to the North. The High-Church party, which was thoroughly identified with the Conservatives, took over the latter's tone of abuse of the North and admiration of the South with no ecclesiastical modification whatever, and, it must be admitted, stuck by their guns after less steadfast souls had yielded to the march of events. After emancipation, after Gettysburg and Vicksburg, their most aggressive organ was still able to say that the ordinary British ideas of slavery had been all wrong, and that the slave, though

[1] M'Neil was a Northern officer in Missouri who was reported to have shot ten Confederate prisoners in cold blood.

'capable, no doubt, of being trained to a higher and nobler life, for the present at least [is] best and happiest, and, in truth, most contented as he is.' Beresford Hope, one of the most prominent laymen of the High-Church party, was one of the three or four most ardent champions of the Confederacy in the realm and never made the slightest attempt to be tactful toward the erstwhile United States. Lord Robert Cecil, also one of the more intransigent defenders of the Church, sympathized with the South in private and in Parliament. This group was not at all influenced by anti-slavery opinions, and can only be taken as a part of anti-democratic conservatism.

In the Broad- and Low-Church sections of the Establishment, slavery figured hardly more conspicuously. Charles Kingsley was considered lost to the North. F. D. Maurice, who was moved by an intense monarchical feeling and dread of democracy, could not, even after the Emancipation Proclamation, see his way to identifying the cause of the North with that of the slave, and protested against the party, that is, Radical, spirit, in which his friends Hughes and Ludlow espoused the side of the Union. The Earl of Shaftesbury, a leader of the Evangelicals, was a friend of the South for all his identification with the chief philanthropic movements of the time. I am aware of very few instances in which ministers of the Establishment avowed open and active sympathy for the North. The biographies of bishops and deans of the period are usually silent on the American question. Bishop Wilberforce, whose deserved reputation has suffered unjustly from his famous tilt with Huxley and from the nickname of 'Soapy Sam,' would have liked to see recognition of the South, while a Suffolk rector published pamphlets in advocacy of intervention, not shirking an actual defense of slavery. It may be noted, too, that the ablest statement of the opinions of the upper and middle classes on the war came from the pen of Archbishop Whately.

An interesting example of the diversity of opinion on America is furnished by the Evangelical Alliance. This international body had been formed in 1846 and was composed of Protestants of various countries united chiefly by hostility to Roman Catholicism. Its British Branch, by far the most important, joined in one work the Evangelicals of the Established Church and of the Dissenting sects; it was always particularly positive in condemnation of slavery. In September, 1861, the Alliance held its annual conference at Geneva, an American delegation being in attendance. The Americans tried to secure a declaration in favor of the Union, while English speakers condemned and defended the apparently general sentiments of their country. The conference was able to go no farther than the adoption of very weak resolutions of sympathy with the United States, entreating God 'to dispose the hearts of his own people in America to use the means dictated by wisdom and Christian principle, for the speedy and complete suppression' of the slave system. By 1862, Americans were complaining that the English organ of the Alliance was siding with the South.

In particular Nonconformist denominations it was equally impossible to obtain positive official declarations, though as a body Dissenting ministers listened more willingly to Northern claims than any other portion of the middle classes. The Wesleyan Methodists, the largest of the sects, included all sorts of views. Before 1861 they had been a good deal exercised about the division of the American Methodist Church and refused to hold any commerce with the 'Methodist Episcopal Church, South'; but the proceedings of their annual conferences in 1861 and 1862 show that pro-Northern partisanship had to be sacrificed to Methodist harmony. At least one able Methodist minister, who was sufficiently interested in the United States to read a good deal in its history, was converted to toleration of the South *after* the Trent affair, and leaned strongly to the opinion that each side was entirely in the wrong. Another preacher, in 'A Watch-Night Homily' delivered on the eve of 1863, took occasion to stigmatize the war in unmeasured terms and charged the Christian ministers of America with having given way to 'the cruellest and guiltiest passions of depraved human nature.'

The Congregationalists, Baptists, and Presbyterians, the most numerous of the remaining Protestant denominations, were in no different case. The Congregational Union, expressly in order to avoid internal trouble, gave no opinion on the merits of the Civil War, and when a prominent American minister addressed its meeting, he was requested to say nothing that would arouse a partisan dissent. F. W. Chesson in his diary gives a peep behind the scene. He wrote on October 9, 1862: 'Attended meeting of the Congregational Union at Weigh-house Chapel with a view to hear the discussion on American affairs. It was brought on by Dr. Massie in a long string of resolutions designed to please both parties, but which gave satisfaction to neither. Mr. J. Spicer delivered a strong Secession speech, altogether infamous. Thought that the anti-Northern party would have gained the upper hand or would, at all events, have shelved the question, but Newman Hall moved a resolution which dexterously expressed the hope that both Slavery and the war would speedily come to an end. This was passed with acclamation.' The Congregational ministry supplied some of the most ardent advocates of the Northern cause during the war, one of whom estimated later that nine tenths of the pastors and churches of the denomination took the same side. But Dr. Robert Vaughan, editor of the 'British Quarterly Review' and historian of English Nonconformity, was notoriously anti-Northern; and one of the ablest and most attractive of the nineteenth-century Dissenters, Robert Dale of Birmingham, was converted only by emancipation.

III

The saying is attributed to Lord Palmerston that 'in the long run, English politics will follow the consciences of the Dissenters'; and in the first half of the Victorian era there is certainly nothing to disprove the assertion. Prior to the fall of the year 1862, the religious bodies were wavering and divided on American questions, and it was only in that year that there was real danger of British intervention. It was not 'conscience' which determined British sympathies toward the American sections, but other and more complex motives. On the other hand, a non-slaveholding South might have fared much better at the hands of European chanceries than was actually the case. All the members of the 'governing classes,' however little sentiment they might themselves have on the subject of slavery, knew perfectly well that slavery was particularly obnoxious to the working men and Nonconformists who wanted a more democratic England, and that they could not afford wantonly to offend these groups. Yet it is the opinion of the present writer that the weakening anti-slavery feeling of England during the first third of the war was not strong enough to have stood seriously in the way of a plausible recognition of the South. It would have been necessary to save face in the manner of interfering; it would not have been possible to ally with the Confederacy; yet it does not seem that, except for a small minority, 'conscience' about slavery positively determined either the opinions or the decisions of the English people.

With the great change in the policy of the Northern Government toward slavery, English opinion entered on a new phase. The transition, however, was very slow. It cannot be claimed that Lincoln's preliminary proclamation of emancipation was issued with especial regard to its results abroad; but its effects in England were ultimately decisive. The very slowness of British response, the need for the clenching argument of the definitive proclamation of January 1, 1863, show the determinant character of the slavery question. The dilemma of a war against slave-holders but not against slavery was at last resolved, and the conflicting feelings of many good folk were now allowed to crystallize into judgment. A great central fraction, not so much of men as of thoughts and sentiments, was by that single act moved to one side in the balance of opinion, and this shift marks a real climax in a story of government by opinion and without votes.

The possibility of emancipation during the war had, of course, been considered by English observers. Bright, Motley, and other friends of the North in Europe, had urged the abolition of slavery as the only means which could be counted on to avert French or English intervention, while the anti-slavery organizations constantly asked for it. The Nonconformist religious bodies, as has been said, confined themselves to prayers that the outcome of the struggle might be freedom for the slave. Friends of the South, on the other hand, were never backward in pointing out the dangers and disadvantages of sudden emancipation, and usually left it to be inferred from their remarks that the enlightened Confederates would ultimately grant to the Negro whatever rights and privileges he was fit to possess in a civilized community. These people, and very many who were more neutrally minded, expressed great anxiety about the possibility of a servile insurrection, in which, coloring their fears with dim reminiscences of Rome, they saw the most hideous visions of crime and destruction. The apprehension was not very valuable to the South unless verified by the event, but for a time it served as a brake on enthusiasm for emancipation.

Rumors of an intention of the Northern Government to proclaim freedom preceded the act and called forth sharp criticism from the Tories, who stigmatized emancipation in advance as an infamous crime, a dastardly instrument of vengeance on the South. However, Lincoln did not shrink from taking up 'such a load of infamy,' and on September 22, 1862, the proclamation was made public which announced the President's intention of declaring free the slaves in all districts in rebellion on January 1, 1863. In England this proclamation had at first none of the prestige of a *fait accompli* and even bade fair to be nearly lost between the reports of the battle of Antietam and the discussion aroused by Gladstone's speech at Newcastle. Yet its importance grew with reflection, and in the course of two or three weeks most of the press had seen fit to comment, stimulated thereto by the jubilant cries of those organs which were already Northern in sentiment. The attitude of the Tories may be gathered from what is already known of the 'Morning Herald' and from a letter from John Stuart Mill to Motley written at the end of October. 'In England,' he said, 'the proclamation has only increased the venom of those who, after taunting you so long with caring nothing for abolition, now reproach you for your abolitionism as the worst of your crimes. But you will find that whenever any name is attached to the wretched effusions, it is always that of some deeply-dyed Tory — generally the kind of Tory to whom slavery is rather agreeable than not, or who so hate your democratic institutions that they would be sure to inveigh against you whatever you did, and are enraged at no longer being able to taunt you with being false to your own principles.'

The proclamation was at first seen as a purely military measure designed to weaken the resistance of the South, and such an impartial critic as 'The Economist,' while denying its atrocity, assured Englishmen that they would be very unwise to give their sympathy to the North on account of it. Those persons in England who cared most about the issue of slavery were won over from this view slowly. 'The Spectator,' for example, whose course on the war had been almost entirely governed by the slave question (and which had lost authority and circulation in consequence), was itself lacking in sympathy. The proclamation, it said, was a hopeful promise but nothing to exult over; a military measure, making no concession to principle. Even those most closely identified with the anti-slavery movement were not in many cases disposed to look favorably on the latest war measure, and repeated in public the obvious remark that Lincoln was proclaiming emancipation to the slaves whom he could not liberate while retaining in slavery those whom he could. J. M. Mason wrote after the proclamation had been known in England for a month that '... even the Emancipation Proclamation... had little other effect than to disappoint the Anti-slavery party here, and met with general contempt and derision.'

Nevertheless a force had been set in motion which was to urge many waverers into the Northern camp. The French Protestants had been much more prompt than the English Dissenters in siding with the North, and their action gave a fillip to the impending agitation in Great Britain. Immediately after the President's proclamation a letter from the Paris branch of the Evangelical Alliance was sent to England announcing the intention of French Christians (i.e., Protestants) to make public their sympathy with the North, and, in effect, asking their English brethren to follow the example. This communication was considered at the sixteenth annual conference of the British Organization of the Alliance, where the speeches showed that the subject was considered too dangerous for frank expressions of opinion. The reply presented to the French was so general as to mean nothing. The British and Foreign Anti-Slavery Society, however, though slower than the French Evangelicals, soon began to move. Just a month after the news of the President's action had reached England, its Committee met, and with some hesitation, due to the pacifist element, drew up a carefully revised public address. An extract will best show the tenor of this document, which stated that its framers,'... while anxious to avoid any opinion likely to be construed into an approval of a war policy, regard it as established beyond disproof, that the South was not only the aggressor, but designedly provoked an armed contest with the United States Government, with the express sole object of founding a Confederacy to perpetuate slavery. On the other hand, the United States Government, embracing the political anti-slavery party of the North — commonly called the Republican party — has initiated and carried into effect measures in furtherance of negro emancipation, which entitle it to the sympathy of all true friends of freedom.' Copies of this address were sent to all members of Parliament and peers, to six hundred newspaper editors, and to two thousand ministers.

At very nearly the same time as this address, a much more partisan movement was started, with the design of organizing the activities in England of all persons willing to come out flatly on the side of the North and the slave. This was initiated by a very small group of old friends of William Lloyd Garrison who, centering about George Thompson and his son-in-law F. W. Chesson, had almost alone been 'right' on the war since the beginning. A preliminary meeting was held at the Whittington Club in London on November 11, an address was at once issued, drawn up by Washington Wilks, a journalist and lecturer connected with the temperance and Radical reform movements, and the organization took the name of 'London Emancipation Society.' The Society at once started active propaganda. Prominent men all over the country were circularized, pro-Northern pamphlets were bought or printed and distributed in considerable numbers, and meetings were held to express sympathy with the new anti-slavery cause of the Union. It was a time of intense activity. Chesson, usually very faithful to his diary, noted of the period from November 22 to December 13 that he was 'too much occupied with the affairs of the Emancipation Society to keep a diary.... We organized a Committee consisting of between one and two hundred members, and including some of the best known names in the country.' By the latter part of January, the names on the general committee numbered nearly three hundred, of whom some of the chief were John Stuart Mill, Goldwin Smith, F. W. Newman, J. E. Cairnes, General Perronet Thompson, Thomas Hughes, and the Honorable and Reverend Baptist Noel. The Society bought three thousand copies of the fourth edition of a lecture of Cairnes at Dublin and proposed sending one to every member of Parliament. It had three thousand copies printed of an address of Baptist Noel, purchased twenty-five hundred of Harriet Beecher Stowe's address to the ladies of England, two thousand of a pamphlet by Washington Wilks, and two thousand of one on England's dereliction from duty in connection with the ship Alabama. Efforts were made to form auxiliary societies in the provinces, and a circular was issued to ministers of 'all religious denominations' requesting them to give prominence to the subject of emancipation in their New Year services. Later a more elaborate organization was devised for the metropolis, by which the secretaries of sub-committees in its various boroughs were given seats on the central executive committee.

Coöperating with the Emancipation Society was a Committee of Correspondence on American Affairs. This Committee was formed by a party in the Congregational churches which was dissatisfied with the failure of the Congregational Union to declare itself at its annual meeting in October. It sponsored an address and two pamphlets prepared to its order and sent twenty-five hundred copies to influential men throughout the country. On December 31 the secretary of the committee wrote to the American Minister his assurance that the anti-Northern tide in England was turning. The C.C.A.A. soon dropped out of sight, its members being absorbed in the main movement of the Northern reaction.

Despite great vigor on the part of the leaders, the movement accelerated slowly. The meetings to express sympathy with the North seem to have been entirely got up by the Emancipation Society, the same speakers are found at them time after time, and it was always Nonconformist ministers who occupied the platforms. Nevertheless, there was no apparent difficulty in securing large audiences for these affairs the purpose of which was known in advance, and the resolutions presented were carried by acclamation. The resolution of a meeting held in Clerkenwell may be taken as typical: 'The Government and people of the United States having freed themselves of the guilt of complicity with slavery, and being engaged in a deadly struggle with the rebellious upholders of the atrocious system, are entitled to the warmest sympathy of the British people.'

The British middle classes were not yet quite certain for what purposes their sympathies were being invoked, and for a time the Southern dam held back the waters. Friends of the Confederacy kept asserting in every possible place that Lincoln's preliminary proclamation was only a threatening gesture designed to intimidate the brave South, and that he would never have the courage to affront the Democrats of the North or to precipitate actual servile insurrection by taking the promised final step on January 1. In November and December, the speeches of members of Parliament to their constituents show little trace of a change in opinion due to emancipation. The same members of the Manchester School defend the North with more spirit than earlier; the same Tories attack the United States and democratic institutions; and the Liberals are still divided between disgust at the duration of the war and admiration for the South. Cobden, speaking at Rochdale late in October, did not trouble even to make a talking point of emancipation. Old Lord Brougham, whose connection with the abolition agitation before 1833 was still remembered, and who had more prestige with the public than with politicians, showed conspicuous aversion to the North and no signs of being affected by the news of September 23. One of the greatest thorns in the side of the friends of the North was Charles Buxton, M.P., son of T. Fowell Buxton. Before 1861 (when he was in large measure superseded by W. E. Forster), Buxton, as the wearer of his father's mantle, formed the chief link between the Anti-Slavery Society and active politics. But in the question of the American war his anti-slavery convictions and his social and political feelings came into conflict, and throughout the war he resolutely declined to give countenance to the North, with the result that he became a sort of bulwark to the Southerners. Bright was so annoyed that he said, 'I should not like to go out tiger-hunting with Buxton; he might leave me to the tiger.' Buxton's attitude in the autumn of 1862 aroused so much attention that one of the old anti-slavery democrats went down to Buxton's constituency at Maidstone in order to hold a meeting at which a resolution approving the emancipation proclamation was carried 'by an overwhelming majority.'

On the whole, English opinion prior to the first of January, 1863, was marking time and waiting for what should come next. But it had stopped marching toward the South. The trend is quite accurately described by two letters of John Bright to Charles Sumner, letters written on October 10 and December 6. In the first Bright wonders what Lincoln's proclamation means, but says nothing about contemporary opinion of it. In the second he is more interested but still not very positive. 'The anti-slavery sentiment here has been more called forth of late, especially since the Proclamation was issued, and I am confident that every day the supporters of the South among us find themselves in greater difficulty owing to the course taken by your Government in reference to the negro question.... The Proclamation... has been misrepresented, but it has had a large effect here, and men are looking with great interest to the 1st January, and hoping that the President may be firm.'

IV

On December 31, 1862, the Northern reaction in England began to gain rapidly in force and extent. The movement is marked chiefly by an alliance of the working classes and of Dissent against the palliators of slavery and the dog in the political manger — against what these elements considered a class monopoly in State and Church. It is impossible to separate even the anti-slavery motive from subjects of domestic controversy.

The political history of Nonconformity in the nineteenth century has still to be written. Here it is only necessary to point out that from about 1835 to 1870 or later, an important party in the Dissenting denominations was closely bound up with the movement for political reform. It is quite possible to agree with a hostile critic that Dissent and Radicalism were allied for the purpose of destroying the Established Church by means of universal suffrage. Edward Miall, the hero or Lucifer of this alliance, established his newspaper, 'The Nonconformist' in 1841 and made it the organ of Joseph Sturge's Complete Suffrage movement; in 1844 the Anti-State Church Association was founded; and from 1852 to 1857 Miall was in Parliament. It was thoroughly understood in the latter fifties that political reform and the abolition of compulsory Church rates were connected, that the Dissenters were Radicals and the Radicals for the most part Dissenters, and that the Whigs could win support from Dissent only by consenting to the abolition of Church rates.

On the other hand, the working classes, including relatively fewer electors in 1860 than in 1832, were not an easily ponderable political force in the decade before the second Reform Act. Other writers have shown how in the fifties and early sixties the trade unions were gradually brought into coöperation with the middle-class protagonists of franchise extension, and this is not the place to recapitulate. What must be observed is the fact that while the laboring men had very little positive power in the state, as measured by votes, their dead weight was great. It was very difficult to initiate any large policy of which the working classes disapproved. This negative influence, in London as well as in the textile manufacturing regions, was from the beginning of the Civil War exerted powerfully against traffic with the South, and, unlike that of the anti-slavery party, in favor of the North. But it is almost impossible to gauge its actual effect on journalistic and parliamentary opinion. One can only say that every contemporary who professed any familiarity with public affairs was aware that the suffering operatives of Lancashire as well as labor elsewhere had a strong fellow feeling for the North and antipathy to the South.

A few meetings were held before emancipation which demonstrated that the feeling of labor underwent no sudden conversion at the end of 1862, and a few autobiographies also testify to the consistency of working men's opinion throughout the war. After the conclusion of the Trent affair, a meeting of working men was held in London which adopted resolutions to be transmitted to the United States Government. These resolutions declared that Mason and Slidell '... are utterly unworthy of the moral sympathies of the working classes of this country inasmuch as they hold property in slaves and are the avowed agents of a tyrannical faction now in rebellion against the Republic in America, and are the sworn enemies against the social and political rights of the working classes of all countries. That in the opinion of this meeting, considering the ill-disguised efforts of "The Times" and other journals to misrepresent public opinion here on all American questions, to embroil us on any pretext in war with millions of our kinsmen, to decry democratic institutions under the trials to which the Republic is exposed, it is the duty of workingmen especially as unrepresented in the national Senate to express their sympathy with the United States in their gigantic struggle for the preservation of the Union; to denounce the flagrant dishonesty and slave-holding advocacy of

"The Times" and kindred journals of the aristocracy...'; and so forth. There were a few, but very few, similar meetings held in 1862, but it would be hard to find a better expression than the foregoing of the fusion of motives which gives the key to the much-touted sympathy of the British operative class.

It was, then, in the ranks of the religious middle classes and of the working men that the main body of Northern supporters was found, while the leaders were men of the Manchester School, Dissenting ministers, and a certain number of professional men — university professors and lawyers. The first really important meetings of the 'Northern reaction' were held in Manchester and in London on December 31, 1862. The date was chosen because of its relation to Lincoln's expected proclamation of the New Year's Day, and the function of both meetings was to adopt resolutions to be sent to America expressing ardent sympathy with the emancipation policy on the part of the laboring men of Great Britain. At the London meeting the hand of the Emancipation Society was very much in evidence. The chairman was an artisan, but the main speech of the evening was that of the Reverend Newman Hall. The affair in Manchester was more interesting. It appears to have been really the result of the feeling of working men themselves. Though they had the use of the great Free Trade Hall, they were not provided even with a chairman in advance; but finding the Mayor of Manchester present, he was prevailed upon to preside — as an individual, not as mayor. As public meetings go, the affair was but thinly covered by 'respectability.' The attendance of a solitary member of Parliament and the reading of a sympathetic but unenthusiastic letter from

John Stuart Mill only emphasize the contrast to meetings where the platforms were adorned with galaxies of notabilities. This first move at Manchester, though it called forth later a well-known reply from President Lincoln, attracted attention only in the philo-Northern portion of the press: 'The Times' was not yet interested.

Immediately after this demonstration, and urged by its success and by the committee in London, steps were taken to form a society in Lancashire for the purpose of forwarding the cause of the Union in the North of England. The new organization, whose name of Union and Emancipation Society is significant of its dual aim, was tied less closely to the slavery issue than its London companion. Its official purpose was '... to give expression, on behalf of the population of this district, to their earnest sympathy with the cause of freedom, and fraternal regard toward their kinsmen of the United States; and to resist all recognition of the Slaveholding Confederacy.'

With the news of Lincoln's definitive Proclamation of Emancipation, the philo-Northern movement was fairly launched. This act, said the 'Weekly Times,'[1] was 'the noblest expression of policy which any American Government has made since the day on which the famous Declaration of Independence was signed.' At last, said the 'Daily News,' the Americans of the free States and their English kindred can enter into a cordial understanding. C. H. Spurgeon, the most popular preacher of his day, thus prayed before a congregation of some seven thousand: 'Now, O God! we turn our thoughts across the sea to the terrible conflict of which we knew not what to say; but now the voice of freedom shows where is right. We pray

[1] A cheap independent paper.

thee, give success to this glorious proclamation of liberty which comes to us from across the waters. We much feared our brethren were not in earnest, and would not come to this. Bondage and the lash can claim no sympathy from us. God bless and strengthen the North; give victory to their arms!' And the great congregation, which did not ordinarily give responses, answered the prayer with a fervent Amen.

The Northern reaction was very largely conducted under the auspices of the two societies in London and Manchester and was potently aided by a friendly portion of the press. There was, however, no such systematic attempt to cover the entire kingdom as had been made by the Anti-Corn-Law League twenty years before. On the whole, the Manchester organization was the more active of the two, partly because Lancashire was a region more fully trained and more manageable for 'agitation' than London and the agricultural counties, and partly because opinions on America in the manufacturing districts were more intense and sharply divided than elsewhere. The methods of the movement were strongly reminiscent of the activities of the Anti-Corn-Law League, the personnel of which was very conspicuous in this later movement. Public meetings were held, lectures were given, and many pamphlets were printed. A certain number of addresses of sympathy and friendship to President Lincoln were circulated for signature, and of course the editorial writers of the pro-Northern press were encouraged. There was even a little political activity, as when the London Society adopted a resolution recommending the electors of Finsbury to bear in mind the need of cordial friendship with the United States when choosing their new member to Parliament. But the situation did not lend itself to much of this sort of thing.

The most conspicuous portion of the Northern reaction was formed by the public meetings which were held in most of the larger cities of England and Scotland. In very many instances it is possible to perceive the hand of one of the two Emancipation Societies, but the evidence in others points to local initiative, while at all the demonstrations one finds the same combination of Dissenting ministers and the leaders of local Radicalism. In Scotland the meetings were relatively numerous and large and were managed largely by men who belonged on the ground. I have noted forty-four meetings in February in England and Scotland; March and April each saw nearly as many. At the same time literature was being distributed. By the first week of February twenty thousand copies of a tract on 'What the South is Fighting For' had been distributed by the British and Foreign Anti-Slavery Society and twenty thousand of its address of November 19, while ten thousand were soon printed of a pamphlet on 'British Aid to the Confederates.' The London Emancipation Society put its imprint on a certain number of pamphlets, and the Union and Emancipation Society of Manchester issued a great many leaflets and tracts. Forty-three titles, published between November, 1862, and the end of 1863, may be definitely connected with one of the two societies or with an author who took part in the work of one of them. At a meeting of the Manchester organization, held after six months of work, it was reported that over one hundred and fifty meetings had taken place under its auspices in the North of England and Scotland, that more than forty local committees had been formed, and that 2,750,000 pages of anti-slavery information had been circulated.

The activity, which was really tremendous, was often compared to that of the Anti-Corn-Law League, though the devices for striking the public eye were less numerous and ingenious. An address of sympathy to the American President received about 13,500 signatures in Birmingham and was presented to the American Minister by Bright and the most important reformers of that city. Lincoln's well-phrased reply to the working men of Manchester was everywhere reprinted in the papers, and in pamphlet form by the Union and Emancipation Society, but it is doubtful if it made any great impression. A Committee of Correspondence on Slavery in America, possibly a revised version of the earlier Congregational Committee, also made a brief appearance with a pro-Northern manifesto signed by over fifty persons, mostly Nonconformist ministers.

Mr. Rhodes has eloquently described the phase of the movement which took the form of public meetings, but some of the more important of the manifestations in favor of the Union may be alluded to separately.

In the middle of January the friends of the North in the Southern stronghold of Liverpool raised their heads and undertook an elaborate agitation. 'There are none like the Liverpool people,' wrote John Stuart Mill with unwonted enthusiasm, 'for making an organization [to influence public opinion] succeed, if once they put their hands to it.' A conference was called, at which pro-Southerners were present, and a number of lectures, sometimes ending in lively debates, were given. Soon the Cotton 'Change was affected, and long before the culmination of the movement an impartial reporter could say that even pro-Southerners among the brokers admitted that 'as long as the proclamation is in existence public opinion in England will never permit our Government to take any action in favour of the South.' The culmination of the local campaign was reached at a meeting of three or four thousand persons on February 19. Several of the speakers stressed the fact that it was only emancipation and not the conduct of the war that they were prepared to applaud, and there was vigorous opposition even to these carefully limited statements. But in spite of a good deal of uproar, there was no difficulty in securing the enthusiastic passage of resolutions condemning slavery and the South and of an address to President Lincoln. An interesting feature of the Liverpool movement is the fact that clergymen of the Establishment played a real part in it.

The most important of all the demonstrations in favor of emancipation was the one held in London at Exeter Hall on January 29. The Emancipation Society was responsible for it and provided the chairman and speakers; but the attendance, estimated at ten thousand, showed that more than a mere clique was concerned. The main hall was not sufficient to contain the crowd, and overflow meetings were held in a lower room and in the street outside. Enthusiasm was tremendous. Fierce attacks on the South were received with wild applause, while the name of Lincoln was hailed as that of a benefactor of mankind. In the midst of the proceedings a telegram was read announcing that four thousand people were simultaneously assembled in Bradford for the same purpose, and the participants in the two meetings plainly felt that at last the nation, the half-hidden masses of the British people, had come out into a limelight where they could not be ignored. The audience was composed of the lower middle and of the working classes. George Jacob Holyoake was on the platform and Randal Cremer, a budding trade-union leader, was conspicuous in the outside meeting. The speeches of the evening were made by Nonconformist ministers, while Thomas Hughes, J. M. Ludlow, and a solitary M.P. completed the tale of men who were known to the public. Judged by the standards of 'The Times' or the 'Edinburgh Review,' the affair lacked prestige and weight; nonetheless it made a strong impression, so that Cobden, who was certainly entitled to an opinion, declared that he knew 'nothing in his political experience so striking as a display of spontaneous public action....'

Besides the Emancipation Proclamation itself, several other occurrences early in the year served to encourage the philo-Northern movement. Lincoln's announcement of freedom to the slaves of rebels was met by President Davis with a violent counterblast very unpalatable to Englishmen. The proposal to execute white officers captured in command of Negro troops stole the thunder of Englishmen who had been freely denouncing the Federal Butlers and M'Neils and took aback all but the most fervent friends of the South. Another move in the South which hurt its cause was the pastoral of a convention of the Southern Episcopal Church, in which the justice and beauty of slavery were affirmed. This caused very severe animadversions. Still further grist was furnished by a large audience of M.P.'s and business men at an official banquet of the Lord Mayor of London: they loudly cheered Commissioner Mason's 'appropriate remarks' and were taken to task therefor not only by pro-Northerners but even by 'The Times.' One of the members of Parliament present thought it wise to assure his constituents of Liverpool that he had not been among those who applauded.

But perhaps the most important bit of aid given to the Emancipation Proclamation was rendered by 'The Times' and the 'Saturday Review.' We have seen that slavery had found occasional palliators before 1863, while private conversation had often considered the question whether the Negro would ever be fit for the white man's freedom. But this had not prepared any one for a quasi-official *defense* of the institution, and it was a great innovation when, on January 6, 'The Times' actually published such a defense in its editorial columns. This article, since notorious, did not go very far; but it went far enough to shock English opinion and to give a handle to the opposition which the Newman Halls and Baptist Noels were quick to grasp. 'The Times' said that in that Bible which is always appealed to by abolitionist fanatics, 'there is not one single text that can be perverted to prove Slavery unlawful'; the story of Paul the Apostle and the runaway slave Onesimus is the most ample statement of the Gospels on the question. Slavery is, indeed, contrary to the spirit of the New Testament, but so also are 'sumptuous fare, purple and fine linen, wealth, ecclesiastical titles, unmarried clergy; good clerical incomes, and many other things.' At the same time the 'Saturday Review' presented a similar case, attacking Lincoln for presuming to do what Saint Paul might not do! Assistance such as this was a spur to pro-Northern agitation.

Another timely influence in strengthening the hands of friendly journalists and of the Union and Emancipation

Society was the aid sent to the Lancashire unemployed from the Federal States by the George Griswold and other ships. The master and chaplain of the Griswold were at once taken off to pro-Northern rallies, and this evidence was particularly valuable as a refutation of the widely held belief that all the Northern Americans were the determined and ferocious foes of England.

It is a temptation, in contemplating the conspicuous details of the Northern reaction, to forget its distinctly limited scope. Those who took part in it were very largely people who had been favorably disposed toward the North from the beginning, but who had been silenced by their environment and by the difficulty of finding strong points in the cause of the Union. Their opinions had been confused because they could not be articulate. This was what Bright and his friends were referring to when in 1861 and 1862 they insisted that 'the heart of the nation was sound.' Emancipation released feelings already in existence, but did not create a new stream.

The governing classes of England were but slightly affected by the initiation of an emancipation policy by the North: the best evidence of this is the nature of the continued discussion on America throughout the year 1863. There was probably a real expectation of servile insurrection, though 'brutum fulmen' and 'a Pope's bull against the comet' were phrases often repeated about Lincoln's proclamations. At any rate, in the columns, say, of the popular 'Daily Telegraph' for December and January, hardly any trace is to be found of the reaction to the North, and editorial articles were concerned with the

Democratic victories at the polls, with American finance, with the sad prospect of the Federals after the defeat of Fredericksburg — with everything, in fact, save emancipation.

It happens that there appeared precisely at this time a quasi-authoritative statement of the opinions of the great majority of educated Englishmen. This was a letter from Archbishop Whately of Dublin in answer to an open address from Harriet Beecher Stowe. The venerable prelate summarized coolly and fairly what he believed to be the English attitude on American affairs, and his points are worth giving in full. Of Englishmen, he said, '... some few sympathize with the Northerns, and some few with the Southerns, but far the greater portion sympathize with neither completely, but lament that each party should be making so much greater an expenditure of life and property than can be compensated for by any advantage they can dream of obtaining.' Furthermore, he stated, it was generally considered that the war was not waged for abolition by the North, in which section Negroes were badly treated, and that the South had as much right to secede as the Americans to revolt from Great Britain in 1775. Englishmen were much and not unreasonably provoked by the incessant railings of Americans at England, and by threats to invade Canada, while many persons thought it would be sound and fair policy to recognize officially 'a people who shall have maintained their independence for two or three years.' Finally the aged archbishop declared that most people thought that in view of British material interests, great forbearance had been shown in withstanding the temptation to break the Federal blockade.

If this description was accurate, it is no wonder that pro-Northern meetings were at first ignored in the metropolitan press, or that the recess speeches of members of Parliament bear such a strong resemblance to those of 1861. A perusal of many of the latter makes one appreciate the description of an American who was in London at the time. 'It is really amusing,' wrote Benjamin Moran, 'to read some of the speeches on our affairs lately made by Tory members and to note the complacent tone of self-glorification and boastful superiority over all mankind which forms their staple. According to some of these gentlemen British institutions have stood unchanged more than a thousand years; are the most perfect known; and never can feel the shock of Civil War. That evil is peculiar only to a Democratic Republic, which always engenders it.'

Impartial estimates of the change that was taking place were very rare. J. M. Mason cited the carping condemnation of the Emancipation Proclamation in 'The Times' as the judgment which would be 'passed upon it by all except the most ignorant classes in England'; and 'The Athenæum' concluded that Lincoln was an abolitionist joke and that English society had no faith in the shifty and illegitimate measures of the abolitionists. The general tenor of the comment of the journals read by the upper classes was to the effect that Lincoln's latest move was either a piece of hypocrisy designed to gull the unsophisticated of all countries, or else a dastardly attempt to incite a servile insurrection of the most hideous nature.

The most lively discussion was aroused by the Exeter Hall meeting. There is some comedy and a good deal of significance in the way in which after that affair the opposing sides vigorously called each other minorities. The 'Saturday Review' dubbed the activities of the emancipation organizations 'a carnival of cant' and the Exeter Hall audience 'good simpletons.' It taunted them with the absence of the Wilberforces and the Buxtons, averring that their performances were not in the slightest degree representative of the intelligent portion of the English people. 'The Times' was entirely agreed, and the whole of the upper-class press seemed unanimous that this meeting of ten thousand persons was absurd, a burlesque, an affair of hired *claqueurs*. Nor was respectability alone in this opinion. That interesting yellow journal, the 'Weekly Despatch,' thus expressed itself on the 'London and Manchester Federal Sympathisers': 'Oh, those canting pulpiteers! Those medicine men and rainmakers of this pagan Christendom! Your Newmans and Beechers, and Noels and Cheevers, and mouthing Massies and shouting Newman Halls, and loud-tongued Mialls!... Here stands Protestant Presbyterian 'unco gude' Newman Hall howling for war, and hounding on Lincoln and his ban dogs to stick by the slot of the Southern heroes, and lap more blood. There Ichabod Crane, self-dubbed Professor Newman, who never knows his own mind on any subject, bellows at Mr. Gladstone for counselling peace, and roars for more slaughter and piteous ruin....'

Federal sympathizers, on the other hand, were equally positive that their movement was broadly based. Cobden wrote: 'The great rush of the public to all public meetings... shows how wide and deep the sympathy for personal freedom still is in the breasts of our people.' And Bright, in his favorite terms, thought that 'in every town in the Kingdom a public meeting would go by an overwhelming majority in favor of President Lincoln and of the North.' E. O. G[reening] wrote to a paper in London that Confederate agents had not been able to find, even by bribery, a single representative working man in Manchester willing to advocate the cause of the South. The 'Daily News' insisted that the Exeter Hall demonstration was representative of the people, even though not of the Church of England and of the nobility. It likened 'The Times' to the mountebank of ancient story who had learned to squeak so much like a pig that when he and a pig were brought into competition the man was adjudged the more natural of the two: 'The Times's' squeak sounded more like public opinion than the cheers of ten thousand Englishmen gathered in London.

Of course a good deal of truth lay in the claims of both parties. 'The Times' represented much more than the sound and fury of an aristocratic minority, and Exeter Hall represented much more than those elements which the 'Saturday Review' would have been delighted to call, in Roosevelt's phrase, 'the lunatic fringe.' It may be noted that 'Punch' was respectful of the Exeter Hall audience, though disagreeing with it. Intelligent persons strongly hostile to slavery were not all reconciled by emancipation to the continuance of civil war. Gladstone, who was no palliator of slavery, lamented the movement in favor of the North because it tended to prolong the conflict, while it was his conviction that no satisfactory emancipation of the Negro could be effected by the bloody hand of war. Samuel Morley expressed a similar belief, refusing, although not a pacifist, to participate in a proposed meeting of the British and Foreign Anti-Slavery

Society on the ground that the contestants in the fratricidal war ought to be rebuked rather than encouraged. He was one of the most influential of the lay Dissenters. F. D. Maurice protested against any sympathy with the South, but felt that the cause of freedom was too sacred to connect with the success of the North; he disapproved of the Exeter Hall meeting.

Opinions such as these show that the Northern reaction was and must remain incomplete. Its strength and its limitations alike are shown in two of the more important of its later manifestations. One of these was the meeting of the London Trades' Unions in St. James's Hall on March 26, 1863, of which Mr. Rhodes and other historians have made much. This meeting is chiefly significant as marking an important stage in the alliance later consummated between middle-class Brightism and organized labor. Though the Emancipation Society paid for the use of the hall, it was W. R. Cremer and other trade-union leaders who entirely ran the whole affair; the audience was exclusively trade-unionist; and what is more surprising, middle-class speakers did not monopolize the rostrum. But from the point of view of America, all that can be said is that this meeting showed that London skilled labor was not, as had been feared, much more inclined to tolerate the South than the same group in the provinces.

Another episode shows from a different point of view the scope of the pro-Northern agitation. This was a sort of mobilization of English Dissent behind the North's emancipation policy. In February the French Protestant ministers carried out the intention which had been foreshadowed in October by issuing an address asking the ministers of all Evangelical churches in Great Britain to call forth a great manifestation of sympathy for the colored race. The only peaceable means of hastening the end of the war, said this address of seven hundred and fifty signers, was to take measures which would assure the slaveholders that they could never hope to receive the right hand of fellowship from the sincere Christians of Europe. To draft a reply to this demand a great deal of pulling and hauling, mailing of printed circulars, consultatory breakfasting, and so forth, was required, the whole being fostered by the two Emancipation Societies. At last a conference of ministers in London formulated the document, which circulated from April to June until the signatures numbered over four thousand. Finally a great Nonconformist conference was held at Manchester on the 3d of June, which, after English efforts to answer the French letter had been explained, adopted an address to all ministers of Christian denominations in the United States. Two ministers were appointed to carry this friendly message to America, whither they sailed in the middle of the month.

The character of this 'Northern reaction' has been sufficiently indicated. What conclusion may be drawn? These matters of opinion, of 'movements' and 'agitation,' are incommensurable; nevertheless, it is possible to judge pretty accurately what was the trend of public feeling in the first six months of 1863. Englishmen became divided in that period quite sharply into three classes. In the first were the open friends of the South, who hoped that the British Government might be brought to recognize the Confederacy, who were willing to see the law and English neutrality stretched to the peril of the blockade and of Northern commerce, and who were inclined to be reckless about the possibility of war with the Federal States. These men were to be found largely among the Tory gentry, among the merchants and shipping men in the large ports, and in the services and the universities. Although not actually very numerous, these 'Southerns' seemed stronger than they were because of their background in that great majority of the upper classes who had no liking or sympathy for any Americans, Yankee or Southern. The second group, numerically larger, were those who hoped that the American Union might be restored. This element was prepared to resist by every means in its power any British countenance or aid to the South. It was weak among electors, very weak in Parliament and in society, but strong in numbers and self-consciousness, and possessed of a leadership and organization which rendered its weight even greater. Political Dissent, skilled laborers, and a large section of the younger 'intellectuals' constituted this class. The greater portion of Englishmen, however — aside from the inarticulate masses — still took an attitude of irritated neutrality. They did not at all like to see the war continue and did not think that it was tending toward a solution; while they were distressed by the suffering resulting from the war in their own country. Yet they did not feel any active hostility toward either side in the once United States, and were easily alarmed by talk of war with the Union, which offended a vague sense of cousinhood and raised visions of high taxation. This great body was being gradually driven by the pro-Northern movement to set its face against the South, for it contained much sincere though not very intense anti-slavery feeling. Emancipation achieved in England a work of no small importance.

7

PROPAGANDA AND THE FAILURE OF CONFEDERATE EFFORTS IN 1863

After the reaction induced in England by emancipation, interest in American affairs began to slacken. Signs of incipient boredom were not lacking, and rivals for public attention made their appearance. The Civil War continued to drag on without conspicuous novelties, and was making no obvious progress toward an issue. On the other hand, the flaming-up of rebellion in Poland enlisted British sympathies in a foreign cause more clearly than either of the contestants in America had ever been able to do, while at home the marriage of the Prince of Wales to Princess Alexandra of Denmark absorbed for many weeks a large share of public curiosity and emotion. In 1864, the Schleswig-Holstein question, or rather the struggle of Denmark against the German powers, was the leading topic of the news. Though the trans-Atlantic conflict did not recede at once into the background, and though discussion of it continued lively, 1863 and 1864 may be touched with a light hand for the purposes of the present study, because English opinions had reached a position of approximate stability and were no longer changing. If it is understood what they were in the spring of 1863, it is understood quite exactly what they were until practically the end of the war.

I

With this fact in mind, it is nevertheless curious to observe that it was these years which saw the highest development of belligerent propaganda, both Northern and Southern. In part this activity was due to the problem of the blockade, which made it essential for the South to secure ships in England and essential for the North to prevent their doing so. The questions connected with the rams, however, were primarily diplomatic, not ones in which the attitude of the public was of the first importance, so that most of the propaganda in the strict sense was focussed as earlier on recognition or intervention.

The task of Northern diplomacy during the Civil War was a far easier one than that of the South, for it was the negative task of preventing English action which would affect American affairs. The South, on the other hand, had to stir up British action at a time when no British interests urgently required that anything be done for them. The North held the interior lines, the forts of formal diplomatic conversations, which the South had to force. The consequence was that much of what the South demanded of England could be attempted only by indirect methods, so that Southern propaganda was more complex than that of its rival.

The problem of the Confederacy so far as it concerned Great Britain was twofold. In the first place, it was hoped that the Government might be persuaded or forced into a recognition of Southern independence; and secondly, Confederate envoys in Europe were to secure as much military aid as they could, whether Southern independence were acknowledged or no. Southern propaganda was always pointed to the one end of creating a pressure on the Palmerston-Russell Ministry which would lead it to give formal recognition to the disunion of the United States.

The course of Confederate emissaries was to a large extent marked out for them by events. We have seen that in July, 1861, Yancey and Mann in London were keeping quiet and allowing the North to sink into greater and greater disfavor with Englishmen of all classes. For a time their hopes were constantly buoyed up by the mirage of an intervention coming naturally from the British and French chanceries; and they did not consider it necessary to do much to 'act on the public mind.' It is probable that Yancey made some efforts to establish relations with London newspaper editors — 'not without a good deal of success,' said C. F. Adams — but no records of the details of this activity appear to have survived.

With the arrival of James M. Mason in London at the end of January, 1862, Southern propaganda entered on an active phase. Mason at once embarked on the task of stimulating the Houses of Parliament to a debate on the Federal blockade. He cultivated acquaintanceship among members of Parliament and peers, supplied information to his friends in the House of Commons, and did all that he could to foster the impression that the South would never give in and that the blockade was not properly enforced and hence was illegal.

This attack was not successful, and the blockade debate of March 7 ended in fiasco. Meanwhile, a regularly appointed propagandist for the South was making his headquarters in England. Henry Hotze, a Swiss commissioned by the Confederate State Department as 'commercial agent,' arrived in London about the same time as Mason, and started to work at once. His method at first was to obtain the insertion in the large metropolitan dailies of editorials which he thought would be useful to the Southern cause. He did not have the disposal of large funds for this purpose: this resource was hardly necessary, since the desire to obtain authoritative news from the Confederacy was great among journalists, and many of them were so favorable to the Southern demands that they had no hesitation in giving space to Southern arguments as their own. One of Hotze's methods was to offer his articles to professional leader writers, who were then allowed to receive the fee for them. He also gave away boxes of cigars, American whiskey, and similar items as 'little personal compliments.'

Hotze was not satisfied with the progress made by these means alone, and did not have enough money to organize agitation in starving Lancashire; so he conceived the idea of starting a Confederate newspaper. This was the weekly 'Index,' the first number of which appeared early in May, 1862. A commercial success was of course out of the question, and the editor did not hope to reach the general public, but rather to influence those by whom public opinion was formed. James Spence was enlisted in support of the organ and Hotze secured the services of another Englishman as his assistant editor; but the major portion of the work he did himself. The 'Index' was also used as the means of securing the alliance of professional journalists who needed a more lively incentive than whiskey and cigars. Up to March, 1863, it had employed the services of seven writers on the London daily press. In addition to J. B. Hopkins, his assistant, Hotze wrote that he was

'... further under obligations to Percy Greg, esq., one of the most talented leader writers of London, who besides being a valuable contributor to the Index is one of our most efficient supporters in the columns of the Saturday Review and other literary and political periodicals of high standing.... These gentlemen are not citizens of the Confederate States and expect no favors of any kind.'

Though advertisers were very few and the 'Index' was costing about forty pounds a week, it was not without success. The fact that ordinary newspaper methods were able to obtain so little direct news from the besieged Confederacy lent the information of the 'Index' an air of authority and caused it to be widely quoted, so that its carefully edited material may have done something to obscure the weak points of the Southern case from English eyes. The editor of the 'Annual Register,' for example, applied to Hotze for information and documents for his 1862 volume. On the other hand, Hotze was expending money and energy on a field which was already well fertilized. His active friends among newspaper men and in society were such in consequence of preconceived conviction and not as a result of his labors, while his skillful handling of the slavery question and use of facts damaging to the Federals served only to strengthen the prevalence of anti-Northern feelings and did not at all increase the pressure for recognition.

A very curious incident was connected with the formation of the Anthropological Society in 1863, on the council of which, enclosed by a forest of names followed by the initials F.Z.S., M.D., M.A., M.R.C.P., and so forth, we find that of 'Henry Hotze, Esq., C.S.A.'! This society was a secession from the Ethnological Society. Its president was James Hunt, who delivered a paper at the 1863 meeting of the British Association for the Advancement of Science in which he stated as an anthropologist that the Negro was more like the apes than like Europeans and that slavery was his proper place.

The greatest single stroke of war propaganda, moreover, is to be credited to Hotze. In the summer of 1863 was issued an 'Address of the Ministers of the Confederate States met in Richmond to Christians throughout the World.' This document, setting forth in familiar terms the claims of the Confederacy to Christian sympathy and constantly hinting at the desirability of slavery under Southern conditions, was published as a pamphlet in England, as well as in the newspapers which took it in the normal course of reporting. Hotze's triumph consisted in arranging for the distribution of this pamphlet by securing the aid of a Presbyterian publishing house to have it stitched up under the same cover with the current numbers of 'every respectable religious publication [in Great Britain], as well as the Quarterly and Edinburgh Reviews.' This, he estimated, meant a circulation of two hundred and fifty thousand copies. The tone of mournful dignity of the Address had an excellent effect, he wrote; and it was certainly called to the attention of nearly every one. Yet it is very questionable whether the move was a valuable one for the Confederacy, since it tended to sharpen an issue the clarity of which could be only detrimental to the South. Anti-slavery advocates were shocked and at once came forth with counterblasts. The friendly 'Christian Observer' was forced to take editorial notice of the Address, and in an article which tried hard to give away the whole game to the Confederates, finally concluded that an unbridgeable chasm lay between it and the authors of the appeal. Nearly a thousand Scottish clergymen subscribed to an indignant answer. Altogether it was true by this time that slavery was past saving in England, so that any additional proof of the identification of Southern independence with slavery could easily be made to fly back at its authors.

There were many Confederates in England during the war period, most of them with official appointments of one sort or another, but all eager to forward recognition by such means as lay in their power. Many of them wrote letters to the papers or communicated private correspondence from the Southern States; some of them published pamphlets; and all cultivated friendly acquaintances, dined out as much as possible, and talked — and talked. There was no correlation of their work, which naturally took the line of least resistance and consequently resulted in very little save a series of pleasant social contacts and conversational pabulum for London and county society.

Robert B. Campbell, for twenty years United States Consul in London, was one of these men. A second was Hiram Fuller, formerly a New York newspaper editor. He published some articles in 'Fraser's Magazine' as a 'White Republican,' and during the Trent incident gave a lecture in London at which Charles Mackay presided and Yancey was present. A third was M. F. Maury, the distinguished Southern naval officer and scientist, who had a short tiff with Thurlow Weed in 'The Times' and the 'Globe' in the last days of 1861 and went the round of many country houses during his later stay. Lucius Q. C. Lamar was in England in 1863, where he made at least one speech, in which he explained that the South was

The list of its committee of organization was really impressive, for it included the Marquess of Lothian, the Marquess of Bath, Lords Robert and Eustace Cecil, Lords Wharncliffe and Campbell, and eight members of Parliament. Membership was one guinea annually. In spite of distinguished auspices, the movement languished, though the volume of its pamphlet literature is considerable. Hotze remarked that want of money and want of moral courage were both to blame; he added that money might be supplied by Confederate agents, 'but unless we could give moral courage as well it would be but an artificial vitality. Associations of this sort, to do us good, must derive their sap from British soil.'

In fact Hotze's 'want of moral courage' was mainly a difference of opinion within the Association which prevented it from making any real effort. Professor E. D. Adams has shown in detail how the political situation in the first six months of 1864 inevitably divided this non-partisan Association into supporters of Palmerston and Russell and Tories who hoped to overthrow them on the Danish question. The result was that in spite of the best efforts of Lindsay and the Southerners it could not be moved to action in time: this was the penalty the South paid for the necessary policy of letting it be an *English* association.

So serious was the situation that another organization was brought forward. This was the Society for Obtaining the Cessation of Hostilities in America, which at the end of May, 1864, addressed to members of Parliament an appeal for immediate action. Nothing further was done, however, until after the critical division of July on the Danish question, when, Palmerston being once more securely in the saddle, it sent a deputation to urge him to make peace in America. The deputation was headed by the Marquess of Clanricarde and the Bishop of Chichester, and its argument was based squarely on the public opinion of the regions and classes where Radicalism and the emancipation societies had no strength. Its evidence consisted of letters received, especially from the rectors of parishes, reflecting the feeling in the country districts; on petitions to Parliament from the clergy and laity in eighteen English and thirteen Irish counties; and on the 'general tone of feeling and conversation in all social circles, meetings, and the public press.' Palmerston, doubtless light-hearted after the recent crisis, gave no encouragement; he feared that premature efforts would only exasperate the North, and quoted the couplet:

> 'They who in quarrels interpose
> Will often wipe a bloody nose.'

The Society did not cease its efforts with this rebuff. Securing one hundred and fifty pounds of Confederate money, it circulated for signature a rather disingenuous appeal from the people of Great Britain to the people of the United States asking the latter to be good and stop fighting, since the South could not possibly be conquered. The Secretary of the organization was the Reverend F. W. Tremlett, whose parsonage in London was known as 'the home of the Confederates' or 'the Rebels' roost.' Twenty thousand copies of one of his sermons were circulated to promote the petition, and finally the large total of three hundred and fifty thousand signatures was obtained. Joseph Parker of Manchester bore the petition in person to America in the autumn. There he hobnobbed with Copperheads and had some difficulty in knowing what to do; for Seward refused to receive him and the Democratic Governor Seymour of New York asked him not to publish the address until after the elections. A year earlier such a demonstration might have made a real impression both in England and the United States; now it was very little attended to.

The fact is that Spence, Hotze, and their English allies did not have the right material for a popular movement. While the emancipation societies could focus all Radicalism for a time on the American question, friends of the South had to be drawn from the upper classes, who were politically divided. Peers, Church of England incumbents, members of Parliament, and some large manufacturers were not unwilling to contribute names, money, and even time to the cause of Southern independence. But they would not take concerted political action, which was the only way in which they could have affected the situation. It did not do Southerners any good to denounce Low-Churchmen and admire the English aristocracy for the benefit of Beresford Hope if Churchmen of all views and the 'gentlemen of England' would not desert Palmerston on account of America. Very many important people, perhaps even a class, would have rejoiced at the spectacle of an independent Southern Confederacy whose existence had been recognized by Europe; but there was very little to impel them to act on their convictions.

II

Northern propaganda was a less vigorous growth than that of the South. No agent corresponding to Hotze was sent to London, though John Bigelow, at Paris, had a somewhat similar commission and occasionally extended his activities across the Channel. Charles Francis Adams, with a recognized diplomatic position, could not emulate J. M. Mason and did not have occasion to risk himself as did Bernstorff and Dumba at Washington in the World War. It does not appear that the American Legation devoted much energy to 'acting on the public mind.' Friendly newspaper writers and members of Parliament called sometimes at the Legation to obtain information for their leading articles or speeches, and in the case of important letters of Northerners to be printed in the London press, the Minister was usually consulted. But of gifts to professional leader writers or of systematic attempts to 'influence' British channels of information, we hear nothing.

There was, however, one field which formed a sort of indecisive battle-ground between Unionists and Confederates in Great Britain. Benjamin Moran and many less informed Americans, believed that Reuter's telegram agency had been bought up by the South, a charge which would involve very important consequences if substantiated. A categorical answer is not possible; but although it seems probable that Reuter himself was no more friendly to the North than most of the powerful newspaper men of the time, it does not appear that he intended to act as a partisan. C. F. Adams learned that American telegrams sometimes were modified at Liverpool by hands hostile to the North; yet all that can be said here is that Reuter himself was perfectly willing to enter into private arrangements with both Northern and Southern agents. He was first of all a business man, and bribes were not offered him from either side; so that such disadvantage as the Union derived from his news was no more than was inevitable in the current conditions of English feeling.

Adams, however, was beset by volunteers, who caused

him a good deal of annoyance. The system of Federal espionage in England in the autumn of 1861 was organized by H. S. Sanford, the American Minister at Brussels; it had only a bad effect on British opinion. Benjamin Moran, in his testy way, declared that, with one half of the money Sanford thus wasted, 'I could have bought the British Press, and I solemnly believe every newspaper writer in London can be purchased, from those of the Times down, including those of the religious world.' The mission of Thurlow Weed and Bishop M'Ilvaine, however, though it was a little galling to Adams's pride, was distinctly useful. Weed was known to be very close to Secretary Seward, so that his arrival in London society just at the time of the Trent affair enabled him more effectively than the Minister to disabuse Englishmen of the idea that the Federal authorities wanted war with England. We have not, unfortunately, Weed's expense account of his European trip, and all that we know of his work consists of his suave letters to the press and his own later remarks concerning the large number of prominent Englishmen whom he was able to see.

A great many other Unionists came to England with more or less official sanction. In 1863, there were John M. Forbes and W. H. Aspinwall of Boston, W. M. Evarts and William Whiting, all sent to work on the problem of the Confederate steam rams. In the last half of the war Robert J. Walker, 'a most interesting old man, although small and shrivelled up,' came to attack Southern credit and to bolster up that of the North in Lombard Street. George Harrington, an Assistant-Secretary of the United States Treasury, was probably bent on a similar mission. Moncure Conway appeared also in the spring of 1863 as the emissary of American abolitionists; he was active in Dissenting and literary circles, but notes candidly that the pro-Northern conferences which he attended had 'an accent of the conventicle about them' which limited their influence. A number of escaped slaves, especially the former coachman of Jefferson Davis, were produced as lions at Unionist meetings; and the Reverend Sella Martin, a Negro who received a parish in London, was one of the most effective of all the workers among the Dissenting bodies.

There was, furthermore, a counterpart to Hotze's 'Index' in the 'London American,' founded before the war but expiring in 1863. It was managed and edited by J. A. Knight and A. Bostwick, quite without success. A mainstay of its columns was formed by the letters and speeches of George Francis Train, a fiery pro-slavery Unionist, who seemed to Englishmen like the 'New York Herald' Yankee incarnate, and who did incalculable damage to British ideas of the Federals. Official sources did not care to aid the 'London American.'

Of all Americans in England during the war, the Reverend Henry Ward Beecher was most in the public eye. A proposal for a trip of Wendell Phillips to that country was not followed up; but his place was most worthily supplied by the other great orator — no less an orator for being a preacher. Beecher's reputation had preceded him, and it was the Emancipation Society people who persuaded him to enter on his great speech-making tour of 1863 because they thought he would be an asset in their work.

He was received with some warmth by both sides. A pro-Southern journalist wrote that an American performer was about to arrive in England — '...the ranting ruffian, the "Rev." Henry Ward Beecher, who is a sort of Spurgeon in New York, and who has been of late amusing himself by preaching perfectly devilish sermons about the war. The fellow will be received with open arms by a large party of tea and muffin-stuffing lunatics here, and will doubtless be planted on the platform of Exeter Hall....Let us hope the man will be treated with indifference.'

Barring hyperbole, this extract indicates very well what happened. Beecher's speeches were made in rapid succession in October in the largest towns of the kingdom, where they rallied the 'American party' in tremendous numbers. Everywhere he was met by urgent opposition. Hostile placards printed in red were posted in the streets abusing him bitterly, and the Tory press was only less vehement in its condemnation. At every meeting the speaker had to overcome a noisy opposition, which at Liverpool very nearly prevented the delivery of the address and turned the meeting into a riot. The crowds were great. At Edinburgh, Beecher's address was given in the Free Church Assembly Hall, which was so crowded that some of the holders of platform tickets failed to secure entrance. At Exeter Hall in London, the speaker himself could hardly be introduced by the aid of the police. The London demonstration was the least divided in sentiment of any, and was more successful, eye-witnesses agreed, than even the famous one of the preceding January.

These were great field days for the Emancipation Societies. Beecher was at his best when handling hecklers and large audiences, and his success with these helped to rally the democrats and anti-slavery people behind the standard of the United States. Prominent politicians kept entirely away,[1] but we find publishers and newspaper men cheek by jowl with the Congregational ministry, such Radicals as Edmond Beales, Justin M'Carthy, and G. J. Holyoake beside Chamerovzow, F. W. Chesson, and George Thompson — practically all the elements of political nonconformity converging on the same platforms.

The demonstration was too hearty to be ignored as Southern sympathizers would have wished. Though it was but a repetition of the movement which had taken place in the first three months of the year, it was enough to show that the friendship for the North released by emancipation was no flash in the pan, and that British favors to the South could be given only in the face of a determined and numerous opposition. 'The Times,' which had withdrawn some distance from its earlier defense of slavery, was clearly disgruntled, as were most of those who agreed with it. Their arguments against Beecher have a slightly discouraged tone. That the preacher made many converts is not to be believed. What he did achieve was to provide new nourishment for a group of leaders who were too few and too much alike not to have worn thin by constant use; he consolidated and rendered more self-confident the ranks of the pro-Northerners. This somewhat vulgar yet essentially noble man was ideally fitted to accentuate the cleavage between the classes and the masses in England. His expedition introduced a fresh breath of religio-democratic oratory to a country where evangelism was still an integral part of popular life, and thus served to sharpen the lines of the social divisions which could be obliterated only by political reform.

[1] October is of course a season when 'no one' is in London.

III

The Beecher speeches, capping the Northern reaction, show that British opinions were not changing substantially in 1863, and the febrile weakness of Confederate propaganda in that year and the following is indicative of the same fact. As Walter Bagehot pointed out, though the mass of Englishmen were singularly divided in their *sympathies*, they were singularly united in their *intentions*, and it is doing no violence to the realities to pass rather lightly over the various alarms and crises of the last two years of the war. What is significant in them is mainly the shifting prognostications of the future in America, and the complications introduced by other matters of international politics.

A certain measure of war prospects as judged in England is afforded by the story of the Confederate cotton loan. That three-million-pound loan was issued on March 19, 1863, in London, Liverpool, Paris, Frankfurt, and Amsterdam. Subscriptions were closed in two days — it was said that fifteen millions were subscribed in London alone — and for a short time trading took place at from two to five points above the issue price of ninety. Business circles were very much interested, and speculators were tremendously excited. Yet, although Confederates and some cotton speculators attempted to make capital out of the loan's initial success and to put it forward as a desirable investment, hardly any one failed to see it for what it was — a pure speculation. A reporter on the Liverpool 'Change said it was 'almost impossible to find any one serious in regard to the Confederate loan.' It was not admitted to listing on the London Stock Exchange, and the powerful financial editor of 'The Times' constantly harped on the point that the loan was not political but a *cotton* speculation. If, said he, the North (which could not sell its bonds in England) were to hypothecate wheat in a manner similar to that in which the South had pledged cotton, it too might obtain subscribers. 'The Economist' at first argued that the loan was a perfectly reasonable proposal, with small chances of loss and great ones of profit; but its reporting columns show that trading was confined to speculators; after two weeks it was saying editorially that 'the cotton loan offers little inducement to the real investor.' Charles Francis Adams and the ecclesiastical and anti-Northern 'Guardian' unexpectedly agree in the opinion that the loan was largely taken up by creditors of the Confederacy. Finally, and most conclusive, is the fact now well known that within three weeks of issue Mason and Erlanger thought it necessary to conspire to bull the market to the tune of a million pounds. There was very slight basis for the opinion of uninformed or Tory writers that the success of the loan showed the confidence of the commercial world that recognition and peace must sooner or later come. Though Lombard Street was at this time very hospitably inclined toward new foreign issues, 'the commercial world' was not represented by their purchasers. On the other hand, the loan was not without some weight as a political demonstration: its flotation stressed, for the layman, the respectability of the Southern cause.

If the cotton loan was not an unmitigated triumph for the Southerners, there were other things at the same period which were far more perilous and annoying for the North. The Alabama and later questions of shipbuilding for a belligerent never became such a burning matter with the English public as Americans have always felt them to be.

It was not until the end of 1862 that American alarm and vexation over the Alabama reached a pitch of intensity which brought the problem to the surface in England. At that time Northern protests were carelessly thrown off with a self-righteous shrug. But continued and vehement American complaint tended to arouse the dormant chauvinism of the British; in March, 1863, the question was brought up in Parliament, where it was mismanaged by the friends of the North; and the diplomats began to fear war. The Union and Emancipation Society soon held a large meeting of protest against further shipbuilding for the Confederacy, but the public in general was only irritated by the ravings of the Federals and objected strenuously to the charge that England did not enforce her own laws. The Foreign Enlistment Act was not very clear: if Unionists bought munitions, why should not Confederates buy ships? In any event, it would never do to allow the North to bully the British lion. The failure of the prosecution of the ram Alexandra was decidedly popular. The mass of the public, however, never realized the seriousness of the ram question, which was the really crucial one of the year.

On the other hand, heat amounting almost to a war scare was generated by two incidents of the spring of 1863. The seizure of the British vessel Peterhoff, which carried mail bags, was unfortunately made by no less a person than Admiral Wilkes. A second damaging occurrence was the action of Charles Francis Adams in licensing two traders to pass freely to the Mexican port of Matamoros because he was convinced that they were loyal American citizens engaged in lawful trade. Some one among the London underwriters started a story which made everybody think that *British* traders had secured the license in question. A portion of the press worked itself up to war temperature over these mistakes, and a rumor got into the papers that Lord Russell was about to dismiss the American Minister. When the Peterhoff's mail pouches were sent to England unopened, and when Adams was thought to have apologized, the atmosphere soon cooled.

Yet some progress toward intervention seemed to be making in May and June. The Southern clubs in the provinces were beginning their activity, in which they were aided by the reports of the battle of Chancellorsville and the very extraordinary sensation made by the death of Stonewall Jackson. The victory of the Union appeared more than ever hopeless, and probably not one in four of the English friends of the North thought reunion more than a bare possibility. Hotze, who had been much depressed, plucked up heart and decided that 'a popular movement which had even the appearance of strength' would be gladly accepted as the excuse for recognizing the South. The attempt was made. Roebuck carried with him a large open-air meeting at Sheffield for a resolution requesting the Government to confer with the other powers of Europe concerning the recognition of the Confederacy. Similar meetings were held at Manchester, at Preston (which was a particular Southern stronghold), and elsewhere. In anticipation of the motion to be made in the House of Commons, Hotze arranged to have every available space in London placarded with representations of the Confederate flag conjoined with the British, and secured a promise from the 'Herald' and the 'Standard' that they would print leading articles in support of the motion at least every other day from June 6 to July 1. Barrel organs all over London played a Southern hymn, 'The Bonny Blue

Flag.' Nevertheless, the movement was lacking in depth and power despite Roebuck's grandiose claims. The two Emancipation Societies combated it with all their strength in a war of posters which made bright the streets of many English cities, while the much-lessened intensity of the cotton famine had already withdrawn the best argument for intervention.

If anything was needed to keep British policy on an even keel, the course of the debate in the House itself supplied it. Roebuck and Lindsay, neither of whom was a person of wide political influence, appeared there in the belief that Napoleon III had authorized them to express his desire to recognize the Confederate States if he could do so in company with England; in fact, they mistakenly understood that he had made actual overtures to the Foreign Office. This was exactly the wrong line to take; for the international situation was again become tense with the Polish rebellion and the early rumblings of the Schleswig-Holstein storm. Stocks were falling; active preparations in arming were going on; and Napoleon was suspected of all sorts of schemes. British politicians were much inclined to stand on a policy of self-sufficient isolation and had no idea of co-operating with the Emperor whose constant friendliness aroused constant suspicions. Roebuck's motion (which came up on June 30) broke down completely, and even more so among the people than in the House. Southerners were thankful to avoid its coming to a vote. He was ridiculed and abused for his intimacy with Napoleon and for expecting to win English support for his scheme. The fact that the South had turned over its fortunes to such an inept leader damaged its prestige not a little. An issue of 'Punch' ridiculed Roebuck on almost every page, and

Henry Adams wrote: 'Mr. Roebuck has done us more good than all our friends.' In the words of Hotze, recognition would in Parliament 'never again receive serious attention, even if a man could be found bold enough to broach it after the experience of the last two weeks.'

The test had been a fair one for the South, since in late June and early July the military situation was anything but auspicious for the Federals. For many months the Vicksburg campaign had concentrated most of the attention which was given to military events, until Chancellorsville had shifted interest back to the eastern seat of war. But Vicksburg was not taken — once, in May, there was a rumor that it had fallen — and while its fate was still hanging in the balance, Englishmen were suddenly greeted with the news that Lee had invaded the North. Excitement was great at the end of June and in the first two weeks of July, and cotton-holders and blockade-runners at Liverpool had to retort to zealous Southerners that the North was not to be conquered as easily as they said. But there was no such general apprehension of the collapse of the North as had helped to check Lindsay's motion a year earlier, and most of the country simply waited in the hope that an opportunity for friendly mediation might at last be forthcoming. With news of the battle of Gettysburg and the fall of Vicksburg, Southern sympathizers were all but silenced. The Confederate loan which, as Professor Adams has said, had become a mere barometer of Southern fortunes, fell off thirty-two points, recovering by the end of August to a net loss of about twenty. For the first time in over a year, English convictions that the North could not win began to be shaken: it is even possible to find direct statements that the cause of Southern independence was hopeless.

Even before the Roebuck fiasco, the Confederates had begun to resign themselves, not without grumbling, to the prospect of continued British neutrality. The Secretary of the Navy wrote in June: 'We have long since abandoned all belief in English intervention, and have learned to regard the settled policy of the ministry as hostile to us.' Mason and his official chiefs decided at almost the same time that his usefulness as embryonic ambassador was at an end, so that in September he officially 'withdrew' from London, firing a parting shot at the impervious armor of Lord Russell. This move created hardly a ripple in English waters. Such remarks as were made show clearly enough that the intervention question was dead — dead unless the Confederacy could win decisive victories in the field. Interference was not rendered impossible by mismanagement. Rather, it is true to say, the Confederate mission was never in a position to influence public opinion at more than a few unimportant points.

For the public in general it remained only to sympathize and predict. In spite of occasional signs of war weariness in the North, there appeared less and less chance of an ending of the conflict within a calculable period. The price of cotton rose steadily from the news of Vicksburg until the end of October, 1863. At Liverpool and Glasgow, blockade-running grew more elaborate and more profitable and drew to itself capital dependent on peace being remote. Some persons were found to prophesy peace after the battle of Chickamauga, which tremendously cheered Confederate sympathizers for a short while; but in general Southern hopes declined, and interest in American events flagged very decidedly. In the last months of 1863, the press, which followed events with a weather eye to the popular trend, shows a slow drift of sentiment toward the North, which is confirmed by the manner in which pro-Southern newspapers commented on happenings like Beecher's tour, Cobden's and Bright's speeches at Rochdale in November, and Grant's victories at Lookout Mountain and Missionary Ridge. Emancipation; the comparative success of Northern forces in the field; the passing of the crisis of the cotton famine and the close economic ties of England with the North; and, finally, increasing fear of European complications, all acted to prevent the development of further hostility toward the Union.

The Polish revolt in 1863, so harshly crushed by Russia, had been somewhat damaging to the North because of the similarity to the attempted conquest of the South and because of Russia's ostentatious friendship for the Union. But it had served even more importantly to divert attention from America, and after all the English Radical friends of Poland were also friends of the Northern democracy. The Continental crisis over Schleswig-Holstein, following shortly, absorbed a further share of interest at a period when the United States was becoming something of a bore. British understanding of this crucial problem was notoriously inadequate, and at first there was no general feeling on the subject except such hostility to Prussian policy as had been aroused by Bismarck's unconstitutional course as Minister-President. But with the beginning of the war against Denmark in February, 1864, sympathy with the smaller country was very general despite the Germanophile British Court, so that in the early months of the year America was very much in the background.

In spite of a total lack of comprehension of the Schleswig-Holstein situation and in spite of the lecturing tone adopted by 'The Times' and British public speakers, there was little popular pressure for interference. 'Non-intervention,' as the English euphemistically called their policy toward Italy and America, was raised to the dignity of a popular principle, and it appears to the present writer that enthusiasm for action in behalf of Denmark was less than had been that for Poland twelve months before. The Cabinet were divided and came near to war; but in this case public opinion, though favoring the Danes, was even more clearly against action than it had been in supporting the far more statesman-like policy of the Government toward the United States. It was this fact which made the Conservative attack on the Ministry more formidable than anything that had occurred since 1859.

Meanwhile America was left alone. Military stalemate there was no longer of much interest. By and large the year 1864 saw the causes of the Union and British Radicalism gaining ground together; yet there was no considerable change. The English pro-Northerners had gradually become converted to belief in the sincerity of the Washington Government, and in the autumn the Emancipation Societies 'came out' for Lincoln's reëlection.

PART II
THE CONTINENT

8

THE CONTINENT AND THE WAR

THE opinion of the Continent with regard to the American Civil War is of scarcely less interest than the opinion of England; and it was vitally affected by the opinion of England. For the Continent, the question was not simply: What shall we think and do in view of the struggle in America? The question was: What is England thinking and doing? The development of feeling in England during the Civil War, and especially the attitude of the British Government, determined, to a very great degree, the course of public opinion and of governmental policy throughout Europe. A similar close connection between England and the Continent had already manifested itself during the Wars of Independence, both in North and South America. As in 1776 and 1825, so in 1861, it became evident that no European government or people could adopt a point of view toward America without first taking into serious consideration that of England.

While no study of Continental opinion would be complete without a previous study of England, it does not follow that the formation and character of Continental opinion were wholly or ultimately determined from across the Channel. The Continent had its own way of thinking about American problems, and its own way of connecting them with European affairs. In France and Spain, moreover, public opinion and government policy depended upon important national considerations. Both countries had a definite stake in America. To both the Civil War presented an opportunity of increasing the power of Catholic Europe in the New World; and both countries at one time or another tried to guide Europe without reference to British opinion.

A brief glance at public opinion in the other and less interested European countries will suffice. The Italian States, closely concerned with their own struggle for unification, could give little attention to the war in America. The Confederacy made much of the Pope's correspondence with President Davis. The fact, however, seems to be that the interest of Pius IX in the struggle was purely humanitarian, and that his leaning was, if anything, toward the North; while publication of his correspondence with Davis actually strengthened Italian Liberals in their good wishes toward the Union. The Government of Piedmont and the House of Savoy, wrote the American Minister at Turin in 1861, were 'entirely by sympathy on the side of the President. Almost every gentleman with whom I have conversed here coincides in these sentiments.' Garibaldi himself even thought of going to America and accepting a command under the Federal Government.

Concerning Turkey, the American Minister in Constantinople wrote in the autumn of 1861: 'Of the one hundred and fifty American Missionaries resident in this Empire, there is not one who sympathizes with the secession rebellion. Owing to their knowledge of the languages of the country and their extensive intercourse with the people, their influence on public opinion is considerable.'

Swiss opinion is neatly summed up in two dispatches in

1863 from the American Minister at Berne, which illustrate also the good effect of the Emancipation Proclamation. 'I know of no public press or public man,' he wrote, 'whose sympathies are not now with the Federal Government. The War is everywhere understood to be a struggle between freedom and despotism. The President of the Confederation agrees with Congress's resolutions against foreign intervention. He referred to the Sonderbund War of 1849, when all Europe believed Switzerland about to fall apart, and when the Confederation Government refused mediation.'

Austria was remote from American commerce and politics, and concerned only indirectly with the Mexican Expedition. In Vienna, however, as Motley, the American Minister, recorded, there was much interest in the Civil War and more sympathy for the North than in any other city in Europe. The newspapers commented continually upon American affairs. 'The ability and knowledge,' wrote Motley, 'of the public here in dealing with foreign affairs, and especially with American matters, is very remarkable.' There were solid reasons for this sentiment. Austria's policy and interest were against recognition of *de facto* governments. Austria, as a federal state, realized the dangers of secession. At the same time, she appreciated the wisdom of emancipation as a means of destroying the barrier between North and South, and wished the experiment success.

Opinion in Germany, which arose from closer ties with the United States, was equally favorable to the North. American trade with the Hanseatic cities was second only to that of England: Germans had migrated to the United States ever since before the Revolution. The Germans in the Northwestern States ensured the loyalty of the grain-growing region to the Union. Carl Schurz, a German-born citizen of the United States, was Minister to Spain, while some two hundred thousand Germans by birth fought in the Union ranks. German aspirations for political unity and religious liberty inclined public opinion further toward the Northern cause. The influence of 'The Times,' of Reuter's telegrams, and of the pro-Southern Galignani's 'Messenger,' published in Paris, can, it is true, be traced in short comments of the German press. But it is now known that the Frankfurt bankers, by purchasing Federal bonds in great quantities at low rates, had a stake in the restoration of the Union. In 1863, indeed, the Confederate press agent on the Continent wrote home that 'the German mind is obstinately bent against us'; while Bright reported that a friend of his, who had recently traveled all through Germany, had not found one man in favor of the South. This was also the impression of Andrew White, later American Ambassador to Germany. Prince Hohenlohe, the best-informed man of his day in Southern Germany, wrote to Queen Victoria that the American Civil War 'profoundly affects the material interest of the land. It is not only our cotton-spinners who are suffering; it is a question of life and death with them. The capitalists who have put their money into American stock also are anxiously watching the progress of the War, and long for the conclusion of peace and the triumph of the Northern States. Besides, the sympathies of the democratic population of South Germany are naturally with the North-American States.'

In Prussia, a considerable portion of the nobility and of the army officers instinctively sympathized with the Southern cause. But the overwhelming majority of the people were decidedly and vigorously in sympathy with the Union. The traditional policy of Prussia was to cultivate friendly relations with the United States, and her traditional attitude toward all revolutionary movements was hostile. When Prussia supported England in the Trent episode, her motive was no more than the desire to see neutral maritime rights secured. Meanwhile, so many people in Berlin wished to join the Northern army that the American Minister was compelled to place on the doors of the Legation a sign to the effect that 'This is a Legation of the United States, and not a recruiting-office.'

Holland, as a trading nation, had a direct interest in American trade as well as in such questions as the blockade and neutral rights. The American Minister at The Hague, therefore, busied himself with observations upon the economic effects in Europe of the Civil War. He found that, while Holland followed England in issuing a proclamation granting the South the status of a belligerent, her interest was purely the commercial one of ensuring protection for Dutch vessels in Southern waters. 'We could not,' said the Dutch Foreign Minister, quoting a British press correspondent's phrase, 'treat five million men who had declared their independence like marauders or filibusters.' In Holland, however, as the American Minister observed, the dearth of cotton was felt less than in almost any other country, for the native staples, wool and flax, were extensively used. Holland, therefore, was but little affected commercially by the Civil War, and the tone of Dutch public opinion was noticeably calm.

Belgium, like Holland, had primarily a commercial interest in the American struggle. Next to England and France, indeed, she was apparently the worst sufferer from the blockade of the Southern ports. In September, 1862, one third of the cotton-spinners in Ostend were out of work, and another third had only part-time employment. But lack of orders as a result of recent overproduction, and not a cotton famine because of the blockade, lay really at the root of the unemployment. The workmen in Belgium, in fact, blamed their distress on the North no more than did those in Lancashire, for there had been less disposition to mislead the Belgians as to the real cause of their misery. The people in Belgium, on the whole, remained true to the North, the land from which, as a well-known churchman wrote in 1862, their constitution, their religious toleration, and their communal and provincial centralization had been copied. The official attitude of the Government was also friendly to the Union; and this attitude was strengthened by Seward's handling of the Trent episode and by Lincoln's policy of emancipation. Once the slavery issue was defined, the leading Belgian newspaper, 'L'Indépendence Belge,' hitherto convinced that separation was inevitable, admitted the justice of the Union cause and took many opportunities to dwell upon the great resources of the North, which would enable her ultimately to win. Meanwhile, the sagacious King Leopold I had contributed to the pro-Northern policy of the Belgian Government by warning the Archduke Maximilian, in view of the certain hostility of the United States, against going to Mexico without a definite guaranty from France.

'In Sweden,' wrote the American Minister in 1861, 'the public voice, represented by a free press, is clearly and emphatically in favour of my government, and views secession as a causeless rebellion. In the Trent episode, the Northern side of the question was taken by one of the most influential papers and discussed with great vigour and ability.' An especially interesting comment on the war appears in the joy with which the news of the battle between the Monitor and Merrimac was received in Stockholm. 'Captain Ericsson,' wrote the American Minister, 'is a Swede, born and educated here; his brother, Colonel Ericsson, is engineer-in-chief of all the railways in Sweden and Norway. Captain Dahlgren's parents were Swedes who emigrated to America; hence the people here say that a Swede invented the Monitor, a Swede invented the guns with which she was armed: *ergo*, how great is the obligation, the debt of the United States to Sweden.'

Russia was obviously a land where public opinion, apart from Government circles, could scarcely be said to exist. The nature of this official opinion, however, is of some importance and much interest.

At the outbreak of the war, the Russian Foreign Minister informed the American Minister at St. Petersburg that Russia had decided, in coöperation with France and England, upon granting Confederate merchantmen a status similar to that of the merchant ships of the still unrecognized Kingdom of Italy. Russia, however, would do nothing to diminish the power of the United States as a counterpoise to England. 'Russia,' wrote the 'Journal of St. Petersburg' in August, 1862, 'considers the prosperity of the Union necessary to the general equilibrium.' Alexander II, furthermore, assured the American Minister in June, 1861, of his lively sympathy for the cause of emancipation, a subject which keenly interested Russia with her serfs. A year later, the Emperor assured the American Minister that his sympathies had always been with the North, and stated that he was only anxious that the United

States should suffer no diminution of power or influence. In the same year the 'Journal of St. Petersburg' published a very friendly article, prepared by the Foreign Office as a semi-official declaration of Russia's attitude toward the American struggle. In October, 1862, the American Minister reported definitely that Russia 'might be relied upon.' 'We are, however, very, *very* anxious,' said the Russian Foreign Minister to him. 'Proposals will be made to Russia to join in some plan of interference. She will refuse an invitation of this kind, but I cannot express to you how profound an anxiety we feel.' The French suggestion of mediation of October, 1862, was, nevertheless, declined on the basis of the inadvisability of chilling public opinion in the North through officious European meddling in American affairs. The same line of reasoning, it may be noted, caused Seward in the spring of 1863 to refuse to join in the protest of the European powers to Russia with regard to the Polish insurrection. The Russian Government was, of course, much pleased with Seward's declaration. Meanwhile, the leading newspapers in St. Petersburg continued to publish well-informed weekly letters on American affairs, probably made up in London, as well as copious comments from the leading newspapers in England and France. They cautioned readers against being deceived by Reuter's telegrams, and even omitted to publish some of them. The 'Journal' published not only articles from the French press on the prosperous condition of the North, but also Seward's diplomatic circulars describing the progress of the Northern armies in the field.

The conspicuously friendly attitude of Russia gave rise to the rumor of a secret Russo-American alliance. A striking event in 1863 seemed to confirm this notion, when, during the winter, the Russian Baltic fleet was sent to visit New York, while the Pacific fleet visited California. The real motive behind these operations was to put the Russian Navy in a favorable position in ice-free water to prey upon British commerce, should war suddenly break out with England over the Polish question. But Europe and the North saw this visit of the Russian fleet as a significant demonstration of Russian friendship for the Union in its hour of need. The Russian officers were dined and toasted in New York and Washington with the utmost enthusiasm; while the presence of the Russian ships helped to raise Northern prestige in Europe. Their departure left a lasting gratitude toward the Russian ruler, 'who was our friend when the world was our foe,' as Oliver Wendell Holmes put it. This feeling was reflected as late as 1919, in the reluctance of the Department of State to recognize the dismemberment of Russia.

9

NAPOLEON III AND THE CONFEDERACY

While most of the European countries, because of their remoteness from the sphere of the struggle in America, remained to a certain extent uninfluenced by British opinion of the Civil War, the governments and peoples of France and Spain showed an anxious concern in the development of British opinion as well as in the course of the war itself. France, especially, was deeply affected by British opinion. In both France and Spain, however, internal politics, combined with exigencies of foreign policy, finally played the dominant rôle in forming opinion. Our task, therefore, in studying the public opinion of these countries, is not so much to show how British opinion was reflected as to show how similar opinions were produced in France and Spain by various other important factors.

We must first probe the obscure attitude and inconsistent actions of Napoleon III; then follow the general trend of French feeling toward the American struggle; and finally see what Spain said and did—or rather did not do—about the Civil War in America.

As the archives of the Quai d'Orsay have not yet been opened for the period of the Civil War, it is impossible to arrive at a definite conclusion about the Emperor Napoleon's feelings and acts. Yet enough is known from other sources to form a tolerably accurate estimate.

Against the background of French and European politics of the time we can appreciate the imperial state of mind at the outbreak of the war. The position of Napoleon III was then uncertain. Imperial prestige abroad, at its zenith in 1855, had since visibly declined. The Empire no longer stood for peace. Napoleon's ambition, shiftiness, and indecision were beginning to cause apprehension at home and abroad. His politics still commanded the general admiration of Europe, but the seeds of decay were visible to experienced eyes. Within France the Imperial régime had definitely lost ground. The Italian expedition, coinciding with awakening interest in politics, had caused the Emperor to relinquish the principle of an *empire autoritaire* based upon the Church, the Army, and the solid conservative elements. He was beginning to court the support of the Liberal opposition. Had Napoleon been younger and stronger, he might have succeeded in playing off the Liberals against the Clericals; he might, to the equal dissatisfaction of both, have solved the Roman question; and he might have succeeded in the establishment of a responsible government, *L'Empire libéral.* But the Emperor's infirmities, combined with his want of able ministers, were beginning to weaken his system and to paralyze his politics, as early as 1861.

So, at the outbreak of the Civil War, the Emperor's first care was to preserve the good will of England, on which he depended for freedom of action abroad and even stability at home. He saw that the Civil War presented a very good opportunity for going hand in hand with England in this direction, and thus laying a claim upon her for future favors in other parts of the world. As early as May, 1861, Seward noted that 'other European states were apprised by France and England of their agreement,' and were 'expected to concur with, or follow, them in whatever measures they adopt on the subject of recognition.' Publicly Napoleon went so far as to declare himself cordially sympathetic to the Union. Privately, he assured the Confederate Commissioner of the futility of seeking European recognition at that moment. But the soundness of this prudent policy was already being outweighed in the Emperor's mind by his belief that the rebellion would inevitably succeed. In this event, would not the South, to whose inhabitants the Emperor was temperamentally inclined, prove itself a closer and more tractable friend to his régime than the demagogic North? Would not a low Southern tariff open up a rich market for French imports? Would not the Confederacy smooth his path in Mexico, a land toward which he was already casting an ambitious eye? Such thoughts of a speculative nature were running through the Emperor's mind in the spring of 1861, as he sat dreamily with half-closed eyes in his little overheated rooms on the ground floor of the Tuileries. He had, indeed, a certain 'complex' toward a country where he had spent four unhappy months of exile — at New York — a quarter-century before. These reveries and imponderabilia probably explain why the Emperor, in June, 1861, followed Victoria's proclamation of neutrality with a rather more dogmatic and emphatic one of his own. America was, however, so much more sensitive to British than to French opinion, and so inclined to believe the worst of England and the best of France, that the tone of Napoleon's proclamation was quite overlooked. Indeed, we know that one misguided American diplomatist contrasted the friendly conduct of France with the hostility of England. Conversely, opinion was far less aroused in France than across the Channel by the American struggle, and was not sufficiently strong to affect the French Government's policy. Russell and Palmerston saw that public opinion demanded a strict interpretation of neutrality. The Emperor, on the other hand, succeeded quietly and unhindered in laying down a pro-Southern policy entirely as he desired; and the stage was thus set for a play of forces in France quite different from that which we have seen in England.

What this play portended soon became clear. As early as May, 1861, the Emperor began to urge the Federal Government to recognize the South. Soon afterward he went further, and began to hint in vague terms that he might have to recognize the South himself. Twice, during the first year of the war, the Emperor sounded the British Government as to the possibility of joint action looking toward recognition; and in October, 1861, he persuaded Russell to propose to Palmerston a peremptory summons to the North and South to make up their quarrel. Palmerston replied, in the language of sport, that 'the only thing to do seems to lie on our oars.' Napoleon, however, only strengthened his policy. He publicly befriended the Southern Commissioner, thus giving the South the distinct hope of early recognition.

So evident, in fact, were Napoleon's pro-Southern feelings in the autumn of 1861, and to such an extent had Southern propaganda increased in France, as well as in England, that Seward persuaded two prominent citizens to undertake an unofficial mission to Paris as well as to London, in order to impress upon public opinion the resources and determination of the Federal Government to win the war. Their immediate task was to prevent the

French Chambers, in their next session, from raising the question of the blockade.

Before this unofficial mission arrived in Paris, an event occurred which proved that the Emperor was still unwilling to take action alone, and still very desirous of going hand in hand with England. This event was the stoppage of the Trent. Captain Wilkes had flouted the Continental doctrine of neutral rights. Napoleon at once seized the pleasing opportunity of acting as spokesman for outraged Europe. That the Emperor's attitude strengthened the British Cabinet in its demand for a disavowal from Seward is made clear from a dispatch of Charles Francis Adams. 'We might,' he wrote, 'have made a strong argument as against Great Britain. But this would leave us not the less exposed to the reproaches of all the other maritime nations which have hitherto accepted our doctrines in good faith. This,' he went on to emphasize, 'was what constituted the strength of the note of the French Foreign Minister to Seward.' The French note, in fact, arrived in Washington, at the most dramatic moment, just before the decisive Cabinet meeting on Christmas Day, and very probably clinched the argument for giving up Mason and Slidell.

Napoleon, however, had no intention of backing up his position in the Trent affair by joining England in fighting the Union. The Northern blockade, it is true, was cutting off cotton and tobacco from France. Riots on the part of the unemployed had broken out in Lyons and even in the suburbs of Paris. But a dangerous deficiency had occurred in the French wheat harvest, and war with the Union would have prevented the importation of the necessary amount of grain from the Northwestern States. Wheat, therefore, aided the North in France even more than it did in England. Napoleon had still another reason for leaving England to fight alone, if she would fight. A British victory would mean an increase of British sea-power. A British defeat, however, would create a maritime balance of power between the United States and England which would be of great advantage to France. The British Ministry knew perfectly well that Napoleon intended to leave them to fight alone, and this knowledge probably made them the more ready to accept Seward's somewhat qualified apology for the Trent affair.

Napoleon, however, welcomed the peaceful outcome of the Trent episode as sincerely as did the British Ministry. His initial firmness and his later moderation had undoubtedly helped to avert the danger of war between England and America, and he had again demonstrated the value of the Franco-British *entente*. He had not, however, furthered his pro-Southern policy. For the first time, indeed, the danger of a break with the Union became visible to the more intelligent classes in France; and the friends of the North in France found in the unexpected moderation of Seward's diplomacy an initial point around which to rally.

But two developments early in 1862 enabled the Emperor again to pursue his pro-Southern tendencies. Distress in the French silk and cotton industries, due to the blockade, began to rise to a dangerous point. And the Emperor finally decided upon his expedition to Mexico.

The aim of the tripartite Mexican expedition, as both the British and Spanish Governments well knew, was to create an empire in Mexico under French auspices. Mexico and Central America had fascinated Napoleon ever since his youth. An empire in Mexico, he thought, would place

France again as a power in the New World. It would also give a new outlet to French trade, and create a bulwark against American aggression southward. Such an empire, Napoleon knew, implied a direct defiance of the Monroe Doctrine, and a definite reliance upon the success of the rebellion. But Napoleon was assured by the Confederate Government, which was quick to grasp his meaning, that a Southern alliance with Mexico and a guaranty of Cuba were to be had for the asking, if only France would recognize the Confederacy. Meanwhile, no danger from the North was to be feared, for Seward, in order to avoid international complications, was certain until the very end of the war to accept Napoleon's assurances of France's disinterestedness.

The distress in the French silk and cotton industries furnished the Emperor with an even stronger reason for helping the South to secure her independence. Slight mention of this distress is found in histories. The Imperial censorship kept the facts almost entirely out of the press. Actually silk production in France sank from 33,000,000 francs in 1859 to 13,000,000 francs in 1861, and the lack of employment affected at least 80,000 people in Lyons alone. While the cotton situation in France was less deplorable than in England, since only one fourth as many spindles were employed, still the outlook was worse. There were reserve stocks, but there were no new sources of supply, and very little cotton succeeded in reaching France through the blockade. Moreover, the cotton industry in France had not overexpanded, as was the case in England. A cessation of the blockade, therefore, would have benefited France at any time after October, 1861. In that month, in fact, the French Foreign Minister, Thouvenel, began to ask Seward to relax the blockade, while to the French Ambassador in London, he wrote that it seemed 'impossible that the question of cotton should not within three months from this time put England and France under the necessity of consulting before all an interest vital to the prosperity and repose of the industrial cities.' In December, Cobden, who always took a keen interest in French affairs, wrote to Sumner that, from all he heard, French trade was 'dreadfully damaged,' and that he 'felt convinced that the Emperor would be supported by the people if he were to enter into an alliance with England to abolish the blockade.' Thurlow Weed, one of the two prominent Americans whom Seward had sent abroad to influence public opinion, wrote from Paris in January, 1862, that France was more restive than England under the blockade, and that the French pro-Southern press was violently agitated over the stopping-up of Charleston Harbor.

When the French Chambers met, at the end of January, the American Minister in Paris wrote that 'an impression was almost universal both in England and here, that the Emperor would indicate a policy hostile to us in his opening speech.' But the French Address, like the British one of the same time, practically ignored the topic of the Civil War. Wheat, and the recent Northern capture of Forts Henry and Donelson, held the Emperor's hand. The Imperial spokesman in the Chamber declared that 'what is true is the friendship of the Emperor for the United States, his sincere desire to see them make up their quarrel, and his willingness to contribute as much as in him lies to this so wished-for reconciliation.' But Cobden described the Emperor's feelings toward mediation and recognition as much more those of 'Barkis is willin''; and Slidell, the

Southern agent in Paris, confirmed this impression from private talks with the Emperor. If, said Napoleon, England would take the first step, however small, he was willing to follow. Meanwhile, it was his intention to continue to urge the North to avoid European complications by being the first to recognize the Confederacy.

In the spring of 1862, the situation in France grew worse and the Emperor more restive. For ten years the country had not been in such a state of unrest. The misery in the industrial districts was increasing, and the distress of the working classes was causing the Government grave uneasiness. The Russian Minister in Washington told Everett that Napoleon was afraid of a general *émeute*, and that the French Minister had confided to him that necessity knew no law, and that France, in self-defense, would have to take action. Furthermore, as Napoleon had been deserted in Mexico by England and Spain, he had now another urgent reason for wishing to secure the maintenance of his new Empire by means of the independence of the Confederacy.

Again Napoleon sounded the British Government unofficially. Again the reply was 'No.' This time the Emperor was genuinely piqued. He deserved better of England, he said, for having supported her in the Trent affair. But the Emperor did not content himself with a mere expression of opinion. He was beginning even to think of acting alone, when the fall of New Orleans, and Seward's alacrity to declare that port open, caused him to stay his hand. Besides, 'we can't afford to be in more haste than England,' wrote the French Foreign Minister to the French Minister in Washington. But no cotton from the South was forthcoming from New Orleans. So all during the summer of 1862 Napoleon and his Ministers kept on urgently pressing the

British Government to join France in recognizing the South. The cotton crisis in France was increasing, and affected now fifteen Départements. Three hundred thousand people were absolutely destitute. In Rouen, thirty thousand out of fifty thousand operatives were without work; while in the surrounding district only one fifth of the hand-weavers could find employment. The Emperor was being besieged with appeals for aid from all the manufacturing centers. At the same time, the Southern Commissioners in Paris were tempting him with the offer of a huge sum of money in cotton, if only he would break the blockade; and they dangled before his eyes the immense field for French imports in the South, where the people had been unable for over a year to buy manufactured goods of any sort.

By reason of this pressure from all sides, the Emperor was brought to the parting of the ways. With characteristic diplomacy, however, he still tried to go in both directions at once. In July, 1862, he wisely refused the Confederate demand for recognition; but he did so only on the ground that it was premature, and he gave Slidell an interview from which the Southerner bore away high hopes. He also allowed a Confederate loan to be arranged for in Paris. On the other hand, the Emperor still waited for coöperation from England. He took the British Ambassador aside after dinner, and 'in a most open manner, said he was quite ready to recognize the South.' He felt, indeed, that it was high time for Palmerston to give him the lead.

By this time the news of the failure of McClellan's Peninsular Campaign had reached Paris. The stage seemed at length cleared for action. Even the French Minister in Washington believed that the moment had come when European mediation was possible. The new French Foreign

Minister, moreover, Drouyn de Lhuys, was much readier than his predecessor to carry out the Emperor's wishes. Gladstone and Russell were known to be urging recognition upon Palmerston. Napoleon, therefore, took no warning from the news of the failure at Antietam of the Southern invasion of Pennsylvania. He entirely disregarded the significance of the new Northern policy embodied in the first Emancipation Proclamation, and he ignored the sound advice of his former Foreign Secretary, to wait for the result of the November elections in America. Obsessed by the distress at home, confident of much support in England, and ambitious to further his Mexican scheme, the Emperor, on October 30, addressed official notes to England and Russia, suggesting a tripartite offer of mediation to the Federal Government in America. 'My own preference,' Napoleon told Slidell, 'is for an armistice of six months. This would put a stop to the effusion of blood, and hostilities would probably never be resumed. We can urge it on the high grounds of humanity and the interest of the whole civilized world. If it be refused by the North, it will afford good reason for recognition, and perhaps for more active intervention.'

This characteristic attempt of the Emperor to unite Europe strikingly failed. The British Ministry refused to budge from its policy of neutrality; Russia refused to antagonize the North. Napoleon was forced to acknowledge a diplomatic defeat. The Emperor had gained absolutely nothing. He had, rather, added to his internal difficulties by incurring the hostility of the Liberals with regard to his American policy, just as he had shortly before incurred their bitter hostility by reason of his Roman policy. In America, moreover, the Emperor had lost all prestige in the eyes of the North, for it was now clear to every one that he was seeking an opportunity to recognize the South.

What could Napoleon do but continue to further recognition? By the beginning of 1863, the distress in France had reached its peak. Private charity, with a subscription list headed by donations from the Emperor and Empress, was of small avail. At the very gates of Paris, as the 'Revue des Deux Mondes' disclosed, one hundred and thirty thousand people were out of work. 'In England,' it wrote, 'the worst is over. Here, the worst is not yet discovered.' Bands of unfortunate people were creeping from door to door in the country asking for bread and shelter. Around Rouen, twenty-six thousand people were estimated to be in utter destitution. Only Alsace, where, early in the war, cotton had been bought from England, had enough material in stock to keep the spindles moving.

Meanwhile, with the November elections and the disaster at Fredericksburg, the North was going through its darkest period of war weariness. The French agent in Mexico was intriguing to detach Texas from the Confederacy as well as from the Union, and Napoleon was sending reënforcements to Mexico to enable Maximilian to fight his way to the capital. So, while the growing pro-Union agitation in England, following Lincoln's Emancipation Proclamation, strengthened the resolve of the British Government to abstain from interference, Napoleon, ignoring the less widespread Liberal opinion in France, not only accepted from Slidell a memorandum asking for recognition, but in February, 1863, renewed his previous offer of mediation directly to the American Government.

Seward's prompt rejection of the Emperor's offer, coming between two staggering Northern defeats, may well be termed the most daring American diplomatic act of the war. The attitude of Congress, moreover, and the pointed references made in the House to the Mexican expedition, made it necessary for Napoleon to give up the idea of any further active interference in the Civil War.

Fortunately for him, the cotton crisis in France began, in the late spring of 1863, to show signs of an improvement. The Cobden Treaty of 1860, had, in fact, increased the volume of French trade with England to such an extent as to offset completely the loss of the American markets. By the summer of 1863, it was clear that French trade as a whole was flourishing, while it was increasingly clear that France more than ever needed American wheat from the West. The outbreak of the Polish rebellion, and the growing difficulties of the French in Mexico, added further to the chain of circumstances which now drove American affairs out of the foreground in France. Napoleon, busy elaborating a Polish policy on much the same basis as his American policy, and with much the same lack of success, still hoped that England might change her attitude toward the Civil War; but he now took great care to assure the North of his friendship. Characteristically enough, however, he privately facilitated the building of Confederate privateers in French shipyards, with the hope that they might break the Northern blockade. And, although only a vague admiration for the South remained in France, the Emperor again encouraged members of the British Parliament in a new effort to bring up the subject of recognition in the House of Commons; and he even went so far, upon the receipt of news of the heavy Northern defeat at Chancellorsville, as to write to his Ambassador in London, 'I wonder if it would not be well to inform

Lord Palmerston that I have decided to recognize the South.'

The overzealous Southern partisans in the House of Commons spoiled their game completely by referring in the House to the Emperor's 'Messages to Parliament'; while the Union victories at Vicksburg and Gettysburg in July, 1863, gave the death-blow to this last attempt on the part of the Emperor to help the South. In September, Slidell was forced to console himself with the pathetic but significant fact that the Empress 'sympathizes most warmly with our cause and so expresses herself without any reserve.' In November, two months after the Laird rams had been stopped in England, the building permits of the nearly completed Confederate ships in France were withdrawn, and the French Government announced that Confederate cruisers which in future entered French ports for repairs would be interned.

By spring of 1864, Napoleon had definitely abandoned the South. With a new rebuff in Europe on account of Poland, and with increasing danger in Mexico on account of the departure of Maximilian, the Emperor was in no position to interfere further in the Civil War. Not only was his own situation more difficult than ever before, but public sentiment in England had turned definitely in favor of the Union. This fact, combined with the Federal victories in the autumn of 1863, encouraged the American Government in May, 1864, at last to venture to protest against the presence of French troops in Mexico. 'Since the occupation of Texas, Chattanooga, and Knoxville,' wrote the American Consul-General in Paris, 'our people are becoming very impatient with France and fearless of everybody.' The wary Seward still restrained the House from 'gasconading about Mexico when we are in a struggle for our existence,' and still warned public opinion that 'the future of Mexico is neither an immediate nor even a vital question for either the United States or France.' But, in reality, Maximilian's fate was sealed before he even reached Mexico City, and the tragedy of Queretaro was a foregone conclusion.

It was now Napoleon's turn to become nervous because of Northern threats. When the French Foreign Minister received the copy of the joint resolutions of the American House of Representatives against the Mexican Empire, he inquired anxiously of the American Ambassador, 'Do you bring us peace or war?' The Emperor, in fact, dared not protest against the Union's recognition of Juarez. 'He was too sagacious,' wrote the Confederate Commissioner in Paris, 'to act in direct contravention of the settled public opinion' in France against the Mexican adventure. The Liberal Opposition in the Lower Chamber in France had by October, 1863, increased from five to thirty-five. And the outbreak of war in Schleswig-Holstein provided a final reason in the Emperor's mind for disentangling himself from Mexico, as he already had disentangled himself from the Confederacy.

The Emperor's final opinion of the Civil War may be judged from a laconic phrase of his quoted by Prince Napoleon: 'If the North is victorious, I should be happy. If the South is victorious, I should be delighted.' The Empress, on her part, was chiefly worried lest the victorious Northern armies might turn South to aid Juarez against Maximilian. When the American Minister informed her that the armies in all probability would be quietly disbanded, she 'expressed her astonishment.'

In summing up Napoleon's attitude and policy during the Civil War, two important facts are worth emphasizing. In the first place, the Emperor definitely lost the good will of the Union, to such an extent that in 1870 popular feeling in America welcomed the downfall of the Empire. In the second place, the Emperor's American policy undermined his position in Europe. England had been his great obstacle in the New World as in the Old. Had England become entangled with the North, French influence might have become supreme on the Continent as well as in Mexico, and the Emperor might have been able to extend the Empire to her 'natural boundary' on the Rhine. Had England joined with him by intervening in the American struggle, Mexico at least would have been French. Moreover, as Cobden put it in 1863, 'had England joined France, they would have been followed by every other state in Europe, with the exception of Russia.' Then, with two rival republics in the New World, each courting European support, the European balance of power would once more have covered the Western Hemisphere, and France would have been able to play an important rôle in the affairs of that part of the world. But England would not move, and the Emperor dared not move without her. This is the key to Napoleon's whole policy during the Civil War. This was the reason for his failure to carry out his schemes, and this is why English opinion is a primary factor both in the Emperor's policy and in the public opinion of his subjects.

10

FRENCH PUBLIC OPINION OF THE CIVIL WAR

THE historical interest of French public opinion of the Civil War lies in the particular perspective in which the war appeared to different classes of Frenchmen. To the Emperor's official circle and to the Imperialists in general, the war seemed to be a struggle for Southern independence. To the Liberal Catholics, the Monarchists, the Republicans, the Liberal Imperialists represented by Prince Napoleon, and the five leaders of the Opposition in the Lower Chamber, the Civil War was a crusade to preserve the Union and to destroy slavery. Each side had its writers and its press, and each side looked at the war from a characteristically French point of view.

The wide body of pro-Southern opinion in France deserves first consideration, for it shows how much sympathy and support the Emperor found for his opinions and acts. Such opinions were held by many of the most important elements of French society. Persigny and almost all the Emperor's Ministers, de Morny and almost all the state officials, were in favor of the South. Thouvenel, Foreign Minister until the end of September, 1862, alone of the Emperor's official advisers, was known to favor the North to the extent of advocating a policy of watchful waiting. 'I think he is with us as to slavery and secession,' wrote the American Minister in Paris to Seward, 'but doubts our power.' Thouvenel did not believe that the South could be beaten. But he thought that war weariness in the North, rather than European intervention, should be allowed to bring about a recognition of Southern independence.

The Imperial Court and the higher banking circles were pro-Southern. Most of the army officers, as in England, preferred the chivalrous Confederate leaders to the Northern generals. The older and stricter Catholics, following the ideas of Joseph de Maîstre, disliked the United States, were jealous of their growing power, and hoped as well as believed in their division. The conservative middle classes, who supported the Empire, also supported the Emperor's attitude toward the South. 'They say the New Orleans people are their brothers,' wrote an English observer.

All these elements united in believing that the Northern Government had no right, as one critic put it, 'under pretext of emancipating four million Negroes, to impose slavery upon six million whites.' Emancipation might or might not be a good policy. European intervention might or might not be wise. In any case, separation was a *fait accompli*, and the longer Europe delayed recognition, the longer would it deprive itself of the advantages of the new state of affairs.

It is not surprising that the Southern agents swarmed to Paris as the best point from which to spread their propaganda. Two circumstances made it especially easy to circularize in France the usual arguments about slavery and separation. Parisian society was well acquainted with the charming type of Southern lady, who with her husband and daughters frequently made her home in Paris. Many Frenchmen, disillusioned Republicans and now strong

Imperialists, had a temperamental aversion to American democracy. The United States aroused in these people a feeling exactly opposite to that held by the *noblesse* who had responded so warmly to the Declaration of Independence. The lawless democracy which America incarnated was to them anathema. The *Empire autoritaire* had, they believed, no lesson to learn from America, but rather a lesson in governmental order and stability to teach the demagogic Union politicians, and a lesson in Latin American statecraft to teach the American filibusters. Indeed, the Emperor's Mexican policy would by itself have made these Imperialists pro-Southern.

In spite of the presence of a large official majority in the Lower Chamber composed of these elements, Parliamentary discussion of American affairs was rare; and when opportunities for discussing foreign affairs came, during the yearly debate on the Reply to the Address, the Corps Législatif showed itself quite temperate. There were no Roebucks and Lindsays in France. Billault, the Government spokesman, was careful to avoid debate on the Civil War, while the wording of the relevant paragraphs in the Emperor's Addresses of 1862 and 1863 was colorless enough to prevent strong argument. Only once, in March, 1862, did a Deputy venture to ask if the Government was prepared still to acquiesce in a blockade which 'cut off the most lucrative export area of European commerce.' Billault, however, hastened to cut short the discussion by stating that both the British and French Governments were satisfied with the conduct of the blockade. Later, in the same vein, he killed a Liberal amendment approving abolition by informing the Chamber that such language did not become a neutral power.

In the debates upon the Mexican Expedition, prominent Liberals like Thiers seized the occasion to express their desire for neutrality and for the eventual success of the North. They made, however, no direct attack upon the Emperor's pro-Southern diplomacy. The Imperialist Deputy Arman, builder of Confederate warships, proposed in February, 1864, an amendment to the Address, looking toward a peaceful separation between North and South. This amendment was withdrawn, but the pro-Southern sentiment of many members of the Corps as late as April, 1865, is indicated by the fact that the news of the capture of Richmond was saluted with cries of *Tant pis!*

If the Chambers were relatively quiet during the American struggle, the official and semi-official press exhibited pro-Southern feelings in a most venomous form. For all the Parisian newspapers, the Civil War was one of the major questions of the day, on a par with those of Germany and Rome, and worthy of an equal amount of investigation and thought. The French press, because of censorship and small circulation, could not accomplish as much mischief as the pro-Southern British press; but it made up for this weakness by raising a more hideous outcry against the Union. As Thouvenel once put it, these newspapers were often 'two hours ahead of the clock,' and their attitude often embarrassed the Government. For, as the Confederate press agent in Paris soon discovered, golden opinions could be bought with Southern money, and Southern propaganda spread with as much speed and fire as the censorship and newspaper circulation permitted.

Besides the official 'Moniteur,' the pro-Southern press comprised 'La Patrie,' edited by La Guéronnière, an influential Senator and Imperial pamphleteer; 'L'Union';

'Le Pays,' under the well-known Deputy Cassagnac; 'Le Constitutionnel,' under Persigny's direct control; and 'La France,' a newspaper founded in 1862 to conciliate Liberal ideas with the maintenance of the temporal power of the Pope. These last four papers were generally supposed to draw their money and ideas not only from the South but from French high officials, and from the Emperor himself.

The 'Moniteur' appears at first glance the most impartial of newspapers, with official news, reports from the Chambers, a *bulletin du jour*, quotations from foreign newspapers, and letters from other capitals — all in an impeccable style of impersonal dignity and disinterestedness. The 'Moniteur' gave, in fact, an accurate representation of English opinion; its American correspondence was unprejudiced and justly attracted the attention of prominent men everywhere; and it never went beyond the views in which a distant neutral state such as France might indulge. After a while, however, one comes upon something important, quoted or stated as received by wire, which one knows is false, and the question arises: Was the 'Moniteur' now and again deceived, or did it deliberately publish an occasional 'canard'? Did it minimize and withhold news? Its news, during 1861 at least, was complete, careful, and impartial in tone; but it criticized what it called the folly of the Federal Government in thinking it could subjugate the South. During the Trent affair the 'Moniteur' gave as much prominence to Cobden's and Bright's speeches, and to the English 'Daily News' as to the resentment and excitement of the anti-Northern 'Times' and 'Morning Post.' During 1862, however, it dwelt on the sinking of the stone ships in the channel leading to Charleston, calling it an act, not of war, but of vengeance; and, while it noted Seward's increasing moderation, and the advantages of the blockade to the North, it minimized the capture of New Orleans by stating that the critical field of battle was in the East; and it dwelt upon the strength of the Confederacy, as shown by the failure of the Peninsular Campaign and by the advance in September, 1862. The amount of attention which the 'Moniteur' paid to Western affairs at this time, and its understanding of the objects of army movements, were remarkable. In 1863, after publishing news of Northern reverses at Vicksburg and Gettysburg, it finally admitted them as *affaires manquées*; but it held to its opinion that no number of Northern victories would bring reunion. In 1864, it dwelt on the unabated vigor of the South and on the resistance to conscription in the North, together with other general signs of Northern war weariness. The seizure, meanwhile, by the English Government of the Confederate ironclads was noted only in a tiny quotation from the 'Evening Star,' under the heading 'Nouvelles diverses, Angleterre.' Later, the 'Moniteur' emphasized again the still unexhausted Southern resources against invasion.

Thus, simply by dealing in facts, by disregarding such events as the Emancipation Proclamation, and by never prophesying Northern success or praising Northern acts, the 'Moniteur' came to be known as the cleverest of the pro-Southern newspapers. Its attitude was undoubtedly inspired by the Government's policy of praising a power which might be recognized. But its untrustworthiness is well illustrated with regard to the Mexican expedition. During the whole of this, the 'Moniteur' flatly and fiercely lied. It used its official access to news in order constantly to magnify French successes, and to paint Mexican enthusiasm for Maximilian in rose colors. Respecting Mexico, in fact, the 'Moniteur' sank to the level of a mere propaganda paper like the 'Index' in London.

The semi-official French newspapers already mentioned were hostile to the North almost from the start. Even before the fall of Sumter, 'Le Pays,' in a controversy with the Liberal 'Opinion Nationale,' not only upheld States' rights, but conceived the whole question as one of natural and inevitable separation; and, while deploring the possibility of war, cast the onus of responsibility for it on the North. This point of view was supported by quotations and adaptations from the London 'Times,' the 'Morning Post,' and the pro-Southern 'Courrier des États-Unis' of New York. 'Le Pays' early adopted an anti-emancipation attitude, not as of principle, but as of wisdom. Emancipation, it contended, must come slowly, peacefully, and with good will. In February, 1861, a series of articles, in agreement with the views of the 'Moniteur,' dealt also with the commercial side of the question. Recognition of the South, they argued, would open the door to free trade, and would strengthen the already formed links of race, culture, and interest between the South and France.

Over the Trent affair, 'Le Pays' waxed eloquent in its defense of England's case and in vituperation of 'American democratic violence.' No sooner had this episode passed than it attacked the Federal Government for its blockade of Charleston by stone ships. Then mediation was brought forward, supplemented by information on the cotton crisis and the loss of the silk market in the United States. At the same time the paper dwelt upon the futility of this *guerre de race* against the Carthage-like energy of the South.

From then on, 'Le Pays' disputed point by point with the pro-Northern 'Siècle,' 'La Presse,' and 'L'Opinion Nationale.' It could not say enough in its effort to blacken the ideas, people, government, and conduct of the North. At one time, indeed, it even made the war out to be 'a Puritan Crusade against the Catholics in the South.' Its Washington correspondent was constantly sending lengthy descriptions of arbitrary acts or wanton demonstrations in the Union. As the war prospered for the North, 'Le Pays' asseverated more and more strongly the impossibility of assimilating the slave South with the commercial North, a land 'full of turbulent immigrants.' The only outcome of a Northern success, it predicted, would be the creation of 'another Ireland, another Venetia, or another Poland.' Up to the end, in a word, 'Le Pays' insisted upon finding all manner of strength in the South, in its defensive position, its natural resources, its extent, its homogeneity of population, and its patriotism; while for the successive measures against slavery no appreciation whatever was shown. They were merely a clear proof of the fact that 'the government of the United States is one of the most barbarous, most ferocious, and most inept which has ever been seen.'

'La Patrie' was equally violent against the North — often, it seems, by deliberate Imperial intention. Aucaigne, the editor, was in the Confederate press agent's pay. He was, in fact, the sort of man who delighted in being paid to hate some one, and who fulfilled this function with no trepidation or variation. While, therefore, his 'American letters' were carefully written, they almost always contained exaggerated accounts of such things as the activities of the Northern peace party, as well as instances of rabid Northern demagogy and Federal tyranny. He vied, indeed, with the 'Times' in the injustice of his attacks, so that again and again the American Minister in Paris called attention to his strong support of the South at critical periods.

The Clerical 'L'Union,' which considered Rome the paramount question, showed much the same spirit as 'La Patrie.' Its carefully written news articles were impartial; but it judiciously condemned the Northern thesis and supported French offers of intervention. It hoped that the Federal Government would recommend progressive emancipation to the South, but believed separation the only conceivable outcome of the war. The last of the pro-Southern group, 'Le Constitutionnel,' hesitated some time before coming out in favor of the South. It maintained that slavery was not the prime issue in the war, and called the Southern cause one of 'individual liberty, freedom of nationality, and freedom of trade.'

These newspapers as a group show how plausible were many of the Southern arguments offered in France. It is interesting to observe how historically just they were in certain particulars. The appalling devastation of modern war, the difference between mere emancipation and the solution of a racial problem, the dangers to which a democracy is subject in time of war, and the economic dependence of the continents on each other — all these are valid reasons to-day for desiring mediation and a quick peace in any struggle, European or American. Indeed, after perusing these papers, one cannot resist the conviction that, to the French reader of the Government press, the Yankee must have somewhat resembled the 'Hun' of 1914. In the one case as in the other, partial information and preconceived opinions, even more than deliberate propaganda, were to blame. The final impression which one takes away from a survey of pro-Southern opinion in France is that Napoleon himself was far less unfriendly to the North than he might excusably have been, and that he represented his supporters a good deal less boldly than they often desired.

Pro-Northern opinion in France represents a very much more refreshing outlook on American events than that which we have just been considering. However interesting may be the different opinions which the Emperor Napoleon expressed in public and in private, however correct in various instances the pro-Southern press proved to be, one gains a more and more cynical and hopeless view of American affairs the more one studies pro-Southern opinion in France. In the opinions we are now to consider, there is a more modern note. The pro-Northerners in France in 1861–64 were, in fact, the spiritual successors of those who had supported American independence in 1775, and the precursors of the American friends of France in 1914. Had Napoleon III been as idealistic as he liked to imagine himself, he might easily have identified himself with this body of opinion and proved himself the greatest friend of the Union in time of need, as in other days a King of France had done.

If the Emperor, his circle, and his adherents took the darker way, it was because the Northern cause and Imperialism were fundamentally incompatible. But this does not mean that the pro-Northern elements in France were unimportant. 'There is unquestionably a strong feeling in a portion of French society in favour of the North,' wrote the 'Saturday Review,' in October, 1863, 'and a majority of the *educated classes* are desirous that the relations of the French with the Federal government should continue amicable.' 'Sympathy for the North,' wrote J. S. Mill from Avignon, 'animated all *liberal-minded* Frenchmen from the start. It was in this moment of trial that in France all the friends of liberty recognized each other. They did not know more about the subject of slavery or secession than the English, but their instincts were truer and the prejudice against slavery was stronger in France than in England.' The educated and intellectual French Liberals very soon decided that a slaveholding Confederacy asking for admission to the society of nations was offensive to the spirit of the age. The causes assigned by the South for its revolt left them cold. Did not parts of France suffer because of centralization, and yet must not each part give way to the whole? Europe would dissolve into chaos if every part marched off by itself. A nationalist cause must have something idealistic about it; it must proceed from racial or religious persecution, or from intolerable exactions. The South was too large to enter either of these pleas. The *raison d'être* of federations, moreover — the existence of differences between the elements composing them — was precisely the reason for not disrupting them. To break up wantonly a federation was as unjust as to try to disrupt a really unitary state. In 1865, the 'Journal des Débats,' summing up the characteristics of the pro-Northern sympathizers in France, defined them thus: 'The political principle which interested enlightened Frenchmen who believed in the maintenance of America's power as being more and more necessary to the equilibrium of the world; the desire to see a great democratic state survive an attempt at dismemberment and continue to set an example of the most complete liberty... the need, finally, of applying somewhere a sympathy, an admiration, and a hope for which the old world offered very little occasion: these assured the Northern cause of numerous friends, eager to uphold, in this point at least, the traditional policy of France and the liberal spirit of our nation.'

These opinions were held by such *gens d'élite* as de Tocqueville and the Liberal publicist Comte Gasparin; by Ampère, son of the famous scientist; by the prominent journalist and Deputy Augustin Cochin; by Henri Martin the historian; by the Senator Professor Laboulaye; and by Laugel, at one time secretary to the Duc d'Aumale, and a director of an important railway. These men were not only sincere but active friends of the North. 'It is impossible,' wrote one of the Confederate agents in 1864, 'to remain blind to the articles which emanate from the best-known names in French literature.' Cochin sustained the Union cause from the very first, when it was very doubtful. Laugel published a book on the Civil War favorable to the North; while Laboulaye gave an important series of lectures on America in 1861, at the Collège de France, which he followed with three books on the United States and their resources. These enjoyed a wide sale. The Liberal Catholics, led by Montalembert, shared the pro-Northern opinions of these prominent men. The French Liberal Coalition Party of 1863 also held pro-Northern opinions, not only out of principle, but because of their opposition to the Mexican expedition. The most widely read magazines, the most independent and progressive newspapers elaborated the pro-Northern point of view. Victor Hugo and Guizot believed in the North. Even in the

Emperor's own family, Prince Napoleon ('Plon-Plon'), though out of office and favor because of his Italian views; openly and liberally supported the North, and gave the cue to his several newspapers and his large circle of political friends. Finally, the Orléanistes and their following were by tradition friends of the North. Articles in the 'Revue des Deux Mondes' by the Comte de Paris and the Prince de Joinville, the Orléanist princes who fought under McClellan, contributed to an accurate knowledge of foreign affairs. When the Comte de Paris' frequent letters to Sumner, sympathizing with 'the liberal and national cause,' were shown to Lincoln, he called them the letters 'of a most sensible man'; while their effect on Sumner was to confirm him in his opinion that thoughtful statesmen in Europe would never recognize 'such a new nation as these slavemongers are building.' Republicans such as Louis Blanc coincided in the Orléanist views. The working classes, in France as in England, steadfastly upheld the Northern cause.

Remembering what has been said of the disadvantages under which public opinion labored in the Second Empire, and remembering the equivocal attitude of the North toward slavery, let us examine these Liberal elements in more detail.

'Prince Napoleon,' wrote Weed in his 'Memoirs,' 'differing widely and boldly from the Emperor, was a warm friend of our Government, and sought occasions to serve us.' The Prince had returned from his journey to the United States in 1861 (which had taken him as far west as Michigan and as far south as the Confederate lines), with an impression of entire admiration for the North and friendliness toward the Federal Government. Seward confirmed the Prince's attitude a few months later in a dispatch to Dayton: 'The general course adopted towards us in what seemed a critical hour by Prince Napoleon made an equal impression in this country' with the action of the Comte de Paris and the Duc de Chartres, 'who have just returned after a year's service in our armies.' In a letter in 1861 to George Sand, whose son had accompanied the Prince in America and who was publishing a book on the journey, Prince Napoleon begged him 'not to forget that true liberty and true progress are represented by the United States.' Writing later, in 1862, to George Sand, *à propos* the policy to be pursued by the 'Revue des Deux Mondes,' Prince Napoleon advised thus: 'As for the Orléans princes, it is very simple. If what they write under pseudonyms is good, well composed, in a good spirit, and in favor of the good cause of the North against the South, let them publish it.' Later, in June, 1863, during the Prince's trip up the Nile, the American Consul at Alexandria, after a long talk with him, reported him as saying that France was very little acquainted with the merits of the Northern cause, although Laboulaye, as well as others, had written excellent articles in the papers on the subject. The Prince added that he had been surprised, when he visited England the year before, at the misconceptions prevailing there as well. He had, however, talked much with Bright, and thought that Bright had the best appreciation of the Northern cause. Later, in 1865, when a friend of Prince Napoleon became Minister of the Interior, the American Minister in Paris noted with satisfaction that the Prince's influence with the Government had 'always been exerted in American affairs in opposition to the Confederacy.'

As a cousin of the Emperor, and as a fearless speaker in the Senate, the Prince's views were widely known. He had identified himself with the Liberals in the Italian war, and counted himself, as in fact he was, an important protagonist of their ideas. Of the so-called Liberal press, two papers — 'Le Siècle' and 'La Presse' — were directly controlled by Prince Napoleon, and both acted as intelligent apologists for the North. 'Le Siècle,' particularly, praised the Emancipation Proclamation and the moderation of the Washington Cabinet. It advocated mediation, it is true, and feared a servile revolt; but it continually aroused the ire of 'Le Pays' by its unabated criticism of the latter's reactionary stand. 'La Presse' published in bold type every few days very well-written news of the war. It was particularly accurate about the movements of the contending armies. Politically, however, it contented itself with praising Palmerston's moderation and advocating a like policy of stubborn neutrality in France, since — as it concluded in 1865 — the Union was indomitable.

The rest of the Liberal press — composed of 'L'Opinion Nationale,' 'Le Temps,' 'Le Courrier du Dimanche,' and 'Le Journal des Débats' — was able to defy the censorship more openly and effectively than the Liberals in the Chamber. These newspapers defended the North openly, warmly, and ably; their admirably written pages give a picture of French journalism at its best; and their opinions strikingly illustrate the doctrines of the Liberal School on the Continent. The chief provincial newspapers, 'Le Journal' and 'Le Courrier' of Havre, the Marseilles 'Sémaphore,' and the Bordeaux 'Gironde,' a widely read Republican paper, were of the same liberal complexion. So was the 'Phare' of Nantes.

In the most independent French newspaper, 'L'Opinion Nationale,' the editor, an intimate friend of Prince Napoleon, was pro-Northern by conviction from the beginning, while the well-known writer, Malespine, one of the principal contributors, was, said the American Consul-General in Paris, 'a faithful and effective friend of ours from the commencement, and the only writer on American affairs for the press here who has never faltered in his republican faith.' 'L'Opinion' published, in fact, abundant news about the Northern armies and commanders, and abundant extracts from the Northern diplomatic correspondence. When it is remembered that Seward's dispatches, especially his circulars with regard to the progress of the war, were written quite as much for public perusal abroad as for the guidance of his diplomatic representatives — the volume for November, 1862, to November, 1863, alone contains more lengthy dispatches than any other Government had published for twenty years — it is not extraordinary that the United States diplomatic correspondence must be counted as having been one of the leading means of awakening and educating Liberal European opinion.

Throughout the war, 'L'Opinion' took every opportunity to insist upon 'neutrality and its profits — the only policy conformable to our traditions, our honor, and our interests.' At the beginning of 1864, it printed with favorable comments a letter of encouragement to the Loyal and National League of New York, signed by Henri Martin and Laboulaye; and it reprinted several of Seward's dispatches giving the attitude of the United States toward Mexico. In March it dared warn the French Government that the departure of the Confederate cruiser

Rappahannock, then docked at Havre for repairs, would seriously compromise Franco-American relations. The next month it emphasized the importance of the Congressional resolutions against the Mexican expedition. It even went so far as to reproduce the documents showing the connivance of the French Government in the contracts for Confederate ironclads. For this 'L'Opinion' was censored, and the official newspapers were forbidden to copy this article. The censorship, however, could not touch a remarkably vigorous article (probably written by Bigelow) commenting on the usefulness, moderation, and openness of expression of the American diplomatic correspondence. Nor could the censorship quarrel with the final judgment of 'L'Opinion,' in 1865, that 'since 1860, when the United States were nothing but a great commercial power, they have become one of the first naval and military powers, and their points of contact with Europe have multiplied.'

The greatest review in France, if not in the world, was the fortnightly 'Revue des Deux Mondes,' whose knowledge of foreign affairs was amazing, and whose articles on the Civil War read like a modern history of the United States. Forcade, the editor of this review, was a man of letters and a leader of that Liberal element which wielded a force far beyond its numbers. His *revues de la quinzaine*, editorial comment on the news, are a valuable record of contemporary French Liberal opinion.

His first opinion was that, although secession was unjustifiable, a war of conquest by the North would only succeed in turning the South into a second Poland or Ireland. At first, in fact, he favored the Mexican expedition as a check to the immoderate expansion of the United

States; while over the Trent affair he praised English rather than American good sense. But he forcefully condemned Napoleon's idea of mediation, and he upheld the Emancipation Proclamation, carefully judging its important effect on Northern and European opinion. His interest in Northern politics, moreover, enabled him to appreciate the meaning of elections. He made a noteworthy study of the election of 1864, the orderly progress and outcome of which seemed to him a stupendous moral victory for liberty.

The articles in the 'Revue' by Forcade's collaborators are equally encouraging and intelligent. In 1860, for instance, an article on the recent political changes and elections in America pointed out the number of anti-secession votes in the South, and emphasized the enthusiasm of the West for Lincoln. A subsequent article reviewed the 'Black Codes' of the slave States and the obnoxious conditions to which Negroes were subjected in the North. Slavery, it concluded, benefited only some ninety-one thousand people in the South at the expense of the poor whites and the Negro himself. The South was, moreover, too weak and lacking in manufactures to secede successfully. Gradual emancipation was her only remedy.

In November, 1861, Laugel wrote on the particular differences between the North and South which had gradually produced the conflict. The Civil War, he thought, sprang from the premeditated plot of an aristocracy of slave masters, who were determined to secede from the Republic rather than give up their controlling situation. 'It is,' he wrote, 'a *coup d'état* by a minority.'

In January, 1862, a writer on the cotton crisis declared that the war would destroy Southern cotton, even if the

South were victorious. He deplored, therefore, the lack of preventive measures in France against the cotton famine, and predicted that the Orient would be the future source of cotton. An article by the Liberal leader, Casimir-Périer, on the Trent affair declared that its peaceful solution was a greater triumph for maritime freedom than the Declaration of Paris. France's rôle, he added, had been well played; in the future, it should remain one of strict and careful neutrality. Casimir-Périer's conclusion is interesting. 'Whatever prejudices, opinions, and individual leanings one way or another there may have been in regard to America; whatever might have been thought of institutions whose duration seemed doubtful to friends of liberty because of the exaggeration of their popular principles; whatever dislike had arisen from the terrible scourge of slavery; whatever judgment might be passed on the crudeness of manners and on the habitual stiffness of international relations — it was impossible that the prosperity of the Union should not have continued to cause in France the most sincere prayers, conformable to the political tradition of our country.'

In October, 1862, the Comte de Paris, under a pseudonym, wrote of the Peninsular Campaign, whose success would, he insisted, have ended the war. The old Union, however, he believed, could not be reconstituted now; either the South would attract all the States save California and the Northwest; or else, by oceans of blood, the North with its immense resources would reëstablish its authority on another basis. The second alternative, as we now know, is what occurred, although American historians until recently have been curiously unwilling to admit it.

The Indian: 'Gentlemen, please — put some ceremony into it. *We* don't butcher each other that way.'

Cartoon in 'Le Charivari,' Paris, March 6, 1862

Other articles on the war were concerned with such topics as cotton cultivation by free Negroes in Beaufort, the various stages of abolition, and the relief organizations created by Northern women. Admiration was shown for the moderation of the Federal Government and for the stupendous military development of the civilian population in the North. About these articles, the American Consul-General wrote: 'The recent articles in the review ... have been everywhere printed and read, and their effect has been all the greater that they emanate from one friendly to our cause.'

Of the other Liberal publications already mentioned, the 'Journal des Débats' is the most interesting. It illustrates both the position of the Liberal but constitutional Opposition, and its sympathy for the North; and its enmity towards such papers as the 'Morning Post' shows how French Liberal support of the North increased as the moral issue of the war became apparent.

As early as January, 1861, the 'Débats' proclaimed the Southern ideas unreasonable and dangerous. Secession, it believed, would find no sympathy in the minds of those in Europe who believed in the principle of nationalities, for secession aimed merely at freedom from Northern protectionist tariffs, at opening of the slave traffic, and at future southward conquests. The South had really, in fact, no cause for war; it had merely been balked in its traditional domination of the National Government and in its former freedom to carry slavery into the new Territories, where it did not belong. The 'Débats' went on from this to describe the situation in these excellent terms: 'On the one hand we have a vast revolt, excited by real but inevitable grievances, mingled with an unjust and mad ambition, prepared with art and executed with courage, but combined above all with the hope of foreign aid, and almost impossible to carry out without such aid. On the other hand, we have a people of double the number, immensely richer in resources of all kinds, controlling the sea and the rivers, resolved to maintain its integrity, and in the event that the energy on both sides be equal, the superiority of its forces gives it the right, if it goes to the bitter end, of hoping for victory.'

Proceeding from these remarkably clear and well-formed assumptions, the 'Débats' called the attack on Sumter inexcusable; doubted the presence of a unanimous spirit in the South; and believed that Lincoln's forbearance would, in any case, allow spirits to cool. 'Time works for the North,' it declared, and for its legal and moral rights. In August, 1861, when fighting had at last begun, the 'Débats' believed that Europe would have to put an end to it sooner or later. It advocated neutrality for the present, but suggested tentatively a 'league of republics' between the North and South. The Trent episode strengthened its stand on neutrality, however, and caused it to point out the dangers to England if she decided upon war. The 'Débats' noted with satisfaction the way in which the American papers moderated their tone; and it praised the language 'at once joyful, worthy, measured and wise,' of the 'Times.' England, it concluded, had brought a striking condemnation by herself on herself, while a clear result of the incident in France was an explosion of sympathy for the Union cause.

By February, 1862, the 'Débats' was attacking the 'Constitutionnel's' argument that slavery was only one cause of the war. In May, it quoted 'The Times' as saying that the fall of New Orleans rendered the Confederate cause hopeless. In July, it argued against the 'pompous assertions' in the pro-Southern press as to Confederate strength and plans for victory. It rejected the idea of French mediation, if not in principle, at least as an inopportune measure. In August, it published a long article by Augustin Cochin to show that slavery was doomed in any event. Having already noted Lincoln's gradual steps toward abolition, it wrote in September, 'the news from America keeps up an interest even comparable with the news of Italy.' Articles by Laboulaye, on 'The United States and France,' then appeared. The news in the autumn of Antietam confirmed the 'Débats' in its belief in Northern victory, while the Emancipation Proclamation, it declared, showed that slavery was without question the great issue. In December, 1862, the 'Débats' gave three columns of praise to Lincoln's annual message with its plan of gradual emancipation.

Turning to England, from which it often quoted the pro-Northern comments of the 'Daily News,' the 'Débats' contrasted with Gladstone's famous speech, Palmerston's opinion of July 18: 'The recognition of the South would not create a nation unless it were followed by a direct or indirect intervention.' It applauded Cobden's speech at Manchester, in which he declared that free trade and non-recognition were part of the same policy. In November, the well-known Deputy, Prévost-Paradol, wrote at length on the folly of the French offer of mediation. 'It is proposed to Europe to intervene,' he concluded, 'either by useless advice which can in no wise modify the war, or by offering to the feebler side, first a peace proposition which it is naturally the only one to wish; then, as an inevitable result, the menace of a foreign intervention calculated to exasperate the stronger side; and finally the force of arms.'

A most interesting comment in 1864 emphasized the chilling effect which the capture of Atlanta had had on the European pro-Southern press. Sensing like a vulture the approaching death of the South, the tone of this press completely changed, noted the 'Débats.' Upon news of Lincoln's assassination, Prévost-Paradol eulogized him as highly as Lincoln's greatest admirers since have ever done. 'We waited for his first words in 1861 with impatience and misgiving. They dispelled all our fears and showed us a man of destiny had come.'

The remaining sector of French Liberal opinion was the Liberal Catholic. This comprehended those who respected the past, but believed in a practical settlement of the relation between Church and State which would free the Church for its great spiritual work. Liberal Catholicism rallied quite early to the North. The Pope probably approved their attitude, for early in 1862 some of the French bishops issued instructions saying it would 'not be objectionable' to pray for the emancipation of the four million slaves whom Lincoln proposed to set free. One of the most influential churchmen in France, moreover, Père Lacordaire, expressed confidence in the United States and their institutions in his discourse upon his election to the Academy. Especially noteworthy, too, is the fact that Montalembert, the foremost figure of the Liberal Catholic Party in France, devoted a portion of his last days to writing a defense of the United States, the land where, according to his ideal, a free church existed in a free state. Catholics, he urged, should uphold a Christian community fighting against the scourge of slavery. 'For the first time in thirty years we can applaud the victors,' he declared, referring to previous European wars. America had never lost her tradition of liberty, he pointed out, during the war. Her treatment of prisoners and wounded was admirable, while her avoidance of military autocracy was a marvelous triumph. When the victory of the Union finally came about, Montalembert believed that it was 'the most considerable event of our days.' America, he declared, now belonged among the great powers of the world.

Montalembert was one of the directors of the principal Catholic organ, 'Le Correspondant' — then as now widely read and second only to the 'Revue des Deux Mondes' in importance. The editor, Augustin Cochin, compiled a long article in January, 1861, in defense of the North and of the Union point of view. Later, he published a book, 'De l'Abolition de l'Esclavage,' which Henri Moreau, a brilliant publicist and formerly secretary to Berryer, reviewed in an article in the 'Correspondant' for October, 1861. In his review, incidentally, Moreau maintained that French industrial suffering was due less to lack of cotton than to the lack of a demand in the North for European products. To aid the South, therefore, was merely to prolong the war and aggravate the crisis.

In an article on 'Mexico, the United States, and Europe' (October, 1862), the 'Correspondant' criticized sharply the impossible burdens which the Emperor's distant expeditions laid on France. The trend of the United States was inevitably southward. If the only way to stop this was by a revival of monarchist sentiment in Mexico, France should have let Spain, whose real interest it was, bear the brunt. In October and November of the next year appeared an especially lucid review in the 'Correspondant' of French policy in America. Friendliness to the Union was emphatically maintained as the only sound policy for French interests. From this point of view it criticized one by one the published dispatches of Thouvenel and Mercier, as well as the attempts of the French Government at mediation.

From the Liberal press we turn finally to the Chamber of Deputies. We have noted in the Chamber the conditions to which debates upon foreign affairs were subjected. We have noted how the Government's cautious tactics in the Chamber prevented any such important scenes with regard to the Civil War as took place in the British Parliament. Yet every year, when Mexican affairs came up for discussion, the Liberal Opposition — an important factor from 1863 onwards — seized the occasion to attack the Emperor's policy in Mexico and toward the United States. It was a Liberal Deputy who suggested to Seward, in 1863, that the best way for him to keep Liberal support in France was to avoid any threat to Maximilian, because an appeal to the Monroe Doctrine would enable the Emperor to rally patriotic support for his Mexican policy. At the same time, Seward was advised to protest in general terms against the undesirability of a foreign régime in Mexico. These ideas coincided, as we have seen, with Seward's actual policy, and they gave the North, as the Liberals desired, the whole-hearted support of their group.

In 1864, in fact, Thiers warned the Government of the danger of departing from its neutrality. 'The United States,' he pointed out, 'which to-day are careful in dealing with you, and flatter you because it depends on you to end the Civil War, will not aid you, once the war is over.' In the spring of 1864, the Liberals probably would have welcomed an opportunity of testing the Government's position by bringing up the question of Confederate ship-building in French dockyards. Berryer was prepared to lead the debate. But the Government withdrew the building permits, as we have seen, and the Corps, as Bigelow informed Seward regretfully, 'may be considered as closed to us this season.' In April, 1865, however, after an angry debate upon a motion 'deploring the blood-shed for a foreign prince in Mexico,' twenty-four members, upon the announcement of Lee's retreat from Richmond, voted to thank the United States for its 'efforts on behalf of Civil Liberty.'

The general impression one takes away from a study of the pro-Northern elements in the Chamber, and from the pro-Northern newspapers, is the freshness of mind of French opinion. The United States stepped forth from de Tocqueville's pages, and presented itself to the Liberal classes in France not in the reflected light of European politics, but in its own terrifying blaze. This by itself is a tribute to the intelligence and imagination of Liberal France. That the moral issue of slavery should have been seen to outweigh the Southern claims to heroism and nationality is a praiseworthy reflection on the cultivation of French society under the Empire.

Foreign reaction to a foreign crisis is rarely entirely detached; and just as Roosevelt and Lodge in defending the Allies were at the same time attacking Wilson and the Democracy, so Laboulaye and Thiers, in defending the Union, were attacking Napoleon III and Imperialism. The Second Empire, for all its misleading docility, was a seething cauldron of struggling ideas, and the Civil War was bound up with the very marrow of Imperial policy.

To attack the Empire or to defend it meant above all to attack or defend its foreign policy. If Mexico was the Emperor's heel, North and South were his heel tendons. They were the most sensitive spots on which to strike, the most vulnerable places to be shielded by loyal Imperialists.

Thus the American Civil War entered that current of European events which kept Liberal ideas alive among the French people. Continental Liberalism rose against the Southern rebellion for the same reason that it rallied to the Greek and Italian revolutions, and in the same exalted manner. From the welter of comment on the war there emerges in France a great and a lucid idea: the United States may perhaps need to be purified, but never must they be overthrown, for if America can experience the horrors of war and still keep her character, she will become the mainstay of all that is progressive in Europe.

11

SPANISH OPINION OF THE CIVIL WAR

IN the rehabilitation of modern Spain, the brilliant Ministry of Leopold O'Donnell from 1856 to 1863 stands out as one of the most interesting periods. It was the first time during the century that one of the series of military leaders who governed the country was backed by a widely diffused political majority. The Union-Liberal Party of O'Donnell represented an attempt to draw together all elements in Spain toward a vivid, grandiose, and thoroughly Spanish policy.

In 1861, however, O'Donnell's brilliant and popular régime was already on the wane. The heterogeneous elements which had given him support on the abstract basis of 'Dynasty and Constitution,' and on the concrete basis of glory for Spain, were drawing apart. The Republican Cánovas del Castillo, O'Donnell's most brilliant follower, had definitely broken with him. The reactionary elements in the country were growing restless of their dependent rôle in the Union-Liberal coalition. Events abroad were also having a definite influence in breaking up the coalition. O'Donnell's policy of doing nothing at home, while attempting everything abroad, after involving Spain in costly expeditions in Morocco and the Far East, had led to a serious undertaking to recover Santo Domingo (March, 1861), and was about to draw Spain into the Triple Convention against Mexico. Both these expeditions belied their hopes. O'Donnell's rival, Juan Prim, retreated in time from Mexico; but Santo Domingo proved O'Donnell's political grave. In 1863 he resigned, and with him Spain ceased to play an active part in the New World.

The situation of affairs in Spain in 1861 explains the attitude of the Spanish Government at the outbreak of the American Civil War. Had O'Donnell's Ministry still been strong, had Spain already been in Mexico as in Santo Domingo, immediate recognition of the South would have been the logical course to take. As things were, however, a more circumspect procedure was advisable.

O'Donnell was undoubtedly glad that the Federal Government would now have to concern itself with other ambitions than those indicated by the Ostend Manifesto concerning Cuba. The Civil War opened the door for his ambitious scheme of bringing Santo Domingo, and possibly Mexico, back into Spain's sphere of influence. But while the Government realized the advantages of the Civil War, and while it estimated the South and North as opponents equal in strength and resources, the prudent course for a secondary power to take was to wait and see what the great powers would do, and what both North and South had to offer in the way of assurances concerning Mexico and Cuba. O'Donnell, therefore, determined to follow the example of England and France by issuing a proclamation of neutrality. But 'this Government,' wrote the American Minister, Carl Schurz, 'does not mean to provoke a difficulty with us, and will, I think, earnestly endeavor to avoid a conflict with us under all circumstances.'

After the first Union defeat at Bull Run, Schurz reported that Spain, because of her exposed West Indian possessions, would still take no initiative in recognizing the South. The South, however, had sanguine hopes to the contrary. Preston, of Kentucky, Buchanan's Minister at Madrid, had so labored in the latter part of his term of office to aid the impending Confederacy that the Court and society, in June, 1861, were 'deeply imbued with the idea of an aristocratic and chivalrous South armed to resist the aggression of a *sans-culotte* North. As the upper classes in Spain were still full of resentment at American filibustering in Cuba, which they connected with the Government of the United States, they believed all the more that the rebels would prove the real friends of Spain. The reactionaries and conservatives in Spain, therefore, welcomed the collapse of the Western Republic. Spanish Liberals, on the other hand, had no vital or even direct interest in the Union.

The South, therefore, thought that Havana might easily be made an *entrepôt* for foreign munitions and a refuge for Confederate vessels. In July, 1861, a Confederate agent was sent to assure the Captain-General of Cuba of the friendly intentions of the South. On August 24, Judge Rost, a distinguished Southerner, was sent to ask for recognition in Madrid, on the ground of the community of the Spanish and Southern social systems, and of the proximity of the Confederacy to Cuba.

Seward answered by asserting the principle of the indivisibility of the Union. He took great pains, moreover, to point out that the filibustering and annexationist designs against Cuba and Mexico had been inspired by the South, and might have succeeded, had they not been restrained by the North. The South, Seward asserted, had, in fact, revolted with the avowed intention of expanding in Mexico and Cuba. In several long interviews with Calderón de Collantes, the Spanish Foreign Minister, the American Chargé d'Affaires drove this point successfully home.

In another way, meanwhile, namely, by its deference to neutral rights in the Trent episode, the North bettered its position even more in the eyes of Spain. The first success of Northern diplomacy in Spain appeared in March, 1862, when Calderón informed Rost that Spain would take no initiative in recognizing the South. A month later, Spain's withdrawal from Mexico, leaving France to carry on alone, removed all apprehension in the North as to her hostile intentions in that quarter. In May, 1862, the American Chargé wrote Seward of the aftermath of Mexican affairs: 'Spain has earned the high regard of the United States by withdrawing from the Mexican scheme, while she has shown that she could assert her rights in America when aggrieved. A limited faction of deputies, officers, men who have been in Paris, and state officers (who represent a considerable coterie) has maintained that a close alliance with France is the only safe and fruitful policy for Spain. The Moderado Opposition believes Napoleon the only statesman in Europe. But they are overborne at present by a majority of all classes, who desire a strictly national and Spanish policy.'

The triumph of French policy in Italy, and the rumor that the United States was about to take several States from Mexico as security for a loan increased the strength of this Franco-Mexican party; and, when exaggerated accounts arrived of Federal reverses before Richmond, pro-Southern feeling in general increased. 'The governing classes here,' wrote the American Chargé to Seward in the early autumn of 1862, 'always desirous of the separation of the Republic, always avowedly in sympathy with the rebels from the beginning, have seized upon these indications with avidity.' An *entente* with France, a new expedition to Mexico, and recognition of the Confederacy now became parts of the same policy, and this policy appeared steadily to gain ground.

Such a state of affairs had been foreseen a year before by the vigorous new American Minister in Madrid, Carl Schurz, and had caused him to return to America, in order to arouse the one thing capable of appealing to Spanish Liberals — namely, abolition sentiment. It was well that he had done so, for in September, 1862, the American Chargé, dwelling upon the alarming state of Spanish opinion, reported that the dark hour had now come. 'Even the more liberal classes,' he wrote, 'wonder why we want to coerce the South, which by its valor and vigor has demonstrated its condition to be a solid, separate nation. Against this, I am using the slavery argument. This is the only point which has told for us, and editors have not ceased to reproduce it. Popular ideas of democratic sovereignty are against us. Nothing, they think, is lost in the Montgomery Constitution. Our cause here wavers as the issue of slavery is more or less clear.'

Spain would not have moved without France; but she would almost certainly have followed France in recognizing the South in the autumn of 1862, or later, had not Schurz's strivings borne fruit. Lincoln's emancipation policy accomplished, and to an even larger degree, the same salutary work in Spain as in France. Reactionary Spain thereafter dared not urge a pro-Southern policy, while Liberal Spain had now the example of the Northern

States to bring forward as a weapon in its campaign for emancipation in the Spanish colonies.

After the downfall of O'Donnell in 1863, the successive governments, while still friendly to the South, had neither the power nor the will to prove their feeling in any practical way. Discussion as to the outcome of the war and as to recognition continued, but it was without practical importance. The Spanish Government shut the Spanish ports to Confederate cruisers, and refused Slidell's offer to adhere to the Cuban tripartite treaty. Distinctly favorable expressions of opinion toward the North appeared in the Liberal papers, and these were reënforced by translation into pamphlet form of Seward's circulars and notes. His conciliatory action in the case of an English ship, pursued by a Federal cruiser into Cuban territorial waters, gained further ground for the Northern cause. Criticism of the Santo Domingo expedition and pessimism regarding the French Mexican Empire came to a head in 1864, just at the time that the Southern cause began to appear as hopeless. By that time the North could congratulate itself upon having won as decisive a victory in the field of public opinion in Spain as it had won in France.

A short review of Spanish newspaper comment brings out vividly this struggle of the North in Spain and its final triumph. The leading newspapers in Spain were six. 'El Pensamiento Español' gave Carlist opinion. 'España,' 'La Época,' and 'El Diario' gave different shades of ministerial opinion; while 'Iberia' and 'La Discusión' expressed the Liberal views of the war. Most of their news was copied from abroad, and their editorial comment on the war was infrequent. Hence the Spanish press affords but meager material for us. But if foreign affairs were seen through the wrong end of an opera glass, they were nevertheless judged in a characteristically Spanish way.

A few quotations will suffice to show what sort of comment was from time to time printed in the pro-Southern papers. 'El Pensamiento Español' considered that 'the war may continue a long time or a short time, but the indubitable result will be the independence of the Southern States.' Shortly afterward, in September, 1862, under the spell of Southern successes and promises, it published a remarkable editorial showing the full measure of the temper and attitude of the average extreme reactionary in Spain. 'In the model republic of what *were* the United States,' it wrote, 'we see more and more clearly of how little account is a society constituted without God, merely for the sake of men. Look at their wild ways of annihilating each other, confiscating each other's goods, mutually destroying each other's cities, and cordially wishing each other extinct! The Federals declare their enemies' slaves free, and the latter refuse to allow Federal regiments of whites and blacks any rights of war. Both muzzle the press; both vie with each other in reprisals; and at the end of a year of war they are both on the road to becoming barbarians. The history of this model republic can be summed up in a few words. It came into being by rebellion. It was founded on atheism. It was populated by the dregs of all the nations in the world. It has lived without law of God or man. Within a hundred years, greed has ruined it. Now it is fighting like a cannibal, and it will die in a flood of blood and mire. Such is the real history of the one and only state in the world which has succeeded in constituting itself according to the flaming theories of democracy. The example is too horrible to stir any desire for imitation in Europe.'

This same paper confirmed Schurz's judgment of the effect on Europe of an anti-slavery policy in the North, by accusing the Spanish Democratic papers of supporting the North solely because of its anti-slavery attitude. 'El Pensamiento,' therefore, played up Northern hatred of the Negro and Democratic repudiation of Lincoln's proclamation.

In the other ministerial pro-Southern newspapers, Northern arms were systematically undervalued and Northern victories usually mentioned without comment. We find 'La Época' for April 28, 1861, predicting and hoping that the Civil War will implant European-like states and monarchies in America. Later on, it expatiated on the endlessness of the war and the need for European mediation, and delighted in giving examples of Northern mob-rule and violence. 'España,' which reprinted much gossip from 'The Times,' 'Morning Post,' and 'La Patrie,' considered the war a proof of the wickedness of the Yankee idea of democracy, and thanked God that Spain had never been sullied by such a heresy. Europe was bound to gain by the exhaustion of the combatants. The Union victory at Antietam was so much propaganda; everything the Union had done had been unsuccessful. The Emancipation Proclamation was a 'first-rate political blunder,' fatal to the Northern cause. Bitter was 'España' against Palmerston's rejection of the French proposal for mediation in November, 1862. 'All Europe felt it to be the right time, and only England's selfish interests have prevented action. The North cannot ever win, and should be stopped before it commits suicide.' 'España' continued through 1863 to believe separation inevitable and advantageous, and still maintained that Europe's interest lay in gaining the South as a friend by recognizing her before the war ended. France should be the first; then Spain; then England.

'El Diario' concurred in this opinion. Separation, it argued, was not only inevitable, but necessary for the security of European possessions in the New World, and for the advance of Spanish prestige in Latin America. 'El Diario' considered that the real aim of the struggle in America was the possession of the Mississippi; the North, it predicted, would conquer the river-bank, but the South would gain its independence. Thus Cuba would be assured to Spain. Slavery, therefore, was merely a subject of agitation: Lincoln's proclamation was only an arbitrary order. But the war, 'El Diario' noticed, in the autumn of 1862, revealed 'our lack of precise knowledge of anything but the *political* scene in America.' This paper, therefore, began to study the social side of the struggle. In an interesting series of articles, it came to the conclusion that slavery as an institution, if left to itself, was doomed everywhere to extinction, because of natural factors. The institution could not, therefore, be considered a political disgrace in lands like the Spanish colonies, where it was dying out. In America, however, after having been admitted into the Constitution, slavery had become the political basis of the South, and had resulted in an aggressive, unscrupulous policy of ambition that would never be satisfied. The South depended on the upkeep of slavery. This artificial Confederacy, 'El Diario' decided, could not attract Spain by offers of alliance. The final opinion of this paper was that the Northern cause was the more just and the more noble. All that remained in 1863 of 'El Diario's' preliminary pro-Southern attitude was the feeling that two ways to peace remained open; Northern triumph, each day more probable; or else an agreement between the North and the South to condemn and circumscribe slavery.

When we come to the Democratic 'La Discusión' and the Progressive 'Iberia' and 'Novidades,' remarkably interesting comments of quite another sort occur. In its news articles 'La Discusión' was uniformly favorable to the North, emphasizing such events as Antietam and Lincoln's Proclamation — 'that policy of salvation which alone justifies the struggle.' In the dark summer of 1862, it was against recognition of the South by Europe, because of its belief that slavery was doomed. It warned France that if she went into the American war, she would meet her Moscow. Separation was inevitable; but the South was the turbulent aggressor, while the North would remain the really first-rate power on the continent. Continuing the discussion of the war, this organ combated the argument of the reactionary newspapers that the war was due to the baneful effect of democracy. Slavery — i.e., lack of democracy — it maintained, was the real cause of the war. 'La Discusión' appreciated the forces which hindered Lincoln from acting quickly with regard to abolition, and as early as August, 1862, called what he had done 'a great attempt, a sublime work.' It refuted 'La Época's' plea for recognition by arguing that the South was an undesirable neighbor, and that her independence would necessitate the formation of a Latin-American protective league. In November, 1862, it devoted an entire page to condemning the Southern thesis in all its details. When the French offer of mediation was published, it sensed at once the commercial pressure behind it. By the end of 1862, 'La Discusión' may be said to have firmly attached itself to the Northern cause in all its aspects.

'Iberia,' the principal Progresista organ, often fined for its political utterances, began by publishing Lincoln's message of July, 1861, as the best summary of the American question. It noted, however, that Prince Napoleon had concluded from his journey in the United States that separation, while disgraceful, was inevitable. In December, 1861, it regretted Lincoln's reserve as to slavery, pointing out that abolition was 'the only way to give character to the struggle, to justify the war, and to arouse the applause of all those who are sincerely interested in the future of humanity.'

'Iberia,' as indeed all the Madrid papers, followed the Trent episode with the utmost attention, and went so far as to believe with the rest that war was inevitable because of Seward's 'stiff, obstinate, and over-confident' attitude. Sooner or later, it thought, the question of cotton would bring England and the North to blows. Nevertheless, in March, 1862, since neither England nor France would move to save the South, 'Iberia' began to see her end. All during the summer of 1862, 'Iberia' followed carefully the Southern efforts on the Continent to create a belief in the success of the Confederacy. It warned its readers against believing everything said about Northern disasters; and, in October, it came to the reassuring conclusion that the North was winning everywhere, and that the Emancipation Proclamation would eternally honor the Washington Government.

Among its later articles in the Northern cause is a very interesting review by General Prim, published in February, 1864, relating to his visit to the United States after the Spanish withdrawal from Mexico. 'I never decried the military possibilities of the United States in time of war,' he stated, 'although Europe looked upon the States as powerless.' He then described his visit to the army of the Potomac: 'As to the number of first-rate soldiers, the United States is the first nation in the world.' In this respect, moreover, Prim pointed out, the North and the South were one people, since 'whenever it is a question of America for the Americans, they will be on the same side, even if distinct States.' In conclusion, he lavished praise on American institutions, especially upon the courts and the rapidity of justice, and dismissed all the scandals about Northern corruption and tyranny as simply untrue.

It is both pleasant and enlightening to end this short résumé of Spanish opinion with the words of her greatest and most sensible leader of the century, Juan Prim.

CONCLUSION

12

CONCLUSION

I

The final triumph of the North and of American national integrity was an important event for Europe. As the drama marched to its close through the winter months of 1864–65, European discussion of events continued much as before, though with an added spice of bitterness which foreshadowed the approaching end. Friends of the South willfully closed their eyes to the facts. The fall of Charleston to Sherman's army, for instance, aroused 'great sorrow in the breasts of all honest and chivalrous gentlemen'; but it was not a military disaster, and possession of this heap of ashes would be of no aid to the Federals. So late as April 17, 1865, the 'Manchester Guardian,' commenting on the abandonment of Richmond, still refused to admit that Confederate collapse was near. On the other hand, fears of Northern military power were at last really aroused. As American confidence grew, threats of revenge for British sneers and Alabamas became louder and more insistent, while hostile attention was also turned to Napoleon's Mexican empire. In England the politicians' alarm about the safety of Canada reached the public mind. Roebuck had paraphrased Shakespeare's Cassius in 1863:

> 'America bestrode the narrow world
> Like a colossus, and we petty men
> Walked under her huge legs, and peeped about
> To find ourselves dishonourable graves.'

By March, 1865, there seemed real meaning in this: not only would American insolence and aggressiveness toward all mankind be released by victory, but the United States had actual grievances, against England in particular. America was no longer a blustering, cowardly bully, but a power proved in the furnace of conflict, equipped with offensive weapons by land and by sea. It was argued in all sincerity that the great American armies could not be quietly demobilized, but would insist on being led against Mexico or against Canada; that a nation habituated to war could not at once resume the ways of peace; and that overweening confidence might soon unleash war against the innocently offending French and British.

England suffered from a small but genuine war scare. Delane of 'The Times,' wrote a friend, 'is quite sure Uncle Samuel is about to finish off the dreadful civil war by another war with us scarcely less horrible.' Charles Francis Adams said that at no time since the Trent had he 'perceived a more general restlessness and distrust.' Observers agreed that the funds were kept depressed by dread of war, and for a few weeks its possibility was freely discussed in press and Parliament.

More significant than fear of American power was the stimulus given to English Radicalism by the approaching success of the Union. As early as May, 1864, Gladstone had, in his biographer's words, 'electrified the political world' by his assertion from the Treasury Bench of every man's moral title to a vote. This explicit sign of progress on the part of the popular Chancellor of the Exchequer was a great encouragement to the Radicals, who were fast coming into a position where Labor could coöperate with them. A general agitation for reform, however, still awaited two events: the end of the American struggle and the passing of Palmerston. The former came first and in a way most favorable to the reformers of England.

Lincoln's second inaugural address attracted a good deal of notice for its Scriptural language and its conciliatory temper. Before long came news of the fall of Richmond and then of Lee's capitulation at Appomattox. Grant's courtesy and generosity to the fallen foe revealed possibilities to which most British publicists had been resolutely blind. Closely pressing this great event, which only die-hards declined to receive as conclusive, came accounts of the assassination of President Lincoln.

The news arrived in London about noon on Wednesday, April 26, and was first issued by the 'Daily News' in a second edition. So great was the interest that three or four shillings each were paid for copies of the paper and all the evening journals were sold at enhanced prices. For two or three days the death of Lincoln was the universal talk of the streets, the clubs, the haunts of business. All London was staggering, wrote Forster in his diary; in Manchester business was entirely stopped. The funds dropped nearly a point; and the press abounded in superlatives to describe the sensation which the event had caused. Not, it was said, since Henri IV was slain by Ravaillac had 'the whole of Europe rung with excitement of so intense a character.'

Expressions of grief, sympathy, and detestation of the crime were prompt, spontaneous, and widespread throughout the British Isles. The leaders of the Ministry in both Houses of Parliament at once announced that they would proffer an address of sympathy to the Americans; Queen Victoria sent a personal letter to Lincoln's widow; a series of public meetings of condolence began, and was not concluded within two weeks.

The apotheosis of Lincoln began at once. Even before his death he had begun to be appreciated, and the time and manner of his end gave a final impetus to the process by which he became, for the common folk of the whole area of Western civilization, a modern saint. For the Scottish crofter who still keeps Lincoln's portrait in his cabin, and the Austrian Serb of whom Michael Pupin tells, Lincoln came to typify some of the most noble ideals of the common man.

England, however, had been deeply divided on the American question, so that the fusion of sentiment in the heat of Lincoln's assassination could not be complete. 'Punch,' to be sure, formally and emphatically abandoned its anti-American tone in the famous recantation verses of Tom Taylor,[1] but 'The Times,' warming at first to the United States, soon relapsed into its former lecturing tone. The Tory 'Standard,' which as late as April 21 was unwilling to admit that there was not still good hope of Southern independence, preferred not to express its views of Lincoln's private character and public policy. The President was a despot, it said, and yet played a small part in the control of affairs. 'He was not a hero while he lived, and therefore his cruel murder does not make him a martyr.' The Earl of Derby's remarks in the House of Lords and the character of James M. Mason's denial that the Confederacy was implicated in the assassination, alike show that America was still a political issue.

The most intense feeling, of course, was among the working men and among those public men who had long since

[1] The vote to print them divided the editorial board.

deserted neutrality for the Union side. The mass of addresses of sympathy sent to the American Legation came from town councils, Nonconformist, temperance, anti-slavery, and working men's organizations, capped by the proceedings of public meetings in many cities and towns. These demonstrations were largely promoted by the Emancipation Societies, and at the meetings the speakers were mostly the same Dissenting ministers and Manchester Schoolmen who had been so active in promoting the Northern cause.

Yet there need be no cynicism about the matter. If the response of Englishmen to Lincoln's death was compounded of mixed elements, it was nevertheless real and general. In not a few instances avowed Confederate sympathizers — though none of the most conspicuous — placed themselves on the platforms of condolence meetings, a proceeding which required some moral courage. While there was some partisan exultation at these meetings, especially those of working men, it was less than one might expect.

Probably the most impressive demonstration was that given in St. James's Hall in London, under the auspices of the Emancipation Society. Seventeen members of Parliament, comprising a large part of the Manchester School, sat on the platform, while the governing classes were represented by Mr. Vernon Harcourt ('Historicus') and the Honorable Lyulph Stanley. Multitudes of the common folk were unable to secure admission, but again, as two years before, trade-union leaders sat side by side with middle-class reformers and Quaker anti-slavery men. The balconies were draped with black cloth bordered with white lace and festooned with white cord, while at the end of the great hall three American flags gave a touch of brightness and jubilation to the scene. The proceedings were long and dignified. Lincoln's tolerance, his kindliness, his capacity to learn from experience were especially stressed. Through all the speeches ran a constant thread of satisfaction that the long conflict was over and of hope for the American future. If this meeting represented England, England wished her cousins well.

II

During the Civil War, Europe and the United States were in closer contact than at any time since Napoleon. Not only was there real danger of intervention during the first two years of the war, but during the whole four years from 1861 to 1865 forces were in motion the effect of which was to change profoundly the relations of the United States to Europe. The Civil War made a nation of the United States: it is equally true that it brought this nation back into the European world, not as an infant republic, but as a first-class power. The proof of this statement is the fact that European opinion divided just as sharply with regard to the American Civil War as American opinion, in the early years of the Republic, had been accustomed to divide with regard to Europe.

We have tried to show the causes and nature of this divided opinion — to show the rôle of American wheat and Northern markets counteracting King Cotton; to show the struggle between the Mexican expedition and Lincoln's emancipation policy for the favor of Frenchmen and Spaniards; to bring out the motives directing the policy of Napoleon III so that his acts might be understood before being condemned; and to show how the questions of democracy and liberalism were part and parcel of all discussion of American affairs.

It is as impossible to avoid mention of slavery as it is easy to overstress it. Until 1863, it was a confusing and complicating element in the welter of European opinion; thereafter the air was cleared. It should be emphatically remarked that the adhesion of the Liberal elements in England, France, and Spain to the Union came in time to defeat the possibility of European recognition of the Confederacy. Northern military successes, backed by Seward's diplomacy and Lincoln's emancipation policy, succeeded in Europe before they succeeded at home. By 1863, no European Government dared defy the sentiments of its people. The North won an earlier and more decisive victory in the contest of opinion abroad than it did in the war of arms at home.

Nor was the Civil War without its aftermath in Europe. It resulted in a prolonged and bitter hostility on the part of Americans of both sections against what they considered the cold and selfish attitude of the Government and people of England and, to a less degree, of other countries, during their great struggle. This hostility embittered relations for years to come and created a diplomatic dispute — the Alabama Claims — of the first magnitude.

Equally interesting is the impetus which the reintegration of the United States gave to European Liberalism. The effect in Great Britain was especially notable. Though Palmerston lived six months longer than Lincoln, the outcome of the war did much by itself to release the forces of reform. The 'unbridled democracy' of the North had shown strength sufficient to compel victory to its side; it had produced a man whom all could respect and many could love; it had not degenerated either to anarchy or despotism. A weapon was thus taken away from the party of resistance and given again to the party of progress.

Hardly had the surrender at Appomattox become known than we read words of exultation in London:

'In presence of the glorious triumph of our principles on the other side of the Atlantic let us take heart. Our opponents told us that republicanism was on its trial. They insisted on our watching what they called its breakdown. They told us plainly that it was forever discredited in England. Well, we accepted the challenge. We staked our hopes boldly on the result.... Under a strain such as no monarchy, no empire could have supported, republican institutions have stood firm. It is we, now, who call upon the privileged classes to mark the result. They may rely upon it that a vast impetus has been given to republican sentiments in England, and that they will have to reckon with it before long.'

Mazzini used even more emphatic terms to describe the benefit of the Union's triumph to his cause. 'You have done more for us,' he wrote, 'in four years than fifty years of teaching, preaching, and writing from all your European brothers have been able to do.' Montalembert, writing in the 'Correspondant,' said that 'an instinct, involuntary perhaps, all-powerful and unconquerable, has at once arrayed on the side of the pro-slavery people all the open or secret partisans of the fanaticism and absolutism of Europe.' Goldwin Smith wrote that if the North had failed, the boast of British reactionaries would have been fulfilled, and Liberalism would have met prompt electoral defeat. In the general election of 1865, the president and

'Well, are you succeeding in patching them together?'
'They're a bit knocked about, but the pieces are sound.'

Cartoon in 'Le Charivari,' Paris, October 13, 1865

three vice-presidents of the Manchester Union and Emancipation Society were returned for the first time to Parliament. This was the Parliament which two years later shot Niagara by passing an extensive measure of parliamentary reform.

THE END

BIBLIOGRAPHY

BIBLIOGRAPHY

ENGLAND

THE authors have profited greatly by the labors of their predecessors in the field, none of whom, however, have attempted quite what they have done. Particular mention should be made of Professor E. D. Adams, *Great Britain and the American Civil War* (New York, 1925, 2 vols.); J. F. Rhodes, *History of the United States* (vols. III, IV, V, New York, 1895–1904); and W. R. West, *Contemporary French Opinion on the American Civil War* (Baltimore, 1924).

The direct sources for the study of English opinion are ample and fall mainly into four classes: official, journalistic, personal, and controversial.

The official documents used in the present work comprised the British *Parliamentary Debates*; the published *Diplomatic Correspondence* of the United States — London did not add anything to what Washington made public; and portions of the two great series of United States Civil War records. Of these the most important volumes are: *Official Records of the Union and Confederate Navies in the War of the Rebellion,* Series II, vol. 3 (Washington, 1922), which includes almost all that has been printed of the archives of the Confederate State Department; and *Official Records of the... Armies...* Series II, vol. 2 (Washington, 1897), which contains interesting information on the Trent affair. Some other diplomatic correspondence has been printed, but the great bulk still lies in the archives, in the Library of Congress, and in private hands in England.

Of course opinion is expressed most fully in the newspapers and magazines, and these have supplied a large part of the raw material for the present work. Many of them have been named when quoted. For the purpose of this study they were selected to cover a wide range of interests: the various types of political thought, financial and business organs, different groups of reformers, a number of Dissenting denominations, parties in the Established Church, were all represented. In addition, journals were drawn from different parts of the country, including manufacturing towns and ports, and agricultural districts. For a discussion of the journalism of the time reference may be made to: H. R. Fox Bourne, *English Newspapers* (London, 1887), vol. 2; James Grant, *The Newspaper Press* (London, 1871–72, 3 vols.); and H. D. Jordan, 'The Daily and Weekly Press of England in 1861,' in *The South Atlantic Quarterly*, vol. XXVIII, pp. 302–17 (July, 1929).

Newspapers and official documents are very partial and formal expressions of their writers' views. To complete and verify and understand them, it seems important to get as near the individuals as possible. A careful scrutiny was accordingly made of British and American biographical materials for comment on the American struggle, with especial desire to find those letters and diaries which bring the historian closer to psychological fact than any other means at hand. The results were satisfactory: some 320 titles referable to individuals writing and thinking at the time yielded each something of pertinence for the present investigation. The larger number of these were British, but a good many Southerners and Unionists who were in Europe during the war have left valuable comment or letters. In addition the writer was enabled to read the manuscript letters received from English friends by Charles Sumner during the war years (in the Harvard College Library); the unprinted portions of the diary of Benjamin Moran, Second Secretary at the American Legation in London (in the Library of Congress); and the diary of Frederick William Chesson, of the *Morning Star*, lent by Mr. W. H. Chesson. Of a less personal nature, but unpublished and important, are the *Minute Books* of the British and Foreign Anti-Slavery Society in the offices of the Anti-Slavery and Aborigines Protection Society in London.

Much of the newspaper comment on the Civil War was naturally controversial, but the newspaper had not at this time by any means supplanted the book and the pamphlet in the field of polemic. Besides a considerable number of titles dealing with parliamentary reform and other controversial topics which cast light on opinion of the American conflict, the discussion of America in England resulted in a large special literature which has not hitherto been gathered together. A list is subjoined of English publications on America in the years 1861–65.

BIBLIOGRAPHY

BRITISH PAMPHLETS AND BOOKS BEARING GENERALLY ON THE CIVIL WAR

ACTON, *Lord*. The Civil War in America: Its Place in History. In the *Bridgnorth Journal*, January 20, 1866, and in his *Historical Essays and Studies*. London, 1907, pp. 123–42.

American Documents. Manchester, 1863.

American Precedents Against the Blockade. London, 1863.

Anent the American War. London, 1865.

Anent the North American Continent. London, March, 1864.

Anent the United States and the Confederate States. London, 1862.

B., R. *A Memoir of Abraham Lincoln, President Elect of the United States*. London, 1861.

BALME, *Rev*. J. R. *American States, Churches, and Slavery*. London, 1863, second thousand.

Letters on the American Republic. London, [1863.] Second thousand, enlarged edition.

The War Crusade. London, [1863.] Third thousand.

BERNARD, MOUNTAGUE. *A Lecture on Alleged Violations of Neutrality* ... London, 1863.

Notes on Some Questions Suggested by the Case of the Trent. Oxford and London, March, 1862.

On the Principle of Non-Intervention. A lecture. Oxford and London, December, 1860.

Two Lectures on the Present American War. Oxford and London, [1861.]

BIRKENHEAD IRON-CLADS. *Correspondence Between Her Majesty's Government and Messrs. Laird Brothers*... London, [1864.]

BRITISH FREED-MEN'S AID SOCIETIES. *Report*... May, 1865. N.p., n.d.

Speech of the Duke of Argyll... on May 17, 1865. London, 1865.

[BURN, J. D.] *Three Years among the Working-Classes in the United States*. London, 1865.

The Case of the Seizure of the Southern Envoys. London, 1861.

CASWALL, HENRY. *The American Church and the American Union*. London, 1861.

CIVIS ANGLICUS. *A Voice from the Motherland Answering Mrs. H. Beecher Stowe's Appeal*. London, 1863.

COBBETT, JAMES PAUL. *Causes of the Civil War in the United States.* London, September, 1861.

COBDEN, RICHARD. *Speech of Mr. Cobden on the Foreign Enlistment Act...* London, 1863, second edition.

COIN, *Colonel* ROBERT L. DE. *History and Cultivation of Cotton and Tobacco.* London, 1864.

COTTON SUPPLY ASSOCIATION. Report of a Meeting at Manchester, May 21, 1857. N.p., n.d.

Third Annual Report. [May, 1860.] N.p., n.d.

The Crisis of Emancipation in America. No title page. [1865.]

DANIELLS, *Hon.* J. M. *The Life of Stonewall Jackson...* London, 1863. Reprinted from the advance sheets of the Richmond edition.

AN ENGLISH MERCHANT. *Two Months in the Confederate States...* London, 1863.

ESTVÀN, B. *War Pictures from the South.* London, 1863, 2 vols.

FISCH, *Rev.* GEORGES. *Nine Months in the United States.* London, 1863.

FISHER, HERBERT W. *Considerations on the Origin of the American War.* London and Cambridge, 1865.

Free Labour Cotton: it can be had. London, n.d. [1863?]

GIBBS, FREDERICK WAYMOUTH. *The Foreign Enlistment Act.* London, 1863, second edition.

Recognition. London, 1863.

GOTTHEIL, *Rev.* DR. G. *Moses Versus Slavery...* Manchester, 1861.

[HARDINGE, *Mrs.*] *Belle Boyd in Camp and Prison.* London, 1865, 2 vols.

HISTORICUS [WILLIAM VERNON HARCOURT]. *American Neutrality.* New York, 1865. Reprinted from *The Times,* December 22, 1864.

Letters to the London Times. London and Cambridge, 1863.

HOPKINS, JOHN BAKER. *The Fall of the Confederacy.* London, n.d. [1867?]

[HOWARD, F. K.] *Fourteen Months in American Bastilles.* London, 1863. Reprinted from the Baltimore edition.

LAWRENCE, G. A. *Border and Bastille.* London, 1863. Third edition.

LAWRENCE, *Rev.* G. G. *Three Months in America in the Summer of 1863.* Huddersfield, n.d.

A Tour in the Southern States in... 1866. London, n.d.

A LAWYER. *The Coming Struggle in America.* Glasgow and Ayr, 1861.

A LAWYER. *Maritime Capture.* London, 1862.

A Legacy of Fun by Abraham Lincoln. London, 1865.

LOCKE, STEPHEN. *English Sympathies and Opinions on the American Civil War.* London, 1866.

LORIMER, JAMES. *The Rights and Duties of Belligerents and Neutrals* ... Edinburgh, 1865.

M'HENRY, GEORGE. *The Cotton Supply of the United States of America.* London, 1865, privately printed.

MACKAY, CHARLES. *The History of the United States of America.* London, n.d., 2 vols.

Life and Liberty in America. London, 1859, 2 vols.

MACKENZIE, ROBERT. *America and her Army.* London, 1865.

MATHEWS, *Rev.* EDWARD. *American Slavery and the War.* A lecture ... Wirksworth, 1864.

MONTAGU, *Lord* ROBERT. *A Mirror in America.* London, 1861.

A NEUTRAL. *Uncle John's Cabin (Next Door to Uncle Tom's Cabin), Containing an Answer to Pro-Slavery Men...* London, 1865.

The Attempt of the North to Subdue the Southerners and the Attempt of Spain to Subdue the Netherlanders... London, 1865.

AN OLD POLITICIAN. *The War in America: Negro Slavery and the Bible.* Stirling, 1862.

PALMER, ROUNDELL. *Speech... on the 'Alabama' Question...* London and Cambridge, 1863.

Speech... on the North American Blockade... London, 1862.

Papers Relating to the Condemnation of the British Barque 'Springbok'... London, 1864, printed for the owners.

PETO, *Sir* S. MORTON. *The Resources and Prospects of America.* London, 1866.

PHILO-AMERICANUS. *The American Struggle: An Appeal to the People of the North.* London, 1862.

A POOR PEACEMAKER. *The Slavery Quarrel, with Plans... of Reconciliation.* London, 1863.

A Protocol for the Settlement of the Strife in North America. London, 1863, leaflet.

REID, HUGO. *Sketches in North America; with Some Account of Congress and of the Slavery Question.* London, 1861.

RUSSELL, WILLIAM HOWARD. *My Diary North and South.* London, 1863, 2 vols.

SALA, GEORGE AUGUSTUS. *My Diary in America in the Midst of War.* London, 1865, 2 vols.

SARGENT, EPES. *Peculiar: a Tale of the Great Transition.* Edited by William Howitt. London, 1864, 3 vols.

The Seizure of the 'Peterhoff.' London, 1863.

SHAFFNER, *Colonel* TAL P. *The War in America.* London, 1862.

SMEDLEY, JOHN. *The Cotton Question.* London and Manchester, 1861, privately printed.

[SMITH, A., *of Nottingham.*] *The Defences of England.* Nine letters by a journeyman shoemaker. London, March, 1862.

SMITH, P. A. *The Seizure of the Southern Commissioners*... London, 1862.

SMOLLETT, P. B. *The Cotton Supplies from India*... Manchester, [1860.]

TALLACK, WILLIAM. *Friendly Sketches in America.* London, 1861.

TAYLOR, CHRISTOPHER. *The Probable Causes and Consequence of the American War.* Liverpool and London, 1864.

[TENNANT, CHARLES.] *The American Question and How to Settle It.* London, 1863.

TROLLOPE, ANTHONY. *North America.* London, 1862, 2 vols.

VIGIL. *American Difficulties,* London, 1861. Letters reprinted from the *Torquay Directory.*

VIGILANS. *The Foreign Enlistment Acts of England and America.* London, 1864.

WILLIAMS, MAURICE. *The Cotton Trade of 1861 and 1862.* Liverpool, 1863.

Seven Years' History of the Cotton Trade of Europe. Liverpool, 1st May, 1868. A reprinting of a broker's annual circulars, including a graphic representation of cotton prices.

WORKS POSITIVELY FAVORING THE NORTH

ADAMS, W. E. *The Slaveholders' War: An Argument for the North and the Negro.* London, 1863.

The Alabama: a Statement of Facts... London, 1863.

An American Citizen [O. J. Victor]. *The American Rebellion: Some Facts and Reflections for the Consideration of the English People.* London, [1861.]

The American Question. London, 1862.

The American Question. London, 1861. Contains a letter of the Reverend William Arthur to the Wesleyan *Watchman*, and the major portion of A. H. Stephens's 'corner-stone speech.'

An Appeal to English Women. London, n.d.

Arthur, *Rev.* William. *English Opinion on the American Rebellion.* Manchester, n.d. [1863?]

Barrington, William L. *The True Origin of the American Rebellion.* Dublin, 1865.

Baxter, W. E. *The Social Condition of the Southern States of America.* London, 1862.

Beecher, *Rev.* Henry Ward. *American Rebellion.* Speech delivered in Free Trade Hall, Manchester... Manchester, [1863.]

Report of Speeches... in England. Manchester, 1864.

Bright, John. *Speech in the Town Hall, Birmingham, December* 18, 1862. Birmingham, n.d.

British and Foreign Anti-Slavery Society. Tracts on Slavery in America:

No. 1. *What the South is Fighting For.* London, 1863, third edition, 30th thousand.

No. 2. *The Crisis in the United States.* London, November 19th, 1862.

No. 3. *British Aid to the Confederates.* London, 1863.

Brown, *Hon.* George. *The American War and Slavery.* A speech... Manchester, 1863.

Cairnes, J. E. *England's Neutrality in the American Contest.* London, 1864.

The Revolution in America. A lecture. Dublin, n.d. Seventh edition, revised and enlarged.

The Slave Power. London and Cambridge, 1863. Second edition, enlarged.

The Case of the Trent Examined. London, 1862.

Channing, William Henry. *The Civil War in America....* An address. Liverpool, etc., [1861.]

CHILD, MARIA. *The Deeper Wrong.* London, 1862.

Civil War and Slavery in the United States. London, 1862. Third edition.

[COBBE, F. P.] *Rejoinder to Mrs. Stowe's Reply to the Address of the Women of England.* London, 1863.

CONWAY, M. D. 'North and South, and Slavery,' in *Pitman's Popular Lecturer and Reader,* August, 1863, pp. 225–36. A separate.

Testimonies Concerning Slavery. London, 1865. Second edition.

COSSHAM, HANDEL. 'America: Past, Present, and Future,' in *Pitman's Popular Lecturer and Reader,* March, 1863, pp. 65–90. A separate.

The American War: Facts and Fallacies. Speech at Bristol, February 12, 1864. Bristol, [1864.]

Mr. Cossham on America: What he Saw and Heard. No title page. Reprinted from *Stroud Journal,* December 16, 1865.

D., B. *Federals and Confederates: For What do They Fight?...* London, [1862.]

DICEY, EDWARD. *Six Months in the Federal States.* London and Cambridge, 1863, 2 vols.

DILL, *Rev. Dr. The American Conflict.* A lecture... Belfast, 1863.

DYER, J. C., *of Burnage. Notes on Political Mistakes,...* Manchester, n.d.

EDGE, FREDERICK MILNES. *The Destruction of the American Carrying Trade...* London, 1863. A second edition, 1864.

England's Danger and her Safety... London, 1864.

Great Britain and the United States... London, 1869.

President Lincoln's Successor. London, 1864.

Slavery Doomed. London, 1860.

A Woman's Example: and a Nation's Work... London, 1864. A description and puff of the work of the United States Sanitary Commission.

ELDER, WILLIAM. *Debt and Resources of the United States...* Philadelphia, 1863. Reviewed in English periodicals.

ELLISON, THOMAS. *Slavery and Secession in America.* London, [1861.] Second edition, enlarged, 1862.

AN ENGLISH LADY [*Mrs.* A. P. BAYMAN]. *Notes and Letters on the American War.* London, 1864.

ESTCOURT, J. H. *Rebellion and Recognition...* Manchester, 1863.

Fallacies of Freemen and Foes of Liberty. A Reply to 'The American War: the Whole Question Explained.' Manchester, 1863.

FEDRIC, FRANCIS. *Slave Life in Virginia and Kentucky.* London, 1863.

GASPARIN, *Count* AGÉNOR DE. *America Before Europe...* London, 1862.

The Uprising of a Great People: the United States in 1861. London, 1861.

A Word of Peace on the American Question. London, n.d. Refers to the Trent affair.

GODDARD, SAMUEL A. *Letters on the American Rebellion.* London, 1870. Letters written during the war by a self-constituted defender of the Union to the *Birmingham Daily Post* and the *London American.*

Reply to Mr. Lindsay's Speech at Sunderland, August, 1864. Birmingham, [1864.]

GOW, DAN. *Civil War in America.* A lecture... Manchester and London, n.d.

HAERNE, *Canon* DE. *The American Question.* London, 1863. Translated by Thomas Ray.

HALL, NEWMAN. *The American War.* A lecture. London, [1862.]

HUGHES, THOMAS. *The Cause of Freedom.* London, n.d.

The Struggle for Kansas. Two lectures delivered in the autumn of 1861 and printed in Ludlow's Sketch of the History of the United States (q. v.).

JACKSON, JOHN ANDREW. *The Experience of a Slave in South Carolina.* London, 1862.

JONES, ERNEST. *The Slaveholders' War.* A lecture... Ashton-under-Lyne, n.d.

KEMBLE, FRANCES ANNE. *Journal of a Residence on a Georgian Plantation in 1838 and 1839.* London, 1863.

KENNEDY, JOHN. *Hebrew Servitude and American Slavery.* London, 1863.

LABOULAYE, ÉDOUARD, *and others. Reply of Messrs. A. de Gasparin, E. Laboulaye... Friends of America in France, to the Loyal National League of New York.* Liverpool, reprinted from the *New York Weekly Tribune,* with a preface for English readers.

LADIES' LONDON EMANCIPATION SOCIETY. Tracts:

No. 1. COBBE, F. P. *The Red Flag in John Bull's Eyes.* London, 1863.

No. 2. CRAIG, ISA (*adaptor*). *The Essence of Slavery*, extracted from Mrs. Kemble's Journal. London, August, 1863.

No. 3. CAIRNES, J. E. *Who Are the Canters?* London, September, 1863.

No. 4. DICEY, EDWARD. *Labour and Slavery.* London, November, [1863.]

No. 5. MOODY, LORING (*compiler*). *The Destruction of the Republic, and of All Constitutional Liberty, the Object of the Rebellion.* London, December, 1863. An adaptation of an American pamphlet.

No. 6. SHIRREFF, EMILY. *The Chivalry of the South.* London, January, 1864.

No. 7. REMOND, S. F. *Negroes and Anglo-Africans as Freedmen and Soldiers.* Not seen.

No. 8. LUDLOW, J. M. *American Slavery.* London, March, 1864.

No. 9. CONWAY, M. D. *Benjamin Banneker, the Negro Astronomer.* Reprinted from the *Atlantic Monthly.* London, April, 1864.

No. 10. TAYLOR, *Mrs.* P. A. (*compiler*). *Professor Huxley on the Negro Question.* London, May, 1864.

No. 11. SHIRREFF, EMILY. *A Few More Words on the Chivalry of the South.* London, June, 1864.

No. 12. *The Humanity of the Confederates, or, the Massacre of Fort Pillow.* London, July, 1864.

A LANCASHIRE ARTISAN. *Cotton!* Broadside, n.d., n.p. A large linen-backed yellow poster. Also distributed in leaflet form.

The Last Address of President Lincoln to the American People. London, n.d., leaflet.

LENG, WILLIAM C. *The American War*... A lecture... Dundee, 1863.

LUDLOW, J. M. *A Sketch of the History of the United States.* London, 1862.

The Southern Minister and his Slave-Convert: a dialogue. Manchester, n.d. Reprinted from *Good Words.*

The Martyrdom of John Brown. The proceedings of a public meeting ... on 2d December, 1863... London, 1864.

MASSIE, J. W. *America*... London, 1864
The American Crisis... London, 1862.
The Case Stated: the Friends and Enemies of the American Slave. Manchester, 1863.
MIALL, CHARLES S. *The Proposed Slave Empire.* London, 1863.
MILLER, *Rev.* MARMADUKE. *Slavery and the American War.* A lecture. Manchester, n.d.
MOTLEY, J. LOTHROP. *The Causes of the American Civil War.* A paper contributed to the *London Times.* London, New York, etc., many editions in 1861. Subtitle varies.
NEWELL'S *Notes on... the Treatment of American Female Slaves.* London, n.d.
NEWMAN, F. W. *Character of the Southern States.* Manchester, 1863.
The Good Cause of President Lincoln. London, n.d.
NOEL, BAPTIST WRIOTHESLEY. *Freedom and Slavery in the United States of America.* London, 1863.
The Rebellion in America. London, 1863.
OAKLAND [*pseud.*] *The Question of Cotton Supply.* Manchester, [1861]. A letter to the *New York Times* by an American writing in Manchester.
PARKER, *Rev.* JOSEPH. *American War and American Slavery.* A speech.... Manchester, 1863.
PARTRIDGE, J. ARTHUR. *The False Nation and its 'Bases'; or, Why the South can't stand.* London, 1864.
PATTON, *Rev.* WILLIAM. *The American Crisis*... London, 1861.
POPE, SAMUEL. *The American War: Secession and Slavery.* Manchester, n.d.
The Problem. No title page.
RAWLINS, CHARLES ED., *Jun. American Dis-Union: Constitutional or Unconstitutional?* A reply to James Spence's *The American Union.* London, 1862.
ROBBINS, E. Y. *An impartial View of the War in America.* London, 1864.
ROCHE, JAMES. *Origin and Progress of the American Republic and the War.* Dublin, n.d.
Earl Russell and the Slave Power. Manchester, 1863.
SARGENT, F. W. *England, the United States, and the Southern Confederacy.* London, 1864, second edition.

Secession Condemned in a Southern Convention. Leaflet published by the Union and Emancipation Society, comprising extracts from A. H. Stephens' speech condemning secession in the Georgia convention of January, 1861.

SIMPSON, JOHN HAWKINS. *Horrors of the Virginian Slave Trade and of the Slave-Rearing Plantations.* London, 1863.

SINCLAIR, PETER. *Freedom or Slavery in the United States.* London, [1863], second edition.

SMITH, GOLDWIN. *The Civil War in America.* An address. London, 1866. An address at the final meeting of the Manchester Union and Emancipation Society on January 22, 1866; the pamphlet includes a report of the meeting and a list of the vice-presidents of the Society.

Does the Bible Sanction American Slavery? Oxford and London, 1863.

England and America. Manchester, 1865. A lecture in Boston, reprinted from the *Atlantic Monthly* with an introduction addressed to the president of the Manchester Union and Emancipation Society.

Letter to a Whig Member of the Southern Independence Association. London, 1864. Includes the Address of the Southern Independence Association.

'Southern Recognition' and 'Real Emancipation.' Manchester, June, 1863, leaflet.

STORY, WILLIAM W. *The American Question.* London, 1862. Three letters to the *London Daily News* at the time of the Trent affair.

STURTEVANT, J. M. *English Institutions and the American Rebellion.* Manchester, 1864.

SUMNER, CHARLES. *Slavery and the American War.* A speech... London, 1865.

TAYLOR, WILLIAM. *Causes and Probable Results of the Civil War...* London, 1862.

THOMAS, ALFRED C. *Prayerful Sympathy Invoked for America.* A sermon... December 21, 1862. London, n.d.

TRAIN, GEORGE FRANCIS. *Union Speeches Delivered in England.* Philadelphia, 1862, two series, two vols.

TRIMBLE, ROBERT. *The Negro, North and South.* London, 1863.
A Review of the American Struggle... London, 1864.
Slavery in the United States of America. London, 1863.

WADDINGTON, JOHN. *The American Crisis in Relation to Slavery.* London, 1862.

WALKER, ROBERT. *American Slavery and Finances.* London, 1864. Reprints, with original paging, of a series of pamphlets published between July, 1863, and February, 1864.

War Ships for the Southern Confederacy. Report of a meeting in Manchester... April 6, 1863. Manchester, 1863.

WHITE, ANDREW D. *Letter to W. H. Russell on Passages in his Diary.* London, 1863.

WIGHAM, ELIZA. *The Anti-Slavery Cause in America and its Martyrs.* London, 1863.

WILKS, WASHINGTON. *English Criticism on President Lincoln's Anti-Slavery Proclamation and Message.* London, [1862?]

The Working Men of Manchester and President Lincoln. Manchester, [1863.]

YATES, EDWARD. *A Letter to the Women of England on Slavery in the Southern States.* London, 1863.

WORKS POSITIVELY FAVORING THE SOUTH

The American Question. No title page. It is 'No. III.,' probably of the Southern Independence Association.

AMERICUS. *Essay on the American War.* Liverpool, 1865.

BLACKMAN, E. L. *Our Relations with America.* Manchester, [1863.]
'Shall We Recognize the Confederate States?' London, 1863.

A BLOCKADED BRITISH SUBJECT. *Life in the South... 1860 to August, 1862.* London, 1863, 2 vols.

CAMPBELL, *Lord* [*Lord* STRATHEDEN]. Speech in the House of Lords ... March 23, 1863. London, 1863.

CHURCH, R. S. H. *The Two Rebellions: A Few Words to C. F. Adams* ... London, 1865.

The Clergy of the Confederate States of America. Address to Christians throughout the World. N.p., [1863.]

COWELL, JOHN WELSFORD. *France and the Confederate States.* London and Paris, 1865.

Lancashire's Wrongs and the Remedy: two letters addressed to the cotton operatives of England. London, 1863.

Southern Secession: letter to Captain M. T. Maury. London, 1862.

[DAVIS, JEFFERSON.] *The Second Annual Message of His Excellency the President of the Confederate States to Congress.* London, 1863.

Third Annual Message of President Davis. London, 1864.

DAY, SAMUEL PHILLIPS. *Down South; An Englishman's Experience at the Seat of the American War.* London, 1862, 2 vols.

AN ENGLISH COMBATANT. [T. E. C.] *Battlefields of the South...* London, 1863, 2 vols.

AN EYE-WITNESS. *The Bastille in America...* London, 1861.

FAIRFAX, L. *The Elopement.* London, 1863. A novel of the Confederate States.

FAIR-PLAY. *The True State of the American Question.* Reply to Thurlow Weed. London, 1862.

For Peace in America. A report from Joseph Parker of Manchester to Sir Henry de Hoghton, on his mission as bearer of the peace address to the United States. N.p., n.d. [January, 1865.]

FREMANTLE, *Lieutenant Colonel* [ARTHUR]. *Three Months in the Southern States, April to June, 1863.* Edinburgh, 1863.

FULLER, H[IRAM]. *The Causes and Consequences of the Civil War in America:* an address... London, [1862.]

The Flag of Truce. Dedicated to the Emperor of the French. By a White Republican. London, 1862, second edition.

North and South. By the White Republican of *Fraser's Magazine.* London, 1863.

GRATTAN, THOMAS COLLEY. *England, and the Disrupted States of America.* London, 1862, third edition.

GREENHOW, *Mrs.* ROSE. *My Imprisonment and the First Year of Abolition Rule at Washington.* London, 1863.

H., M. B., [*of Arkansas*]. *Confederate Notes for English Circulation.* London, [1863?]

HOPE, A. J. B. BERESFORD. *Address upon the Political Questions of the Day...* Hanley, [1862.]

The American Disruption. London, 1862, sixth edition.

A Popular View of the American Civil War. London, 1861, third edition.

Social and Political Bearings of the American Disruption. London, 1863, third edition.

HOPKINS, JOHN B. *Peace or War? An Unbiassed View of the American Crisis.* London, 1861.

HOPKINS, JOHN H. [*Bishop of Vermont.*] *The Bible View of American Slavery.* London, 1863.

HUDSON, E. M. *The Second War of Independence in America.* London, 1863.

HUNT, JAMES. *The Negro's Place in Nature.* London, 1863.

JORDAN, THOMAS. *The South: its Products, Commerce, and Resources.* Edinburgh, 1861.

KERSHAW, T. BENTLEY. *The Truth of the American Question...* Manchester, [1864.]

KIRKE, EDMUND [*pseud.* JAMES R. GILMORE]. *Life in Dixie's Land.* London, 1863.

L., E. *Notes on American Affairs.* London, 1863.

A LATE AMERICAN STATESMAN. [C. F. MERCER.] *The Weakness and Inefficiency of the Government of the United States...* London, 1863.

LEMPRIÈRE, CHARLES. *The American Crisis Considered.* London, 1861.

LONDON CONFEDERATE STATES AID ASSOCIATION. *Address to the British Public and all Sympathizers in Europe.* London, 1862.

LOTHIAN, *Marquis of. The Confederate Secession.* Edinburgh and London, 1864.

M'HENRY, GEORGE, AND RALSTON, GERARD. *The African Race in America...* being a correspondence... between two Pennsylvanians. London, 1861, privately printed.

MCHENRY, GEORGE. *The Cotton Question.* N.p., n.d., revised edition.

The Cotton Trade... London, 1863.

MALET, *Rev.* WILLIAM WYNDHAM. *An Errand to the South in the Summer of 1862.* London, 1863.

MAXSE, *Captain* [F. A.], R. N. *Pro Patria...* London, 1863.

MITCHELL, D. W. *Ten Years in the United States.* London, 1862.

MOREHEAD, CHARLES S. *Southern Confederation...* Speech at the Southern Club, Liverpool. Liverpool, 1862.

A NATIVE OF PENNSYLVANIA. *Why Pennsylvania Should Become One of the Confederate States.* London, 1862.

NEMO. *Remarks on the Policy of Recognizing the Independence of the Southern States...* London, 1863.

NICHOLS, *Dr.* THOMAS L. *Forty Years in America.* London, 1864, 2 vols.

A NORTHERN MAN. *Curiosity Visits to Southern Plantations.* London, 1863.

AN OLD ACQUAINTANCE. [EDWIN DE LEON?] *A Familiar Epistle to Robert J. Walker...* London, 1863, fifth thousand.

ONESIMUS SECUNDUS. *The True Interpretation of the American Civil War.* London, 1863, second edition.

O'SULLIVAN, JOHN L. *Peace the Sole Chance Now Left for Reunion...* London, 1863.

Recognition. A letter to Lord Palmerston. London, 1863.

Union, Disunion, and Reunion... London, 1862.

OZANNE, *Rev.* T. D. *The South As It Is....* London, 1863.

POLLARD, EDWARD A. *The First Year of the War in America.* London, 1863. Reprinted from the Richmond edition.

A RECENT TOURIST. *The Right of Recognition...* London, 1862.

Recognition of the Southern Confederacy Indispensable for Resolving the American Question. London, 1863.

REED, WILLIAM B. *A Northern Plea for Peace...* London, 1863.

Refutation of Fallacious Arguments Anent the American Question. London, April, 1863.

REID, H. *The American Question in a Nutshell...* London, 1862.

The Right of Recognition. London, 1862.

A SOUTHERN LADY. *The Woes of War...* London, 1862, second edition.

SPENCE, JAMES. *The American Union; Its Effect on National Character and Policy, with an Inquiry into Secession as a Constitutional Right, and the Causes of the Disruption.* London, 1862, fourth and revised edition.

On the Recognition of the Southern Confederation. London, 1862, third edition.

Southern Independence: an address. London, 1863.

Three Letters from a South Carolinian Relating to Secession, Slavery, and the Trent Case. London, 1862, privately printed.

TREMLETT, *Rev.* FRANCIS WILLIAM. *Christian Brotherhood: Its Claims and Duties; with a Special Reference to the Fratricidal War in America.* London, n.d. [1864.]

VAN EVRIE, J. H. *Negroes and Negro 'Slavery': the First an Inferior Race, the Latter its Normal Condition.* New York and London, 1861.

WARNEFORD, *Lieutenant* R. N. *Running the Blockade.* London, 1863.

Skedaddle, by 'Our Own' Special Correspondent. London, 1865.

WILLIAMS, JAMES. *The Rise and Fall of 'The Model Republic.'* London, 1863.

The South Vindicated. London, 1862.

WORKS DEALING WITH CONTROVERSIAL SUBJECTS, MOSTLY POLITICAL

ADDERLEY, C. B. *Europe Incapable of American Democracy.* London, 1867.

Letter to Disraeli on the Relations of England with the Colonies. London, 1862.

ALISON, A. *Government Reform in England and America.* London, 1861.

AUSTIN, JOHN. *A Plea for the Constitution.* London, 1859, second edition.

AYTOUN, JAMES. *Real Reform and Sham Reform...* London, 1864.

BAGEHOT, WALTER. *Parliamentary Reform:* an essay. London, [1859.]

BEALES, EDMOND. *Speech... at St. Martin's Hall, May 13, 1865.* London, 1865.

BEESLY, E. S. *Letters to the Working Classes.* London, 1870.

BLANC, LOUIS. *Lettres sur l'Angleterre,* [1861–1865.] Paris, 1866, 2 vols. in 1; deuxième série, Paris, 1866, 2 vols. in 1.

CECIL, *Lord* ROBERT GASCOIGNE. *The Theories of Parliamentary Reform,* in *Oxford Essays,* 1858, pp. 52–79.

Essays on Reform. London, 1867.

GREY, *Earl. Parliamentary Government... and Reform.* London, 1864, new edition.

HARGREAVES, W. *Revelations from Printing-House Square...* London, 1864.

HILL, FREDERIC. *Parliamentary Reform...* London, 1865.

HOLYOAKE, G. J. *The Liberal Situation...* London, reprinted from the *Newcastle Weekly Chronicle,* March, 1865.

Jones, Ernest. *Democracy Vindicated...* Edinburgh, etc., 1867.

Lewis, *Sir* George Cornewall. *A Dialogue on the Best Form of Government.* London, 1863.

M., H. F. *Look to the End.* A lay sermon. London, 1864.

Masheder, Richard. *Dissent and Democracy: Their Mutual Relations and Common Object.* London, 1864.

Murchison, J. H. *The Conservatives and 'Liberals'...* London, 1866.

Nemo. *Earl Russell and the Foreign Office.* London, 1864.

Newman, Francis W. *English Institutions and Their Most Necessary Reforms.* London, 1865.

Non-Intervention in the Danish War. Report of a meeting.... February 14, 1864.... Manchester, 1864.

Partridge, J. Arthur. *On Democracy.* London, 1866.

S[tephen] L[eslie]. *The 'Times' on the American War: a Historical Study.* London, 1865.

Smith, Goldwin. *The Empire.* A series of letters. Oxford and London, 1863.

The Traditional Policy of the 'Times.' Manchester, [1864].

Vandenburgh, O. *An Inquiry Answered: the Democratic Institutions of America.* London, 1859.

FRANCE

Though the French foreign office archives are not open after 1851, there are printed works which throw enough light on the opinions of the Emperor and his circle to enable us to form an accurate estimate of the character and development of French policy. Besides the *Diplomatic Correspondence* of the United States and that of the Confederacy (in the *Official Records of the... Navies*, Series II, vol. 3, Washington, 1922), the most important sources of information on the diplomatic side are:

Bancroft, F. *The Life of W. H. Seward.* New York, 1900, 2 vols.

Bigelow, John. *France and the Confederate Navy.* New York, 1888.
Retrospections of an Active Life. New York, 1909–13, 5 vols.

Bulloch, J. D. *The Secret Service of the Confederate States in Europe.* London, 1883, 2 vols.

Callahan, J. M. *The Evolution of Seward's Mexican Policy.* Morgantown, West Virginia, 1909.

Pecquet du Bellet, Paul. *The Diplomacy of the Confederate Cabinet of Richmond and its Agents Abroad, being Memorandum Notes Taken in Paris... 1861–65.* Typescript, Library of Congress.
Richardson, J. D. *Messages and Papers of the Confederacy.* Nashville, 1906, vol. ii.
Sears, L. M. *John Slidell.* Durham, North Carolina, 1925.
Thouvenel, E. *Le Secret de L'Empereur.* Paris, 1889, 2 vols.

The French part in the Mexican expedition is well handled in Martin, P. F., *Maximilian in Mexico* (London, 1914); and La Gorce, P. de, *Histoire du Second Empire* (Paris, 1896–1905, 7 vols.).

For the study of French opinion certain American sources are useful:

Adams, C. F. *Charles Francis Adams.* Boston, 1900.
Rhodes, J. F. *History of the United States,* vols. iii, iv.
Sears, L. M. 'A Neglected Critic of Our Civil War,' in *Mississippi Valley Historical Review,* i, 532–45 (March, 1915). A study of the editor of the most important of the French magazines, the *Revue des Deux Mondes.*
The Life of Thurlow Weed. Boston, 1884, 2 vols.

The activity of the Liberal opposition to the Emperor played an important part in forming French opinion. It is described and illustrated in:

Gasparin, *Comte* A. de. *The Uprising of a Great People.* New York, 1862.
Laboulaye, Édouard. *Discours Populaires.* Paris, 1869.
Oliphant, *Mrs. Memoir of the Count de Montalembert.* Edinburgh, 1872.
Ollivier, Émile. *L'Empire Libéral.* Paris, 1895–1914, 17 vols.
Picard, E. *Discours Parlementaires.* Paris, 1882.
Thiers, Adolphe. *Discours Parlementaires.* Paris, 1879–83, 15 vols.

The newspapers and magazines used have been indicated when named.

SPAIN

In the study of Spanish diplomacy and opinion, the diplomatic correspondence at Madrid, interesting also as showing the relations of France and Spain with reference to the Mexican expedition, is of especial importance. A clear understanding of Spanish parties and party leaders may be obtained from various historical sources, but the expressions of opinion are chiefly to be sought in the newspapers. The press, however, furnishes less abundant comment on American affairs than that of France. The following works are particularly useful:

BENOIST, CHARLES. *L'Espagne, Cuba, et les États-Unis.* Paris, 1897.
CALLAHAN, J. M. *Cuba and International Relations.* Baltimore, 1899.
The Reminiscences of Carl Schurz. New York, 1907–08, 3 vols.

OTHER CONTINENTAL COUNTRIES

Information on opinion of the American conflict in other countries is very scattered. A good deal was gathered from the dispatches of American Ministers at different capitals, and there is good gleaning in such works as Hobson, J. A., *Richard Cobden, the International Man* (London, 1919), and the Bright-Sumner Letters in the *Proceedings* of the Massachusetts Historical Society, vols. XLV, XLVI. For Austria the richest source is *The Correspondence of John Lothrop Motley*, New York, 1889, 2 vols.; and for Germany, and the cotton situation in particular, Hohenlohe-Schillingsfürst, Prince Chlodwig of, *Memoirs*, vol. I, London, 1906.

For Russia, where public opinion counted for little, American students have cleared up the official attitude:

CALLAHAN, J. M. *Russo-American Relations during the American Civil War.* Morgantown, West Virginia, 1907.
GOLDER, F. A. 'The American Civil War through the Eyes of a Russian Diplomat,' in *American Historical Review*, XXVI, 454–63 (April, 1921).
GOLDER, F. A. 'The Russian Fleet and the Civil War,' in *American Historical Review*, XX, 801–12 (July, 1915).

In Switzerland the files of the pro-Northern *Journal de Genève* are interesting, while in Belgium opinion friendly to the North — that of the majority of the thinking people — may be seen in the *Indépendence Belge*.

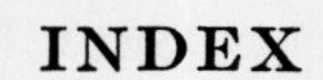
INDEX

INDEX

All newspapers named were published in London, Paris, or Madrid unless otherwise indicated.

Abolitionists, *see* Anti-slavery party
Acton, Sir John (Lord), 29, 60, 76; on significance of American democracy for England, 51
Adams, C. F., U.S. Minister at London, 166, 175, 206; comments on English opinion, 26, 111, 260; attacked for licensing traders to a Mexican port, 183
Adams, Henry, quoted, 21, 70, 186
'Alabama,' ship, 182 ff.
Albert, Prince, death of, 41
Alison, Sir Archibald, 68, 98
Allingham, William, 77
Alsace, cotton supply in, 213
America, an experiment in government, 24, 51–55, 58
American Revolution, referred to, 11, 13, 23, 103, 193
Americanization of England, 51, 62, 66, 68
Ampère, J.-J., 229
Annual Register, 168
Anonymity, journalistic, 79
Anti-Corn-Law League, referred to, 150, 152
Anti-slavery party, in England, 5, 10, 60, 125 ff. *See also* British and Foreign Anti-Slavery Society
Anti-Slavery Reporter, 126, 129
Appomattox, Lee's capitulation at, 261
Arbitration of Trent affair, proposed, 38–40
Argyll, Duke of, 87
Aristocracy, in England, 68–70. *See also* Democracy
Arman, J.-L., builder of Confederate ships, 221
Army and Navy Gazette, 82
Arnold, Matthew, 29, 76, 90–91
Aspinwall, W. H., 177
Athenæum, The, on emancipation, 158
Atlanta, capture of, 240
Atrocities, Northern, 111 ff., 132, 154, 225
Aucaigne, editor of *La Patrie*, 225
Austria, interest in U.S., 195

Bagehot, Walter, 87, 181
Baines, Edward, 41, 92
Bath, Marquess of, Confederate sympathizer, 173
Battles, Antietam, 113, 125, 212, 239, 252; Bull Run, 18 ff., 80; Chancellorsville, 186, 214; Chickamauga, 187; Fredericksburg, 157, 213; Gettysburg, 186, 215; second Manassas, 113; in Peninsula of Virginia, 102, 104, 107, 211, 236, 248; Shiloh, 102; in Tennessee, 100. *See also* Monitor, Vicksburg
Beales, Edmond, 180
Beecher, Rev. H. W., in England, 178–80
Beesly, E. S., 94
Belgium, influence of Civil War on, 197–98
Bennett, James Gordon, 28, 33. *See also* *New York Herald*
Beresford, Major William, 57
Beresford Hope, A. J., Confederate sympathizer, 90, 133, 172, 175
Berryer, Antoine-Pierre, 243
Bigelow, John, U.S. Consul General at Paris, 36, 175, 234
Billault, Adolphe, 220
Birmingham, 44, 152; opinion on Trent affair, 39–40
Birmingham Daily Post, on Trent affair, 41
Blackwood's Magazine, 85, 172
Blanc, Louis, 230
Blockade of Southern ports, 7, 25, 44, 64, 96 ff., 165; debated in Parliament, 99–101; of Charleston by sunken ships, 111, 209, 222, 224
Blockade-running, 90, 114, 187
Borthwick, Algernon, of the *Morning Post*, 86

Boucicault, Dion, quoted, 131
Bradford, pro-Northern meeting at, 153
Bradlaugh, Charles, 94
Bright, John, 16, 56, 62, 91–92, 97, 231; quoted, 144, 145, 159; and Trent affair, 37; America as a model for England, 54
Brighton, public meeting on Trent affair, 40
British and Foreign Anti-Slavery Society, 10, 126–27; on Trent affair, 128; on Emancipation Proclamation, 140; publications of, 151
Brougham, Lord, 144
Browning, Robert, 77
Bucks Herald (Aylesbury), on Trent affair, 30; cited, 104
Butler, Gen. B. F., in New Orleans, 104, 112
Buxton, Charles, 144

Cairnes, J. E., 74, 94, 142
Calderón de Collantes, Spanish foreign minister, 248
Cambridge University, 77
Campbell, Lord, *see* Stratheden
Campbell, R. B., Confederate in London, 170
Canada, possibility of invasion by U.S., 12, 25, 27, 34, 122, 259
Carlyle, Thomas, 72–73
Casimir-Périer, J.-P.-P., quoted, 236
Catholic Church, Rome, 194; France, 219, 240–41
Cavendish, Lord Frederick, 87
Cecil, Lord Robert, 85, 90, 133, 173; quoted, 17
Chamerovzow, L. A., 129, 180
Cheetham, John, 62
Cheever, Rev. G. B., 127
Chesson, F. W., 86, 93, 141–42, 180; quoted, 128, 135
Chichester, Bishop of, Confederate sympathizer, 174
Christian Observer, 169
Church of England, attitude toward slavery and the war, 132–34
Clanricarde, Marquess of, Confederate sympathizer, 174
Clay, Cassius M., U.S. Minister to Russia, remarks by, 14; referred to, 84, 112, 204
Clay, J. Randolph, 36
Cobbe, Frances Power, Northern sympathizer, 94
Cobden, Richard, sympathizes with North, 92; on Trent affair, 38; remarks and opinions of, 15, 105, 121, 144, 154, 159, 209
Cochin, Augustin, Northern sympathizer, 229, 239, 241
Committee of Correspondence on American Affairs, 142
Confederate agents in Europe, *see* Hotze, Mann, Mason, Rost, Slidell, Yancey
Confederate loan, 181–82, 186
Confederate ship-building in Europe, 165, 183, 214, 215, 234, 243
Congregational Union, for arbitration of Trent affair, 39; divided in sentiment, 135, 142
Conservative party in England, 49, 53–54, 88, 95, 104, 108
Conservatism, *see* Democracy
Constitutionnel, Le, 222, 226
Conway, Moncure D., 177
Cooper, Charles, journalist, 86
Correspondant, Le, 241
Cossham, Handel, Northern sympathizer, 92
Cotton, 33, 43, 45, 64, 96, 114–15, 187; in Germany, 196
Cotton famine, in England, 104–05; 107, 120; severity of in Belgium, 198; in France, 208, 211, 213, 235–36; improvement, 214. *See also* Blockade, Lancashire, Manchester
Cotton Supply Association, 62
Courrier, Le (Havre), 232
Courrier du Dimanche, Le, 232
Cowen, Joseph, 92
Cremer, W. R., trade union leader, 154, 161
Crimean War, influence on newspapers, 3; Anglo-American friction over, 16
Cuba, 246 ff.

Daily News, 41, 61, 85, 149, 160, 261; quoted in France, 239
Daily Telegraph, 83, 132, 156; on Trent affair, 33
Dale, Rev. Robert, 136
Darwin, Charles, 78
Davis, Jefferson, 154

INDEX

Delane, J. T., editor of *The Times*, 80, 83; fears war with U.S., 256
Democracy, English views of, 51, 55, 59, 62, 66; French views, 220
Denison, Ven. G. A., Archdeacon of Taunton, 68
Denmark, British sympathy with, 188–89. *See also* Schleswig-Holstein
Derby, Earl of, 88, 96, 99, 108, 262
Despotism in U.S., 21, 58, 61
Diario, El, 250, 253
Dicey, Edward, Northern sympathizer, 83
Dickens, Charles, 78
Discusión, La, 250, 254
Disraeli, Benjamin, 88, 99; *Lothair* quoted, 69
Dissenters, *see* Nonconformists
Donoughmore, Earl of, Confederate sympathizer, 90
Drouyn de Lhuys, French foreign minister, 212
Dufferin, Lord, Northern sympathizer, 87
Dunckley, Henry, journalist, 86
Duncombe, W. E., Confederate sympathizer, 90

Economist, The, 87, 98; on the blockade, 96; on Emancipation Proclamation, 139; on Confederate loan, 182
Edge, F. M., journalist, 84
Elections, English in 1859, 48; South Lancashire, 1861, 61–64; Carlisle, 1861, 64–65; U.S. in 1860, 4; 1862, 117, 213; 1864, comment in France, 235
Ellice, Edward, 88
Emancipation of slaves, 11; compensation for, 102, 129; proclaimed by Lincoln, 137 ff., 149, 195, 198, 235, 239, 249, 252. *See also* Slavery
Emancipation Societies, 148, 150 ff., 179, 183, 189, 267; meeting on Lincoln's death, 263; Ladies' London Emancipation Society, 91; London Emancipation Society founded, 141–42; Union and Emancipation Society of Manchester founded, 92, 149
Época, La, 250, 252
Ericsson, John, designer of 'Monitor,' 199
España, 250, 252
Eugénie, Empress, 216
Evangelical Alliance, 134, 140; Trent affair, 39; French branch, 140, 161
Evans, William, Northern sympathizer, 93
Evarts, W. M., 177
Examiner, The, quoted, 58
Exeter Hall, meetings at, 153, 158–59, 179

Fawcett, Henry, Northern sympathizer, 94
Fergusson, Sir James, Confederate sympathizer, 90
Fitzgerald, W. R. Seymour V., 109
Forbes, J. M., 177
Forcade, Eugène, editor of *Revue des Deux Mondes*, 234
Forster, W. E., spokesman for North in Parliament, 90, 101, 108
France, British opinion of, 14; Confederate sympathizers in, 218–20; cotton famine in, 208–09, 211, 213; Northern sympathizers in, 227–31, 240 ff.; parliamentary discussion of U.S., 220–21, 242; proposes an armistice, 116, 212; pro-Northern press, 232–42; pro-Southern press, 221–27; Trent affair, 42. *See also* Napoleon III
France, La, 222
Freeman, E. A., 77
French Protestants, 140, 161
Friends, Society of, 38, 94; mainstay of anti-slavery movement, 126
Froude, J. A., 77
Fuller, Hiram, 170

Garibaldi, 4, 92, 94; offered command of U.S. army, 24, 194
Gasparin, Comte de, 229
'George Griswold,' ship, 156
Germany, sympathy with Union, 195
Gironde, La (Bordeaux), 232
Gladstone, W. E., 49, 93, 103, 160; speech at Newcastle, 114 ff.
Grain, American, needed in Europe, 45, 108, 206, 214
Grant, James, journalist, 86
Granville, Earl, 122
Green, T. H., 76
Greg, Percy, pro-Southern writer, 168
Gregory, W. H., spokesman for Confederacy in Parliament, 89, 99–100, 108

Grey, Earl de, Under-Secretary for War, 27, 87
Grote, George, 76
Guardian, The, 182
Guizot, F.-P.-G., 229

Haliburton, T. C., Southern sympathizer, 90
Hall, Rev. Newman, Northern sympathizer, 40, 93, 135, 148
Hamber, Capt., editor of *The Standard*, 87
Hamley, E. B., 85
Harcourt, W. V., author of 'Historicus' letters, 117 ff., 263
Harrington, George, 177
Harrison, Frederic, 94
Hartington, Marquess of, 88
Hill, Frank H., journalist, 86
'Historicus,' *see* Harcourt
Hodgson, W. T., candidate for Parliament, 64
Hohenlohe-Schillingsfürst, Prince von, quoted, 196
Holland, little affected by Civil War, 197
Holyoake, G. J., Northern sympathizer, 94, 154, 180
Hooker, Sir J. D., 78
Hope, A. J. Beresford, Confederate sympathizer, 90, 133, 172, 175
Hopkins, J. B., pro-Southern writer, 167
Hopwood, J. T., Confederate sympathizer, 90
Hotze, Henry, Confederate agent in London, 125, 184; founds *The Index*, 166 ff.; quoted, 186
Huddersfield Examiner, letter on Trent affair in, 40
Hughes, Thomas, Northern sympathizer, 93, 142, 154
Hugo, Victor, sympathizes with North, 229
Hunt, James, anthropologist, on the Negro race, 169
Hutton, R. H., of *The Spectator*, 69, 85, 86
Huxley, T. H., 78

Iberia, 250, 255
Indépendence Belge, L', 198
Index, The, 167–68
Intervention, by England, 8–9, 96, 103 ff., 117, 121 ff., 184 ff.; by France, 185, 212; by Russia, 200. *See also* Propaganda, Recognition
Ironclad ships, *see* 'Monitor'
Italy, attitude toward U.S., 194; English interest in, 4

Jackson, Gen. T. J., death of, 184
Jerrold, W. Blanchard, editor of *Lloyd's Weekly*, 85
John Bull, 56
Journal, Le (Havre), 232
Journal des Débats, Le, 232, 237–40; quoted, 228
Journal of St. Petersburg, quoted, 199, 200
Journalists, English, 79–87. *See also* Newspapers
Jowett, Benjamin, Northern sympathizer, 77

Kerrison, Sir E. C., Confederate sympathizer, 90
Kingsley, Charles, 133

Labor, *see* Working classes
Laboulaye, Édouard, Northern sympathizer, 229, 239
Lacordaire, Père J.-B.-H., 240
Ladies' London Emancipation Society, *see* Emancipation Societies
Lamar, L. Q. C., 170
Lancashire, 96–98, 119, 172. *See also* Cotton, Manchester, Propaganda
Laugel, A.-A., Northern sympathizer, 229, 235
Leeds Mercury, on Trent affair, 41
Lempriere, Charles, Confederate sympathizer, 171
Lewis, Sir G. C., Secretary of State for War, 29, 87; speech at Hereford, 116; memorandum against recognition, 118
Liberal party, in England, 48–49; in France, 203, 212, 216, 228 ff.; in Spain, 250, 254. *See also* Elections, Manchester School, Radicals, Reformers
Liberalism, European, favors Union, 228, 244; French, 227 ff., 244; English, 265; stimulated by outcome of war, 265–67
Lincoln, Abraham, election, 4; inaugural address, 7; first annual message, 42;

second inaugural address, 261; death, 240, 261–64
Lindsay, W. S., spokesman of the Confederacy in Parliament, 89, 100, 106–08, 173, 185
Liverpool, 43, 102, 111, 114–15, 155; pro-Northern agitation in, 152–53; Southern Club in, 171. *See also* Blockade-running, Cotton, Election in South Lancashire
Liverpool Chronicle, 41
Liverpool Courier, 56
Liverpool Daily Post, 86
Lloyd's Weekly Newspaper, 86, 103, 110
London American, 178
London Confederate States Aid Association, 171
London Emancipation Society, *see* Emancipation Societies
Lothian, Marquess of, Confederate sympathizer, 90, 173
Lucas, Samuel, editor of *Morning Star*, 86
Ludlow, J. M., Northern sympathizer, 93, 154
Lyell, Sir Charles, 79
Lytton, Sir E. B., 77

M'Carthy, Justin, 86, 180; quoted, 19
McIlvaine, C. P., Bishop of Ohio, 36, 177
Mackay, Charles, 170; correspondent of *The Times* in U.S., 82
Malespine, pro-Northern writer, 233
Manchester, 43, 46, 98, 105; public meeting at, 148. *See also* Cotton, Emancipation Societies, Lancashire
Manchester Examiner, 41, 86
Manchester Guardian, 109, 119, 259
Manchester School, 49, 56, 62, 92, 144, 263; on Trent affair, 37, 41
'Manhattan,' *see* Scoville
Mann, A. Dudley, Confederate agent, 166
Martin, Henri, Northern sympathizer, 229
Martin, Rev. J. Sella, 128, 178
Martineau, Harriet, 109; leader writer of *Daily News*, 85; quoted, 58
Martineau, James, 94, n.
Mason, J. M., Confederate commissioner, 69, 100–01, 154, 166, 262; captured, 28; withdraws from England, 187; quoted, 140
Massie, Rev. J. W., Northern sympathizer, 94, 135
Maurice, Rev. F. D., 133, 161
Maury, M. F., 170
Maximilian, Archduke, *see* Mexican expedition
Mazzini, Giuseppe, 91, 94; quoted, 266
Mediation, *see* Intervention
Mexican expedition, 198, 207, 215–16, 242; Spanish withdrawal from, 248. *See also* Napoleon III
Miall, Edward, 146
Mill, J. S., 58, 67, 94, 142; discusses American affairs, 73–74; quoted, 139, 152, 228
Milnes, R. M. (Lord Houghton), Northern sympathizer, 35, 77
Moniteur, Le, 222–24
Monitor and Merrimac, 102, 199
Montalembert, Comte de, Northern sympathizer, 229, 240, 266
Moran, Benjamin, Secretary of U.S. Legation, quoted, 57, 158, 177
Moreau, Henri, 241
Morley, John, 86
Morley, Samuel, 160
Morning Advertiser, 86
Morning Herald, 84, 110, 184
Morning Post, 86, 115; on Trent affair, 33
Morning Star, 41, 84, 86, 93
Morny, Comte de, 218
Motley, J. L., 67; defense of Union, 13; on Viennese opinion, 195

Napoleon III, policy toward U.S., 203 ff.; relations with England over America, 105, 116, 185, 203, 210; proposes mediation, 212; direct proposal to U.S., 213; significance of his policy, 217
Napoleon, Prince, 230–31
Nationality, 11, 23, 61
Neutrality of England, 9, 20, 109. *See also* Intervention
New Orleans, capture of, 102, 210, 239; Gen. Butler in, 112
New York Herald, 13, 16, 67
New York Times, 13
Newcastle, Duke of, report of Seward's pugnacity, 26
Newcastle Guardian, 21

Newman, F. W., Northern sympathizer, 94, 142
Newspapers, English, 4, 53, 59, 103, 115, 117; writers and editors of, 79–87; on Trent affair, 32, 41; on slavery, 132; venality of some, 87, 167, 177, 221, 225; influence of London on Continent, 196, 200, 238; French, 221 ff., 226; Spanish, 250 ff. *See also* Reuter, names of individual papers
Noel, Rev. B. W., Northern sympathizer, 94, 142
Nonconformists, for peace in Trent affair, 39; friends of North among, 93, 162, 177; on slavery, 134–36; political activity of, 145–46. *See also* Evangelical Alliance
Non-intervention, *see* Intervention
Northcote, Sir Stafford, 88

Observer, The, 86; quoted, 109
O'Donnell, Leopold, 245 ff.
Opinion Nationale, L', 232–34
Orleanists, favor Union, 230
Oxford University, 77

Pakington, Sir John, desires intervention, 115
Palmer, Roundell (Lord Selborne), 101
Palmerston, Viscount, ministry of, 48–49; declines to intervene, 101, 109, 115, 122, 174, 205; protests about Gen. Butler's order, 112
Paris, Comte de, 230, 236
Parker, Joseph, bears peace address to U.S., 174
Parkes, Joseph, 78
Parliament, discussion in, 8, 57, 95–96, 99–101, 106–09, 185, 215
Parliamentary reform, 50 ff.
Patrie, La, 119, 221, 225
Pays, Le, 224–25
Peace Society, 38, 129. *See also* Friends
Peacocke, G. M. W., Confederate sympathizer, 90
Peel, Frederick, Confederate sympathizer, 90
Pensamiento Español, El, 251
Persigny, Comte, 218, 222
'Peterhoff,' ship, seized by U.S., 183
Phare, Le (Nantes), 232
Poland, rebellion in, 164, 188, 200
Potter, Edmund, 64
Potter, T. B., Northern sympathizer, 92
Press, *see* Newspapers
Press, The, 39
Presse, La, 232
Prévost-Paradol, L.-A., against intervention, 239
Prim, General Juan, 246; quoted, 256
Prince Consort, *see* Albert, Prince
Propaganda, 164–89, *passim*; Unionist, 13, 36, 91, 175 ff., 234; Confederate, 165 ff.; in Lancashire, 171 ff., 184; in France, 221
Prussia, attitude to U.S., 196–97
Punch, 18, 160; on Trent affair, 35; quoted, 5, 22, 101; verses on death of Lincoln, 262

Quakers, *see* Friends
Quarterly Review, articles on America in, 85

Radicals, English, 54, 94, 146, 180, 260
Ramsden, Sir John, 57
Recognition of the Confederacy, 8, 20; Gladstone's speech, 114 ff.; defeated in House of Commons, 185–86. *See also* Intervention, Napoleon III, Propaganda
Reformers, English, 50 ff., 58, 60, 94
Republican institutions, *see* Democracy
Republicanism, English, *see* Mazzini
Reuter's telegram agency, 176, 196, 200
Revue des Deux Mondes, 231, 234–37
Ripon, Marquess of, *see* Grey
Robinson, J. R., of the *Daily News,* 85, 86
Roebuck, J. A., spokesman of the Confederacy, 89; motion of June 30, 1863, 184 ff.; quoted, 113, 259
Rogers, J. E. T., Northern sympathizer, 94
Rossetti, D. G., 77
Rost, Pierre A., Confederate agent, 247
Ruskin, John, 78
Russel, Alexander, editor of *The Scotsman,* 87
Russell, E. R., journalist, 86
Russell, Earl (Lord John), 10, 108; diagnosis of American war, 24; proposes intervention, 115

Russell, W. H., war correspondent, 80–82; on Bull Run, 19; on Trent affair, 35; quoted, 59
Russia, official opinion in, 199; visit of fleets to U.S., 201; rejection of proposal to mediate, 200, 212. *See also* Poland

St. James's Hall, meetings at, 161, 263
Sala, G. A., correspondent of *Daily Telegraph,* 83
Salisbury, Marquess of, *see* Lord Robert Cecil
Sanford, H. S., U.S. Minister at Brussels, 177
Santo Domingo, 245–46
Saturday Review, 15, 90, 159; connection of English politics with American events, 56–57; defends slavery, 155
Schleswig-Holstein question, 164, 173, 188, 216
Schurz, Carl, U.S. Minister at Madrid, 196, 246, 249
Scotland, pro-Northern meetings in, 151, 179; Scottish clergymen on slavery, 170
Scotsman, The (Edinburgh), 86, 87
Scott, Gen. Winfield, public letter on Trent affair, 36, 42
Scoville, Joseph A., New York correspondent of *Standard,* 35, 84
Secession, 5 ff., 10, 17, 237
Sedgwick, Adam, 79
Sémaphore, Le (Marseille), 232
Seward, W. H., U.S. Secretary of State, 12, 22, 46, 121, 177; suspected of wishing war with England, 15, 26 ff.; refuses to protest to Russia, 200; rejects French offer to mediate, 213; policy in regard to Mexican Empire, 215–16; policy toward Spain, 247, 250
Shaftesbury, Earl of, 39, 133
Shipowners, British, 44, 89. *See also* Blockade-running
Shipping Gazette, 44
Sidgwick, Henry, Northern sympathizer, 29, 76
Siècle, Le, 232
Silk, distress in French industry, 208
Slave trade, Anglo-American treaty, 102
Slavery, 265; influence of, in England, 10, 16, 60, 98, 102, 119, 129 ff.; Trent affair, 43; J. S. Mill on, 74; W. E. Forster and, 90–91; *El Diario* on, 253; *La Discusión* on, 254
Slidell, John, Confederate commissioner, captured, 28; in France, 209, 211, 212, 215
Smith, Goldwin, Northern sympathizer, 93, 142, 266
Snow, Joseph, editor of *The Observer,* 86
Society for Obtaining the Cessation of Hostilities, 173
Southern Independence Association, 115, 172
Spectator, The, 84, 85, 99, 114, 119, 139
Spence, James, pro-Southern worker, 75, 119, 167, 172
Spencer, Herbert, 77
Spurgeon, Rev. C. H., prays for the Union, 149
Standard, The, 87, 184, 262; its New York correspondent, 84
Stanley, Lord, 88
Stanton, E. M., U.S. Secretary of War, 80–81
Stephen, Leslie, 67, 83
Story, W. W., 36
Stowe, Harriet Beecher, address to the ladies of England, 142
Stratheden and Campbell, Lord, Confederate sympathizer, 173
Suffrage, extension of in England, *see* Democracy, Parliamentary reform
Sumter, Fort, 7
Sunderland Times, 41
Sweden, favorable to Union, 198
Swinburne, A. C., 77
Switzerland, sympathy with Union, 195

Taylor, P. A., Northern sympathizer, 91, 108
Temps, Le, 232
Tennyson, Alfred, 77
Teynham, Lord, Northern sympathizer, 87
Thackeray, W. M., 11, 78
Thiers, L.-A., 221, 242
Thompson, George, anti-slavery agitator, 93, 127, 141, 180
Thompson, J. R., Confederate, 171
Thompson, T. Perronet, Northern sympathizer, 86, 142

Thouvenel, Édouard, French foreign minister, 208, 218
Times, The, 4, 8, 27, 57, 103, 180; discussed, 80–83; attacked, 160; on Trent affair, 29, 32; on intervention, 97, 99, 104, 105, 107, 109; 'Historicus' letters, 117 ff.; on cotton loan, 181; defends slavery, 155; on emancipation, 158; on death of Lincoln, 262; quoted, 6, 11, 16, 61, 63
Tocqueville, Alexis de, 51, 78, 229
Tories, English, 46, 56–57, 138–39, 158, 173. *See also* Conservative party
Townsend, Meredith, of *The Spectator,* 85
Trades unions, meeting in St. James's Hall, 161
Train, G. F., 178
Tremlett, Rev. F. W., Confederate sympathizer, 174
Trent affair, 28–47; French note on, 206; French comment, 222, 224; Spanish opinion, 248, 255
Trollope, Anthony, 78
Tupper, M. F., Northern sympathizer, 78
Turkey, American missionaries in, 194
Turner, Charles, candidate for Parliament, 61

Union, L', 221, 226
Union and Emancipation Society of Manchester, *see* Emancipation Societies
Unitarianism, 64, 94
United States bonds, in Germany, 196

Vansittart, W., Confederate sympathizer, 90
Vaughan, Rev. Robert, 136
Vicksburg, fall of, 186, 215
Villiers, C. P., 88

Wakefield Journal and Examiner, quoted, 30
Walker, Thomas, editor of *Daily News,* 85
Walker, R. J., 177
Weed, Thurlow, 36, 45, 177, 209, 230
Weekly Dispatch, 39, 139
Weekly Times, 149
Wesleyan Methodists, attitude on America, 134
Wharncliffe, Lord, Confederate sympathizer, 90, 173
Whately, Richard (Archbishop of Dublin), 134; diagnoses English opinion, 157
Wheat, *see* Grain
Whewell, William, Northern sympathizer, 77
Whiteside, James, 90, 108
Whiting, William, 177
Whitty, M. J., of *Liverpool Daily Post,* 86
Wilberforce, Samuel (Bishop of Oxford), 133
Wilkes, Charles, of U.S. Navy, 28 ff., 183. *See* Trent affair
Wilks, Washington, Northern sympathizer, 86, 141
Williams, Commander, 34
Wilson, George, of the Anti-Corn-Law League, 92
Wolseley, Garnet (Viscount), 85
Working classes, in England, 70, 92, 97, 108, 110, 146 ff., 161, 262; Trent affair, 39–40; in Belgium, 198; in France, 230
World, The (New York), 13

Yancey, W. L., Confederate agent, 23, 166, 170